HOMOPHOBIAS

Homophobias

LUST AND LOATHING ACROSS TIME AND SPACE

EDITED BY DAVID A. B. MURRAY

DUKE UNIVERSITY PRESS
Durham & London 2009

Printed in the United States of
America on acid-free paper ∞
Designed by Jennifer Hill
Typeset in Minion Pro by Keystone
Typesetting, Inc.

Library of Congress Cataloging-
in-Publication Data appear on the
last printed page of this book.

Permissions/Subventions:
Chapter 7, "The Emergence of
Political Homophobia in Indonesia"
by Tom Boellstorff, was previously
published in *Ethnos* 69(4) (2004):
465–486. Reprinted by permission of
the publisher (Taylor & Francis Ltd,
http://www.informaworld.com).

THE IMPETUS to the formation of this volume emerged
gradually, during the late 1990s and early years of the new
millennium, mostly through informal travel talk with stu-
dents, colleagues, and friends, but also through my gradual
recognition of a trend in North American gay and mainstream media coverage of "gay life" elsewhere around the
globe. In these contexts, I noticed a tendency for places—
mostly nations, but sometimes states, provinces, regions, or
cities—to be evaluated as "gay-friendly" or "homophobic."
For example, a series of controversial events in the Caribbean in the late 1990s, including the refusal of the government of the Cayman Islands to grant docking permission to
a gay cruise ship, received increasing amounts of gay and
mainstream media coverage which, I assume, were responsible for the increased number of questions and cautionary
advice I received about how bad homophobia was "down
there" when I was planning to do fieldwork in that region.
Many other regions around the globe, ranging from the
Middle East, Africa, and China to rural Queensland in Australia, the Midwest in the United States, or "the 905" (the
telephone prefix for the suburban area surrounding the city
of Toronto) have also been classified as places that gays and
lesbians should avoid as tourists or residents.

Of course when a place is labeled homophobic, it is the people of that place who are being identified as such. What struck me was the way in which this term was being used as a sociocultural trait, or more accurately, a sociopathological cultural trait, in which a group of people's sexual attitudes were being judged and the (Euro-American) speaker's sociosexual culture and place were generally compared favorably (implicitly or explicitly) to that of the "other" culture and place. An example of this could be found in newspapers' travel sections, which contained lines like "While the Caribbean lags behind most of the Western world in terms of openness toward gay visitors, signs of change are coming into view" (*Miami Herald* 2007). Homophobia, in other words, was no longer something attributed to individuals or institutions of one's own community or society. Homophobia had gone global, and to be accused of being homophobic was to be accused of something more than just not liking homosexuals; furthermore, this accusation now carried potentially serious economic and political repercussions. I started to wonder about the effects of utilizing homophobia as a sociocultural trait or pathology which is increasingly attached to moral, political, and economic agendas around the globe. But I also started to wonder about the meaning and existence of homophobia itself: What exactly is it? How and why does it exist in the first place? Is it problematic to speak of groups, communities, regions, or nations as "homophobic"? Is it a universal prejudice? If so, on what basis? Or does it operate differently across social, political, and economic terrains? If so, then how is it located in and generated in and through these terrains? Why does it still exist in places where there has been sexual rights activism for over forty years? Why does it seem to be appearing in places where it ostensibly didn't exist before? How do we get rid of it?

This volume is hopefully an initial step toward answering some of these questions. It began with a group of anthropologists who were invited to a panel sponsored by the Society of Lesbian and Gay Anthropologists (SOLGA) at the American Anthropological Association Meetings in 2002. I asked them to think about the questions listed above in relation to their ethnographic research but also in relation to the ways in which (homo)sexuality and sexual prejudice have been framed in sexuality studies and activism beyond anthropology. My hope, albeit a naive one, was that in developing a cross-cultural examination of homophobia we would begin to uncover, expose, and critically analyze the particular logic(s) of antihomosexual discourses and in so doing expose the cultural, political, and economic underpinnings that work to reinforce their position of hegemonic privilege. I tried to bring together researchers from a diverse range of ethnographic sites in order to demonstrate how homophobia is a phenomenon that has no center or origin, but more importantly, to examine how or if a transnational, comparative, and ethnographically informed perspective might extend, challenge, or change our understandings of homophobia.

A quick glance at the table of contents reveals that the ethnographic coverage of this phenomenon is very partial; however, there is certainly enough material here to begin to think through some of the questions about homophobia's logic(s), universality, and relevance as a conceptual framework of sexual prejudice. Not surprisingly, there are no simple answers to these questions; in fact, there are substantially divergent approaches to thinking about and investigating homophobia in the chapters of this volume. This, I would argue, is a good thing for two reasons: (a) such divergent approaches demonstrate how complex this prejudice is, and (b) given this complexity, more analytical and theoretical work is necessary in order to begin to dismantle the tangled webs of power which work to create the illusion that this prejudice is natural and/or legitimate. Nevertheless, the contributors to this volume represent a step forward in their dedication to finding new ways of conceptualizing and addressing a form of social prejudice that continues to oppress, silence, and marginalize millions around the globe today.

This volume owes a great deal to Ken Wissoker and the reviewers at Duke University Press. Their inciteful, challenging, and often provocative suggestions and criticisms raised the bar for all the contributors and myself, and I thank them for pushing us to revise, refine, and clarify our arguments. I would also like to thank Anne Meneley and Don Kulick for helping me get through some of the more challenging moments of the editorial process. I would like to acknowledge the Faculty of Arts at York University for their generous support for the publication of this volume.

I dedicate this volume to "Edward" (see the epilogue) and the many, many others like him who have shared their stories of suffering, struggle, and hope; they are precious gifts to each and every one who reads or hears them, helping us to learn more about ourselves and our relations to each other in all their beautiful, brutal complexity.

Introduction

David A. B. Murray

THE LAST FIFTEEN to twenty years have witnessed the movement of sexuality out of relative obscurity into relative acceptance in anthropological research (Boellstorff 2007b; Lancaster and di Leonardo 1997; Lyons and Lyons 2004; Weston 1993, 1998). Anthropology has contributed toward a better understanding of same-sex sexual practices and/or identities beyond the Euro-American "gay-lesbian" framework, albeit in an imbalanced manner with the majority of work focusing on male homosexuality. In his review article "Queer Studies in the House of Anthropology," Boellstorff (2007b) notes that anthropologists have shifted toward investigating the role of political and economic forces operating through national and global contexts in the construction of sexual subjectivities. There has also been an increase in work on "normative heterosexualities," much of it drawing from, inspired by, or in collaboration with, feminist anthropological research. However, while this latter category includes important topics ranging from romantic love to masculinity, female-male sexual relations in the context of tourist economies, and heterosexuality's articulations with nationalism (Boellstorff 2007b), there does not appear to be any sustained interrogation of what might be thought of as normative heterosexuality's ugly offspring, homophobia. Such is the case as well in anthropological literature focusing on violence and discrimination (e.g., Merry 2006; Mohanty 1988; Schlee 2002), where the structures and forces contributing to gendered hetero-sexual (male on female), ethnic/racial and/or state violence are being investigated but violence against sexual minorities in different sociocultural contexts has not received the same sustained attention.[1]

As Don Kulick points out in the opening chapter to this volume, the anthropological take on homophobia has been, for the most part, a (Margaret) Meadian "look how open-minded they are" approach, emphasizing how sexual diversity is accepted in certain non-Western societies and that "we" Westerners could learn something from "them." In fact, the implicit moral-political positioning of much anthropological research on same-sex sexuality has tended to follow two, often related paths: first, that there are societies where gender and sexuality are organized in very different ways from Western gender and sexual categories and prejudices, proving that these categories and prejudices are not natural or universal; and second, if we do more research on oppressed, subaltern, and/or misunderstood "victims" of sexual prejudice, we will better understand their "world(s)," and therefore their humanity, which will help their and our struggles for inclusion as equals in their/our society. While these may be noble and worthy motivations for research, they have created a significant lacuna in understanding how and why certain sexuality and gender categories and practices come to be taboo, excluded, and/or repellant. We must, in other words, focus on the other side of the coin, that is, do research that focuses on understanding the causes, dynamics, forces, structures and "logics" which work to create, oppress, marginalize, and/or silence sexual alterity.

This volume represents an attempt to address this lacuna in the anthropology of sexuality and sexuality studies more generally. It critically examines homophobia as an analytical concept and as a cross-cultural, transnational phenomenon. The goal of this volume is to initiate an analytical dismantling of the essentialist, naturalizing, and ethnocentric assumptions contained in much of this term's everyday use when applied to individuals and groups both at home and abroad. This volume's contributors approach homophobia first and foremost as a socially produced form of sexual discrimination; they are interested in examining the historical, social, political, and economic processes that contribute to its various formations. Our objective is to destabilize taken-for-granted assumptions of homophobia's intractability by generating more accurate analytical frameworks and vo-

cabularies which situate this prejudice in historically grounded relationships of inequality produced through the intersections of local and global
social, political, and economic forces.

Rethinking Homophobia

Despite significant differences in the following chapters' approaches to dismantling and destabilizing the concept of homophobia, all authors are
united on two simple but fundamentally important points: First, the term
homophobia is, for the most part, located in a psychological, individualized
framework which is deeply problematic on a number of levels.[2] In many
cases discrimination and/or violence against homosexuals is not due to an
"irrational" fear, nor can it be understood from a purely psychological
framework, that is, as a fear or hatred that resides in an individual's psyche.
The chapters in this volume uniformly demonstrate that homophobia is a
socially produced form of discrimination located within relations of inequality. Furthermore, it is a form of discrimination that is not always or
only couched in terms of hatred or fear: discrimination against homosexuals
can be conveyed through a range of attitudes: from indifference to dismissal,
"scientific" logic, "tolerance," or even a carefully delimited embrace (as in
"love the sinner, not the sin"). That said, some authors continue to use the
term *homophobia* with this revised definition in mind while others choose to
replace it with terms like *antigay prejudice* or *gay-hatred*. Clearly, the term is
inadequate both in analytical capacity and cross-cultural utility, but there is
not yet a uniform position on if and how it should be replaced.

Second, these essays demonstrate that the relations of inequality in
which homophobia is produced are arranged differentially in relation to
local contexts and global forces. That is, antihomosexual prejudice is produced through intersections of discourses of inequality which are in turn
generated through intersections of local and global forces. Thus, although it
might appear that homophobia is always about homosexuality, this volume
demonstrates that this is only partly true, or to put it more accurately,
homophobia is rarely ever just about (homo)sexuality. Furthermore, what
appears to be the same thing around the world—the persecution of mostly
male homosexuals—may not in fact be due to the same factors and may not
even be primarily about homosexuality but is rather a phenomenon produced through a complex nexus of gendered, classed, and raced inequalities

which are in turn tied to long term local and transnational political and economic relations of inequality.

The fact that most authors of this volume apply socioculturally nuanced intersectional frameworks to understanding the production of antihomosexual prejudice speaks to the influence of gay, lesbian, and feminist scholarship on the issue of sexual and gender discrimination, notably the problem of assuming "a notion of gender or sexual difference (or patriarchy) which can be applied universally and cross-culturally" (Mohanty 1988; see also Alexander and Mohanty 1997; C. Cohen 1997; Cornwall and Lindisfarne 1994; Lancaster and di Leonardo 1997; Merry 2006; Povinelli and Chauncey 1999; Yanagisako and Delaney 1995). The same problem applies to same-sex sexual discrimination: it is a culturally complex phenomenon that is structured through locally significant categories of gender, sexuality, race, class, nation, and/or religion; these categories are not static and may be influenced by or reactive to globally circulating discourses and social, economic, and political change. Following this framework, the contributors to this volume question what appear to be "obvious" cases of mostly male homophobia happening around the globe and refocus their analytical lenses on the discursive contexts through which a particular formation of sexuality or sexual practices come to be named, known, and deemed morally problematic.

But this is not to say that all of the contributors situate homophobia at identical intersections, and here is where things get complicated, as we are presented with significantly different approaches to the organization, dynamics, and meanings of same-sex sexual discrimination. These investigations of homophobia in different locations and/or at different times raise a number of issues and problems about the production, location, and intersectionality of homophobia with other relationships of dominance. These issues can be addressed through a series of questions that identify fundamental themes and tensions running throughout much of the material in this volume.

Is Homophobia a Universal Prejudice?

Research on same-sex sexualities around the globe past and present demonstrates that there have been many places and times in which homosexual practices were not categorized as a social problem and were acceptable if not respectable aspects of a group's sociosexual worldview. As noted earlier, feminist and gay and lesbian research has convincingly demonstrated the arbitrary and diverse ways in which human bodies, pleasures, and desires are organized and sanctioned. Thus, if the homosexual is not a universal category, then how can homophobia, a prejudice premised exclusively on the dislike of homosexuals, exist as a universal form of discrimination?

We might even argue that it is only in places where the category of "the homosexual" has developed that we will find homophobia. This line of reasoning would require us to pay close attention to processes of globalization and their effects on local discourses of sex and gender. Thinking about the relationship between globalization and homophobia raises important issues regarding the latter's mobility. Some analysts argue that homophobia is "spreading" and has the potential to become universal: Jon Binnie writes, "One could make a very good case for stating that it is homophobia that has been most successfully globalized, not global gay consumer culture" (2004:77). He identifies the genesis of this globalization in colonialism, in which particular constructs of gender and sexuality, especially the homo/heterosexual binary, were exported through a variety of ideological structures (medical, religious, governmental, economic) and often forcibly imposed on colonized societies. This raises the important corollary point that *heterosexuality* is also an imported concept in many societies, but that fact is lost in nationalist claims made by political and religious leaders of their societies' "natural" heterosexual inclinations and the need to keep out immoral, decadent Western sexual customs like homosexuality. This identification of homophobia as part of the legacy of colonialism also helps us to recognize how a racial politics informs much, if not all, talk about homophobia (a major point of Martin Manalansan's chapter exploring how homophobia obfuscates racial, class, and other social hierarchies in transcultural situations).

Yet I think this volume, as a whole, troubles the claim that homophobia is universally the result of the exportation of eighteenth- and nineteenth-century Euro-American models of gender and sexuality which are now festering away in various places around the globe, illustrated through nasty statements of leaders of former colonies turned "developing nations." We should also be suspicious of the claim that homophobia is simply produced in relation to the rise of gay and lesbian activism around the globe which in turn results from the arrival of the foreign sociosexual category "the homosexual" via various modalities (tourism, migration, media, the Internet). Although some authors in this volume make a convincing case that a society's homophobia must be understood in terms of its colonial past, others note the relatively recent development of violence against queers in former colonial states such as Indonesia, arguing that it is possible to have developed a form of postcolonial heterosexism unaccompanied by homophobia (Boellstorff 2007b). However, given changing gendered representations of the nation brought about through recent political and economic upheavals, coupled with the ways in which other moral discourses (for example, religious) are being politically engaged, homophobic violence is now on the upsurge. Globalization or colonialism alone are too simplistic and overly general terms with which to explain the ways in which same sex-sexual discrimination takes root and spreads in different societies.

Thus while I would not discount the importance of acknowledging the significance of the concept of "the homosexual" in relation to understanding the presence of "homophobia" wherever it is said to exist, I would suggest that instead of framing the problem as one of universally similar causes and effects (a problem that often leads to a rather tired rendition of the blame game), we would do better to follow Don Kulick's advice (in this volume) to explore "hatred and violence against people associated with same-sex sexuality as a historical and political process that is empirically investigable and understandable in terms of both local political struggles and wider scale processes of change."

Is Homophobia Produced through Nationalism or Globalization (or Both)?

In the opening chapter, Don Kulick observes that most authors in this volume situate at least part of their analysis of sexual discrimination in relation to the nation-state. At the very least, we can see that each chapter's subject matter is, for the most part, clearly demarcated through national boundaries. We have Constance Sullivan-Blum exploring religious Protestant fundamentalists and Martin Manalansan discussing gay activists' accusations of homophobia in the United States; Suzanne LaFont investigating why homophobia is so popular in Jamaica and Brian Riedel examining its relatively recent "arrival" in Greece; Steven Angelides investigating a moral panic over pedophilia and homosexuality in Australia in the 1980s and my exploration of a similar antigay panic in contemporary Barbadian media; Lawrence Cohen analyzing violence against queers in Lahore, India, and Tom Boellstorff discussing the relatively recent emergence of violence against nonnormative men in Indonesia.

However, there are significantly divergent positions among the authors on the role and significance of the political, ideological, and bureaucratic machinery of the nation-state; it is by no means identified by all as the primary or most significant factor in the production of homophobia. Some authors remind us that nationalism (whether official, oppositional, popular, or diasporic) structures and is structured through gendered and sexualized tropes. These tropes do have their local particularities. As Parker et al. remind us in their volume *Nationalisms and Sexualities* (1992), not all nationalisms are alike in their framing of proper (and improper) gendered and sexual citizenship. Recent research demonstrates how numerous contemporary nationalisms now embrace certain incarnations of the homosexual as emblematic of a progressive, liberal, democratic and "tolerant" nation, often contrasted to "less-developed" (that is, less civilized and progressive) nations known to be hostile toward homosexuality (Giorgi 2002; Hoad 1999; Larvie 1999; Puar 2006). More work is necessary on how it is that the homosexual is becoming the new model citizen in some nationalist discourses while occupying the role of pariah in others.

Furthermore, we need to problematize thinking about homophobia only in relation to an "official nationalism" produced by the institutions of the nation-state; that is, we need to acknowledge how homophobic discourses produced in and through popular culture, religious communities, political organizations opposed to those in power, and a range of other sites attempt to legitimize their position and agenda through various associations of sexuality to (im)proper modes of national belonging. Thus homophobia is not a concept to be analyzed only in relation to official discourses of the nation-state, a reminder that highlights the importance of carefully examining who is producing antigay discourses when they are associated with the nation's interests, identity, or well-being. Additionally, some of the essays in this volume illustrate why we must examine the ways in which social and political changes *within* national boundaries have produced an intensification of antigay sentiment among certain sectors at certain historical junctures, revealing the importance of process and contingency in any analysis of the formation of prejudice. I think it is notable that in this volume, this emphasis on process and contingency within national boundaries tends to be applied to Western settler nations like Australia and the United States.

However, as noted above, other essays in this volume demonstrate that we must also factor in the influence of globalization in the production of homophobia: interrogating homophobia, in other words, requires us to examine not only local and/or nationalist ideas, statements, and claims of knowledge about gender and sexuality but also relations of material production, capital mobility, political alliances, juridical structures, and discourses of race, class, and modernity which circulate across and through national borders and intersect, fuse, mutate, or spawn new formations in local gender/sex hierarchies. For example, international human rights groups like Amnesty International and Human Rights Watch have recently added sexual minorities to their list of groups whose rights require protection and advocacy. In some cases their attempts to pressure governments (often, but not exclusively of developing nations) to change laws on homosexuality have created a backlash, with popular pundits and politicians asserting that they will not bow to foreign pressure. In other contexts, the rise of "gay identity" constructed through transnational commodity aesthetics, political activism, and new modes of electronic communication has come to represent, for some, a more cosmopolitan and modern nationalism but has simultaneously created a backlash against this figure who represents, for others, "foreign" sexual values imported through foreign nongovernmental organizations and popular culture. Or we might consider the massive surge in global gay tourism and how differently positioned gay men may utilize homophobia as a concept to describe the "culture" of exotic destinations, and how this may convey racist, classist, and sexist assumptions simply because these destinations don't display the same forms of "acceptance" or perform "gay" in the same way as these men find in their "liberated" gay ghettos. Numerous other examples are presented throughout this volume which demonstrate the unpredictable effects and outcomes of globalization on sexual subject formations and moral economies.

Thus we can divide this volume into two analytical frameworks located on the national-global continuum which appear to be related to their objects of study. Homophobia in Euro-American settler nations is examined primarily through an insular lens emphasizing process and contingency within a particular sociocultural and political context, whereas homophobia in non-Western nations (or among any group that is not white, male, and middle class) is examined through a more global lens in which the circulation of Euro-American gay identities and politics as well as other external influences are analyzed for their impact on local gender and sexual cultures (Brian Riedel's work on the recent "importation" of homophobia as a category of discrimination into the Greek lexicon is perhaps the main exception to this division). I am somewhat uncomfortable with the ways in which each analytical framework is aligned with its object of study as they risk reproducing a problem identified in much of the research on globalization and its earlier incarnation, world systems theory, whereby there is an assumption of unidirectional movement and influence of sexual ideologies, practices, and identities, from "central," powerful, developed nation-states to "peripheral," powerless, developing nation-states. As Cruz-Malave and Manalansan note in their important volume *Queer Globalizations,* to assume this kind of static, unidirectional relationship in the analysis of sexualities anywhere is not just overly simplistic but also, in most cases, downright imperialistic (2002). Clearly there needs to be greater emphasis on the ways in which local, national, *and* global discourses and practices influence gender-sex hierarchies in any place where antigay discrimination is claimed to exist.

Is Homophobia a Gendered Discourse?

In this volume, most of the case studies are of anti*gay* discrimination; that is, this prejudice appears to be mostly targeting male homosexuals. Does this mean that homophobia is primarily about men? It would seem that in the realm of public institutions like media, government, international development, law and justice, popular culture, and even less publicly visible arenas like HIV/AIDS education and gay activism, the answer would be a qualified yes, the exception being Sullivan-Blum's chapter, which indicates that that antihomosexual rhetoric in mainline Protestant churches is "equal opportunity" in its focusing on lesbians and gays as sinners who shouldn't be allowed to marry. (LaFont also briefly discusses antilesbian violence in Jamaica.)

Unfortunately, as Kulick notes, the reasons for the focus on men in public, institutional antihomosexual discourses remain undertheorized. Some of the essays discuss the masculinist, patriarchal, and heterosexist underpinnings of nationalist and global liberal economic discourses in which "the homosexual" is feared and/or loathed because his "effeminate" identity threatens the "legitimate" (read: heterosexual, patriarchal) models of citizenship of the nation-state. This threatening "other" may be located within the nation or "forcibly" imposed on or imported into the nation through international political and economic alliances. This position builds on the arguments of numerous scholars of nationalism who have noted its heterosexual, fraternal, and patriarchal frameworks in which unruly women (often defined in terms of having a problematic heterosexuality, that is, one that is not based on monogamous marriage and heterosexual intercourse for the express purpose of bearing children) and homosexuals are construed as the greatest threats to the (re)productive fantasies of the nationalist imaginary (Elliston 2004; Mosse 1985; Parker et al. 1992; Yuval-Davis 1997).

However, we might want to think more carefully about what is being emphasized in these gendered, nationalist discourses of fear and loathing: Is it the sex between men (most often the act of anal penetration is presented as the prima facie example of homosexual practices) that disgusts or is it that this kind of sex involves men who are being penetrated and thus occupying a feminine sexual role? In other words, is nationalist (male) homophobia more a product of the threat to a normative nationalist hegemony of gender roles, relations, and hierarchies than it is of sexual practices and identities per se? As has been noted by many feminist and sexuality studies scholars, the concepts of gender and sexuality cannot be analytically separated easily, if at all. Keeping this troubled relationship in mind, we must explore further how homophobic (nationalist) discourses are also/always about the ways in which gender is being (re)configured in relations of domination in particular social and political contexts.

Nevertheless, it would be highly problematic to assume that because most of this volume concentrates on discrimination against male homosexuals there is less prejudice against lesbians or that female homosexuality is less of a "problem" than male homosexuality. As Boellstorff noted in his review of queer studies in anthropology between the years of 1993 and 2006, there continues to be a paucity of work on female nonnormative sexualities (and, I would add, on women's nonreproductive sexuality more generally). This may in part be reflective of the difficulties in accessing these individuals and communities due to the barriers that women in many parts of the world face in accessing public and private spaces away from male control;

but it may also be reflective of institutionalized academic prejudice and disciplinary politics in which such research is considered too narrow or marginal (a position which reveals, of course, the ongoing masculinist and heterosexualized structures of academia) (Boellstorff 2007b).

How Do We Eliminate Homophobia?

While this volume hopefully succeeds in its primary goal of providing new approaches to analyzing the formation and production of homophobia in different sociopolitical contexts, it is in many ways only a first step toward fulfilling what should be the main objective of any research on social discrimination: how to dismantle it. In the epilogue to this book, I introduce Edward, a gay refugee from Uganda now living in Canada, whose amazing voyage from Kampala to Toronto reminds us of the ever-present everyday reality of violence and discrimination against homosexuals and the ways in which this violence and attempts to mitigate its effects are produced through discursive relations of inequality that operate within and across national borders with unpredictable outcomes. If the essays in this volume present different approaches to locating and analyzing the meaning, production, and significance of homophobia, then we cannot assume that there will be a simple formula to eliminate its existence. If same-sex sexual discrimination is produced in and through the intersection of global, national, and local relations of inequality (gendered, raced, religious, national, ethnic, classed, caste, and so on), then strategies of resistance, whether in the form of laws, education campaigns, international human rights activism, or public demonstrations, must acknowledge this density and complexity. Of course homophobia can be eliminated—there are many examples of its demise that we could draw on from around the world—but a great deal more research is necessary to better understand how and why this particular form of change occurs.

Organization of the Volume

This volume is divided into two sections which reflect the underlying objectives of this project as outlined above. The contributors to the first part, "Displacing Homophobia," critically engage with the concept of homophobia and homophobic discourses. They challenge the analytical and popular purchase of homophobia as a taken-for-granted category of discrimination without negating the violent effects of same-sex sexual discrimination. Don Kulick initiates this critical interrogation with an etymology of homophobia in Euro-American medical discourses, revealing its conceptual limitations through illustrations taken from the various ethnographic studies presented throughout this volume. However, Kulick doesn't let anthropologists off the hook: he argues that there is a history of disciplinary ambiguity toward engaging in research on homosexual discrimination in cross-cultural contexts, and that what is needed are more sophisticated analytical frameworks in order to develop "an anthropology of hate."

Martin Manalansan also critically interrogates homophobia's meaning and utility but does so from a very different standpoint. Manalansan observes how homophobia (and its dismantling) has become part of the empowerment agenda of queer activist groups and nonprofit organizations in ways that often obfuscate racial, class, and other social hierarchies which maintain and prop up particular privileged and hegemonic groups. Through a series of events occurring during his fieldwork among gay Filipinos and other queers of color in New York City in the 1990s, Manalansan reveals the unsettling ways in which deviations from particular acceptable attitudes and narratives are labeled homophobic and how this accusation reveals more about the accuser's racial, classed, or gendered privilege(s). In deconstructing homophobia's "natural" power through statements of those who are supposedly its victims, this chapter powerfully demonstrates how we must approach this term with caution and think about the ways in which its operations may reinscribe certain existing relations of inequality even as it works to challenge others.

Constance Sullivan-Blum introduces us to a well-known American site in which homophobia has great purchase, Christianity. However, her ethnography of the debates over homosexual marriage in American mainline Protestant churches in upstate New York also challenges taken-for-granted assumptions about groups who are accused of being homophobic, and what homophobia means to them. Her interviews reveal that most evangelical Protestants are not afraid of nor do they "hate" homosexuals; rather they believe that homosexuality is sinful and must be rejected as morally wrong. We also learn that the debate over the acceptability of gay marriage in these churches is not just about homosexuality: it is part of a much larger and more fundamental discussion of the role and significance of Christianity in relation to modern discourses of scientific rationality. Sullivan-Blum also outlines how there is a significant component of this religious community who are actively working to integrate homosexuality as an acceptable part of their theological ontology; her essay thus complicates any attempt to gloss over religion as an 'obvious' site of homophobia.

With Steven Angelides' essay, we shift in time and space to another English settler society, Australia in the late 1980s. Angelides analyzes the ways in which homosexuality and pedophilia were conflated in public discourse via the explosive case of Alison Thorne, the spokesperson for the Gay Legal Rights Coalition who defended the Australian Pedophile Support Group whose offices were raided and members arrested by the police. Shortly after her comments were made public, Thorne was persecuted on the front page of a Melbourne newspaper and by radio talk-show hosts, hounded by other national and state newspaper syndicates, and removed from her position as a secondary school teacher. By any estimation this was a homophobic trial by media, but Angelides' analysis carefully situates the event in the broader context of rather profound social and political changes occurring in Australia and most other Western societies in the 1980s with regard to sexuality in general and homosexuality in particular. Angelides' essay demonstrates the importance of foregrounding process and contingency in understanding how and why particular forms of sociosexual discrimination are produced.

Brian Riedel's examination of the "arrival" of homophobia or *omofovia* as a new term in the Greek lexicon in the mid-1970s is another example of the importance of locating sociosexual discrimination (including its terms of reference) in historical and sociopolitical context. Riedel's discussion of the unpopularity of *omofovia* in popular, everyday Greek talk and why it is usually replaced by *ratsismos* (roughly translated as "racism") not only complicates any master narrative of homophobia's meaning in Western societies but also reveals ways in which forms of social inequality which North Americans often assume to be distinct and separate may be related and organized differently.

The essays in part 2, "'Transnational Homophobias," explore the interrelationships of complex social, political, and economic dynamics operating at local, national, and transnational levels which produce forms of exclusion, violence, and/or criminalization of sexual minorities. Colonization, globalization, the nation, and citizenship are themes which figure prominently throughout these chapters.

This section begins with Suzanne LaFont's ethnographic study of Jamaica, a nation that has, over the past ten years, received an inordinate amount of media coverage focusing on its widespread homophobic attitudes and actions. LaFont argues that in order to understand why this form of discrimination is so acceptable, we must first recognize how sexualities in Jamaica have developed through the influence of multiple, intersecting African and British sexual meanings which have, in turn, been shaped by the interrelatedness of slavery, colonization, class, race, gender, and religion. In her discussions with a cross-section of Afro-Jamaicans, LaFont demonstrates how a powerful regime of heteronormativity is produced through various discourses generated in multiple sites, from narratives of a mythologized heterosexual morality of the past to contemporary dancehall lyrics and the actions of political leaders and the police force. LaFont also makes an important observation about the uneven effects of homophobic discourses: wealthy gays, lesbians, and bisexuals in Jamaica have a level of immunity which is often unavailable to their poorer counterparts.

Tom Boellstorff's chapter takes us to another nation-state forged through colonialism, Indonesia, where, in contrast to Jamaica, violence against nonnormative men was, until recently, rare to a degree unimaginable in many Euro-American societies. This, however, has changed since the fall of the Soeharto regime in 1998, and attacks and threats explicitly directed at homosexuals and transvestites have become increasingly common and increasingly violent. Boellstorff's discussion of this novel genre of violence hinges on a distinction he makes between heterosexism and homophobia; he argues that it is possible for a society to be heterosexist without being homophobic. Indonesia, for example, is a place where heterosexuality has been the doxic mode of being without the presumption of its naturalness and superiority leading to or depending on violence against people who engage in same-sex sexuality. However, at certain moments or periods, heterosexist values can move from being unreflected-upon doxa to being visible and therefore open to challenge and contestation.

My chapter is concerned with a similar phenomenon, the sudden surge of homophobic references in Barbados's feedback media (radio talk shows, letters to the editor sections of daily newspapers, and online bulletin boards) over the past eight to ten years. I argue that these antihomosexual references in Barbadian feedback media are produced through a heterosexist patriarchal logic originating in a colonial framework of gendered, sexual, racial, and classed hierarchies which have been reproduced *and challenged* through the turbulent, uneven processes of economic, political, and cultural globalization over the past twenty years. For a variety of historically contextual reasons, "homosexuals" have come to be, for some Barbadians, the bogeymen of a turbulent and stressful modernity.

The final chapter of the volume is Lawrence Cohen's fascinating inquiry into the rape and murder of six young men in 1994 in the north Indian city of Lucknow. Cohen's analysis of these crimes, and the local discussions about them, serves as a cautionary tale for anyone inclined to make sweeping statements on the universality of homophobia. According to Cohen, "homosex," to use the vernacular term that moves between Hindi, Urdu, and English, was less the object of panic: it was, rather, the preeminent figure of the political *tout court*. In other words, "homophobia," may not be the most helpful or at least not the only generative concept to understand these murders. What is at stake, rather, is what Cohen calls "the feudal." Cohen argues that the elite media frenzy over the killing of gay men in Lucknow was not so much about blaming the immorality of (imposed Western) homosexuality as it was a way to represent a generalized state of feudal relations in local social hierarchies where sodomitical excess is a potent component of the rhetorical arsenal aimed at local elites.

In the epilogue, I present Edward's story of escape from his home in Kampala Uganda to his arrival in Toronto as a "gay refugee" in order to remind us why critical engagement with homophobia continues to be necessary and timely. I also remind us why this ending is only a beginning, as much remains to be done in order to better understand the operations of this form of discrimination, its material and symbolic effects, and efforts to dismantle it in all their diverse local, national, and transnational contexts.

Notes

1 A notable exception is *Sexual Inequalities and Social Justice*, edited by Teunis and Herdt (2007), which explores the processes through which social inequalities are produced, in particular how sexuality operates with other axes of social inequality.

2 *Homophobia* is popularly assumed to be a term derived from Latin, meaning "fear of the same," but in fact it is a neologism: in Latin, *homo* equals man/human/humankind and *phobus* equals phobia, therefore a Latin homophobe is someone who does not like humans/humankind.

1 Displacing Homophobia

Can There Be an Anthropology of Homophobia?

Don Kulick

THE END OF 2004 was marked by a horrific tragedy. An undersea earthquake off the coast of the Indonesian island of Sumatra set into motion a massive tidal wave, a tsunami, that smashed into coastal areas across the Bay of Bengal and the Indian Ocean. Over 160,000 people, most of them local inhabitants, but many of them tourists, are known to have perished. In the midst of this devastating human loss, the Westboro Baptist Church in the American state of Kansas posted this notice on its home page, www.godhatesfags .com:[1]

> . . . Do you realize that among the dead and missing are 20,000 Swedes and over 3,000 Americans? . . . We sincerely hope and pray that all 20,000 Swedes are dead, their bodies bloated on the ground or in mass graves or floating at sea feeding sharks and fishes or in the bellies of thousands of crocodiles washed ashore by tsunamis. These filthy, faggot Swedes have a satanic, draconian law criminalizing Gospel preaching, under which they prosecuted, convicted and sentenced Pastor Åke Green to jail— thereby incurring God's irreversible wrath [Sweden's law prohibiting hate speech extends to speech that denigrates or incites violence against homosexuals. In 2004, pastor Åke Green, who in his sermons used language not unlike

that found in this Internet posting, was convicted of hate speech against homosexuals and sentenced to a month in prison[2]].

. . . America . . . is awash in diseased fag feces & semen, and is an apostate land of the sodomite damned.

. . . Let us pray that God will send a massive Tsunami to totally devastate the North American continent with 1000-foot walls of water doing 500 mph—even as islands in southern Asia have recently been laid waste, with but a small remnant surviving. God Hates Fag America!

. . . Thank God for the tsunamis & we hope for 20,000 dead Swedes!!!

Meanwhile, in another place and time, Zimbabwean president Robert Mugabe opened the 1995 Zimbabwe International Book Fair with these words:

I find it extremely outrageous and repugnant to my human conscience that such immoral and repulsive organizations, like those of homo-sexuals who offend both against the law of nature and the morals of religious beliefs espoused by our society, should have any advocates in our midst and even elsewhere in the world.

If we accept homosexuality as a right, as is being argued by the associa-tion of sodomists and sexual perverts, what moral fibre shall our society ever have to deny organized drug addicts, or even those given to bes-tiality, the rights they may claim and allege they possess under the rubrics of individual freedom and human rights? (Engelke 1999:299)

And meanwhile, in another place and time, the following brief notice ap-peared on Friday, November 19, 2004, unobtrusively at the bottom of page six in the *Oakland Tribune*, a local newspaper from the city whose main claim to fame is as the referent of Gertrude Stein's aphorism "There is no there there":

Philadelphia

11-year-old boy charged with rape

An 11-year-old boy sexually assaulted another boy in a middle-school stairway after chasing the victim from a bathroom, authorities said. A school officiate said they would try to determine where employees were at the time of the attack Tuesday meaning. The suspect was charged as a juvenile with involuntary deviate sexual intercourse.

This last example might not, at first glance, seem to have much in common with the other two. The report consists of three one-sentence paragraphs reporting on a sexual assault. It is written in dry, telegraphic Associated Press prose that is unremarkable—save for one malignant word occurring right at the end. Deviate.

Grammatically, *deviate*, like the word *involuntary* that precedes it, is an adjective, qualifying the type of "sexual intercourse" that occurred. "Involuntary" clearly refers to the will of the victim and signifies that the intercourse was unwanted. But what is the meaning here of "deviate"? Was the intercourse "deviate" because it was an assault, and to assault someone is to deviate from a statistical norm? In that case, one might wonder why rapes, say, or armed robberies, or murders—never committed by the overwhelming majority of people—are generally not qualified with "deviate" in press reports. Could it be that the word *deviate* refers to the fact that both persons involved were male, as in the familiar derogatory collocation "sexual deviate"?

The occurrence of the word *deviate* here signals a denigrating stance toward same-sex sexuality so banal (and gratuitous) that it might easily pass unnoticed. It is a far cry from an American church's ecstasy over the supposed deaths of "filthy, faggot Swedes" or an African despot's insistence that homosexuals have no human rights. In the *Oakland Tribune*, the word *deviate* is subtle. It functions more as a diacritic than an assertion, gently reframing the modality of the report from a straightforward journalistic account of a sexual assault to a distasteful commentary less on the assault itself than on the idea that the object of the assault should be another male.

What links all these three examples, then, even though they occur at different times and in different places (and in different registers), is a denigration of same-sex sexuality. This kind of denigration is a phenomenon often referred to by the word *homophobia*. Homophobia is a Western concept, coined in the early 1970s by George Weinberg, an American psychologist, to describe what he defined as "a disease . . . an attitude held by many nonhomosexuals and perhaps by the majority of homosexuals in countries where there is discrimination against homosexuals"(1972:n.p.). But even though it was the West that named it, the denigration of persons associated with same-sex sexuality, and hatred and violence against them, is hardly limited to North America and Europe. A chapter in this book recounts how, a few years ago in central Java, a social gathering of mostly gay men and transvestites was stormed by 150 men who assaulted those present with knives, machetes, and clubs. Another discusses how in Jamaica on any given week, at least three of the top twenty musical hits promote violence against queers with lyrics like "Bang, bang into the gay man's head / Homeboys will not tolerate their nastiness / They must be killed." Another reports on a brutal murder of a gay man and his lover in 2004 in Lucknow, India, where subsequent media accounts were much more interested in detailing the supposed sexual proclivities of the victims than in urging the apprehension of the killers. When it comes to homophobia, it seems, it's a small world after all.

As a cultural phenomenon of seemingly global scope, homophobia ought to be an obvious target for anthropological attention. And indeed, individual anthropologists have done important work showing how antigay prejudice affects how lesbian and gay anthropologists position themselves both in the discipline of anthropology and as fieldworkers in different societies (Blackwood 1995a; Bolton 1995; Leap and Lewin 1996; Newton 1993; 2000; Seizer 1995). This anthology differs from that approach in that it is less interested in how anthropologists experience homophobia than in how local people in particular ethnographic contexts are affected by it. In this sense, the book continues and extends the work of those ethnographers who have documented how violence against people associated with nonnormative sexuality is an integral part of heterosexist social, cultural, economic, and political systems that reward some people and punish others (Bunzl 2004; Kulick 1998; Lancaster 1992; Manalansan 2003; D. Murray 2002; Prieur 1998; Valentine 2003). The question this book asks is, in effect: Can there be an anthropology of homophobia? And the answers it gives to that question are developed in chapters that focus on the particular manifestations of hatred and violence faced by people who engage in same-sex sexuality. The different chapters each discuss "homophobia," but they do so without making the elementary error of taking the concept as an unproblematic, transcultural given. On the contrary, each chapter engages with "homophobia" in ways that interrogate and modify our understanding of it. This means that the book is about speech and acts that are generally glossed as "homophobic" even as the individual chapters simultaneously decompose and reframe that concept.

Homophobia, everyone seems to agree, is a problematic word. A few years ago, the historian Daniel Wickberg (2000) published a concise and helpful history of the concept. Wickberg points out that homophobia is nowadays regularly featured in Western liberal discourse as one of the "big three" obstacles to social justice—the other two being racism and sexism. But in addition to being a much more recent concept than racism (which appeared circa 1935) and sexism (circa 1965), homophobia differs from them in two important ways. The first difference is a semantic one and concerns the fact that homophobia specifies the direction of prejudice in a way the other two do not: while the targets of racism and sexism are overwhelmingly people of color and women, respectively, there is nothing in the concepts themselves that prevents whites and men from claiming victimhood from race or gender prejudice. They are, in this sense, equal-opportunity concepts. Reverse-homophobia, on the other hand, cannot exist.

A second, more significant difference between homophobia, racism, and sexism is that homophobia appears to locate the source of prejudice against homosexuals not in social structures but in the individual psyche. The stress on individual reactions to homosexuality links the concept, in ways suggested but not discussed by Wickberg, to a much older psychiatric concept by the name of "homosexual panic." But in contrast to how both homophobia and homosexual panic are generally thought about today, homosexual panic in its original formulation did not refer to a fear of homosexuals. Instead, it referred to cases where men who had been in intensively same-sex environments became aware of homosexual desires that they felt unable to control and unable to act on. The original formulation of the disorder was based on a diagnosis of a small number of soldiers and sailors in a U.S. government mental hospital after World War I (Kempf 1920). These men were not violent—they were, on the contrary, passive. The disorder was characterized by periods of introspective brooding, self-punishment, suicidal assaults, withdrawal, and helplessness. So homosexual panic was generally understood not as a temporary, violent episode but, rather as an ongoing illness that comprised severe bouts of depression. Patients suffering from it were catatonic, not violent.

During the course of the 1900s the original understanding of this condition shifted, and it came to be applied even to men who reacted violently in situations where homosexual desire was made explicit. In the psychiatric literature, there is no consensus that the concept of homosexual panic should or can be used to explain sudden violent outbursts like these. But in the popular mind, homosexual panic has come to be perceived as a surface manifestation of homophobia, a concept that in only three decades arguably has been naturalized as a set of understandable psychological structures that everyone has (even homosexuals) but that reasonable people resist and try to come to terms with.

This pathologizing framework has been criticized by many people, perhaps most trenchantly by the literary scholar Eve Sedgwick (1990), who has noted that the very existence of such a concept rests on an assumption that hatred of queers is a private and atypical phenomenon. But think about it, she says. To what extent would anyone accept race-phobia as an accountability-reducing illness for a German skinhead who bludgeoned a Turk to death? Or gender-phobia for a woman who shot a man who made an unwanted advance to her? (Think for a moment of how many bodies would be swept out of bars and clubs every morning.) On the contrary, the fact that a concept like "homophobia" exists at all indicates that far from being an individual pathology, hatred of homosexuals is actually more public and more typical than hatred of any other disadvantaged group.

For these reasons, every chapter in this book takes some issue with the term *homophobia*. One of the strongest positions is taken by Lawrence Cohen. He suggests that "homophobia as such may not be what is at stake in accounting for specific institutions and practices that punish persons recognizable under the globalizing gaze of LGBT/queer." Cohen's chapter on India discusses a situation in which "the policing of sex between men through arrests, blackmail, sex on demand, and rape is ubiquitous in many Indian towns and cities, but no organized public apparatus of homophobic punishment, interdiction, and shame exists in India to the extent it has in the United States of the last half century." In this context, crimes and arrests involving homosexuality have different resonances than they do in places like the United States—resonances that Cohen analyzes as "feudal" rather than homophobic. On the other hand, there is some indication that a shift may be underway. The final case discussed in Cohen's chapter—a violent murder of a gay man and his lover in August 2004—was reported in the press in a partly novel way; one which may indicate that same-sex desire is being thought about—and punished—in ways that until now have not been imaginable.

Tom Boellstorff's chapter is specifically about this kind of shift. It discusses recent attacks by Muslim groups on gatherings of homosexuals and transvestites in Indonesia. Indonesia, like India, lacks what Cohen calls an "organized public apparatus of homophobic punishment"; indeed, Boellstorff explains that "historically, violence against non-normative men in Indonesia has been rare to a degree unimaginable in many Euro-American societies." This, however, has changed since the fall of the Soeharto regime in 1998, and attacks and threats explicitly directed at homosexuals and transvestites have become increasingly common and increasingly violent. The anthropological question is: why? What has occurred to make this new genre of violence seem conceivable and logical?

Boellstorff's discussion of this novel genre of violence hinges on a distinction he draws between "heterosexism" and "homophobia." This is a distinction that suggests an important general point. Recall that one of most recurring criticisms of the word *homophobia* is that it focuses attention on the psychological rather than the structural dimensions of hatred of and violence toward queers. It is arguably possible to direct a similar kind of criticism at the terms with which *homophobia* is most frequently contrasted on this count: *sexism* and *racism*, both of which direct us to social structures. A problem with terms like *sexism* and *racism* (or the alternative often proposed for *homophobia*, *heterosexism*) is that while they do indeed lead us to pay attention to social structure, they background an exploration of the emotional involvement that people come to have in those structures. To be sure, different kinds of -isms reproduce inequality and foster prejudice and discrimination against minorities, women, and queers. But what is their emotional resonance? How do -isms come to be invested with emotional significance that moves people to think and act in particular ways?

This is where Boellstorff's distinction between heterosexism and homophobia is useful. Heterosexism is the belief that heterosexuality is the only natural or moral sexuality. Homophobia, on the other hand is the fear and hatred of nonnormative sexualities and genders. In Boellstorff's terms, it is possible for a society to be heterosexist without being homophobic. Indonesia, for example, is a place where heterosexuality has been the doxic mode of being without the presumption of its naturalness and superiority leading to or depending on violence against people who engage in same-sex sexuality.[3]

Boellstorff's main point with his distinction is to suggest that at certain moments or periods heterosexist values can move from being unreflected-upon doxa to being visible and therefore, as Bourdieu taught us, open to challenge and contestation. At this point, a hitherto unreflexive relationship to heterosexuality may crystallize into a panicked allegiance to it. This is the moment at which people can come to invest emotionally in heterosexist structures in ways that transform heterosexism into homophobia.

One spark that seems to light this fuse is the rise of gay and lesbian movements. Several of the chapters in this volume note that the establishment of such organizations in various countries has corresponded with increasingly overt hatred toward gay men and lesbians. To note this, however, is not the same as saying that sexual rights activism is to blame for increased violence against queers. It is to make the more interesting observation that hatred and violence against people associated with same-sex sexuality is a historical and political process that is empirically investigable and understandable in terms of both local political struggles and wider-scale processes of change. Anthropological study of these processes is a necessary complement to more recent psychoanalytically or linguistically grounded accounts that suggest that the expression of distaste for or hatred of homosexuals is a resource people draw on to secure a sense of themselves as heterosexual (Butler 1993; Cameron 1997).

The meaning and power of people's senses of themselves as heterosexual leads directly to another theme present in virtually every chapter in this book, namely, the link between same-sex sexuality and the nation-state. In case after case, the nation emerges rhetorically through an engagement with and rejection of homosexuality. As David Murray's chapter reveals, Barbadian public discourse frequently compares the morality of Barbados to that of the United States, which is held to be in a "moral morass" because of its "pro-homosexual stance." Suzanne LaFont notes that the Grammy winner Beenie Man's hit song "Damn" includes the lyrics "I'm dreaming of a new Jamaica, come to execute all the gays." Lawrence Cohen relates that the murder of gay men in Lucknow provided a newspaper columnist with an opportunity to dilate about how India is being corrupted by "a nexus between employees of international aid agencies and the gay underworld." The perception by some that the post-Soeharto Indonesian nation has become embattled electrifies the figure of the effeminate male in novel ways, resignifying him as a kind of metonym for the fragile state of the nation and justifying violent attacks on him by men who feel that he materializes their shame that their nation is no longer strong and virile. In each of these instances, homosexuals are figured as the despised contrast in opposition to whom the nation can exist and thrive. And in each case, the crucial anthropological question is the processes through which particular forms of sexuality become more than acts or identities. How do particular configurations of sexuality emerge as salient and emotionally engaging symbols of the nation?

A related question, not addressed in this book but in dire need of more ethnographic research, is the way in which a supposed tolerance of homosexuality is increasingly being invoked by both conservative, racist political parties and spokespersons *and* by liberals and progressives in the global north as a means of demonizing Muslims. The campaign in 2002 of the extravagantly gay Dutch politician Pim Fortuyn was a harbinger of this kind of discourse, which reached one horrific nadir in the U.S. soldiers' torture of prisoners in Abu Ghraib. Throughout his campaign, Fortuyn stressed the difference between the permissive and modern Netherlands and the conservative and backward countries from which immigrants to the Netherlands originated. His own homosexuality, he argued, both gave him insight into oppression and highlighted the progressiveness of the Dutch state. "In what country could an electoral leader of such a large movement as mine be openly homosexual?" Fortuyn asked the newspaper *Volkskrant* in 2002. "How wonderful that that's possible. That's something that one can be proud of. And I'd like to keep it that way, thank you very much" (Poorthuis and Wansink 2002). Fortuyn specifically targeted Muslims, dubbing Islam a "hostile religion" and "backward culture," writing a book titled *Against the Islamisation of Our Culture* (Fortuyn 1997), advocating the adoption of legislation that prohibits more Muslims from entering the country, and purposely provoking conservative Muslims, "because each time they responded with some diatribe about unnatural behavior and Western decadence, his supposed progressiveness only gained" (Asselberghs and Lesage 2003). And gain he did—before he was assassinated in May 2005, only six days before the national elections, it was widely speculated that Fortuyn might end up being the next prime minister of the country. His eponymous party Lijst Pim Fortuyn went on to win an unprecedented debut of twenty-six seats (of 150) in Parliament (van der Veer 2006).

Fortuyn's strategy of portraying Muslims as the dark repressive homophobic shadow threatening to eclipse the bright freedoms of a sexually progressive West is a consummate example of what the queer scholar Jasbir Puar (2007) has recently termed "homonationalism." Homonationalism is the form that homosexual identities and discourses about homosexuality have been developing in the global north during the past thirty years. It is a "brand of homosexuality [that] operates as a regulatory script not only of normative gayness, queerness, or homosexuality, but also of the racial and national norms that reinforce those sexual subjects" (2007:2). In other words, homonationalism is an understanding and enactment of homosexual acts, identities, and relationships that incorporates them as not only compatible with but even exemplary of neoliberal democratic ethics and citizenship. The problem, of course, is that even while this incorporation widens the scope of citizenship, it also does less happy kinds of work: it secures particular racial and class privileges for only a minority of homosexual subjects (many or most of whom, as Puar points out, are in fact not embraced by this discursive and juridical magnanimity of the neoliberal Western state) and it simultaneously produces whole populations of sexual and racial others whose rhetorical function is to provide a backdrop against which countries like the Netherlands or the United States can appear as progressive, democratic, desirable, and humanitarian. Through these kinds of processes, homophobia at "home" can be downplayed and disavowed because it is projected onto other spaces and other bodies, which emerge as both uncivilized and threatening. The complicated interplay between homonationalism, imperialism, racism, misogyny, and homophobia, in Puar's analysis, is key to understanding how the torture in the Abu Ghraib prison was framed, enacted, and responded to. The power of Puar's analysis in this context is her insistence that any critical engagement with homophobia will always necessarily be marked by squalid and destructive histories of race, gender, class, and Orientalism. Those histories inescapably shape anything we have to say about the topic. And for that reason, they have to be acknowledged and incorporated into any analysis of homophobia that we might wish to pursue.

Anthropology and Homophobia

In 1992, in an anthology called *Homophobia: How We All Pay the Price*, the anthropologist Walter Williams contributed a chapter titled "Benefits for Nonhomophobic Societies: An Anthropological Perspective." Williams's anthropological perspective was a bracing spoonful of Margaret Mead. Surveying the globe, he noted that "the majority of other cultures that have been studied by anthropologists condone at least some form of same-sex eroticism as socially acceptable behavior" (257). He then described the various ways in which acceptance of homosexuality enriches society. Drawing on his own research among Native American groups, Williams claimed that social acceptance of homosexuality results in better religion, better families, better relationships to children, better friendships, and a better society generally, because, as he put it: "The suppression of sexual diversity *inevitably* results in social turmoil" (272; emphasis in original).

My invocation of Margaret Mead when describing Williams's text is not meant facetiously. Personally, I think that we could do much worse than to follow her snappy, "Listen, cookie . . ." advice on how we might more humanely organize society. However, the time is surely past when we can hope to move or influence anyone out of intolerance and prejudice simply by reaching into our anthropological top hat and pulling out examples of traditional societies that do things differently than "we" do. That Boasian argument at the best of times has always been a double-edged sword. On the one hand, it did show us that our way was not the only way of doing things. On the other hand, precisely because the societies from which the examples were drawn were considered to be primitive, they could always be dismissed as precisely that—backward, irrelevant, uncivilized, ripe for and even desirous of colonial domination and exploitation, and proof that our way of doing things was in fact more advanced than theirs.

If we are going to enlist anthropology in the struggle against hatred and violence against queers, then we are going to have to go beyond Boas and Margaret Mead, even as we reaffirm their fundamental insight that distaste at the thought of same-sex sexuality or hatred of people who engage in it are cultural phenomena that can only be comprehended through careful ethnographic fieldwork. The chapters in this book approach prejudice against people associated with nonnormative sexuality as a research problem in its own right, and they focus on the way that local forms of those prejudices are structured and disseminated. The goal is partly to understand how distaste, hatred, and violence are locally configured. But because the texts in this book are examples of critical ethnography, all authors also share a commitment to combating the phenomena they describe.

The problem is that the link between understanding a phenomenon and changing it is never straightforward. Constance Sullivan-Blum, for example, discusses how the resistance and vitriol that evangelical Protestants express toward homosexuality is understandable once it is realized that they have made homosexuality an icon of modernity, which is to say of all those social processes that challenge the epistemological underpinnings of a particular Christian doctrine. If, as Sullivan-Blum stresses, "for evangelical mainline Protestants the stakes over same-sex marriage could not be higher," then it will do little good for anthropologists to hope that Protestants might change their minds and become more reasonable if we share with them a sensitive cultural analysis of why they behave the way they do. In this and other cases discussed in this book, the key to change lies not in anthropologists coming to the rescue but rather on an emphasis that homophobic attitudes and practices are not completely hegemonic or unchallenged. Murray observes that many Barbadians are more tolerant of homosexuality than mainstream media discourses would lead people to believe. And Sullivan-Blum emphasizes that although they get more airtime and have more political influence and power, evangelical mainline Protestants are continually being challenged by other Protestants who argue, from a Christian perspective, that LGBT people should be accepted and welcomed by the church.

Hatred of people who are associated with same-sex sexuality is not a happy topic, and one of the reasons why this is the first anthology to discuss it is that anthropologists are still generally trained to expect to like the people with whom we work. The reasons for this are partly practical: few people would willingly choose to live for a year doing fieldwork among people they hate—or, rather, crucially, among people who hate them. But the problem is also epistemological: anthropology is rooted in a humanist legacy that extends back to Boas's and Malinowski's project of de-exoticizing primitive people. This sense of anthropology as a kind of defender of the powerless was reinvigorated most recently by the Writing Culture moment in the discipline, when the epistemological project itself was attacked from within as colonialist and self-serving. Arguably, the doubt that this criticism sowed within anthropology weakened its critical ability to engage with pernicious social forms. It is striking, for example, that until very recently anthropology has had relatively little to say about phenomena like the rise of the New Right in Europe, or of the rise of fundamentalist movements in the postmodern world; it is also noteworthy that the kind of hatred documented in this book has largely eluded substantive anthropological examination.

But at the risk of sounding a bit like Margaret Mead myself, we need an anthropology of hate. Anthropologists need to ethnographically extend the work being done by cultural studies scholars like Sara Ahmed, who in a recent book discusses the social structure of hate and explores "how hate works as an affective economy" and how it "circulates or moves between bodies and signs" (2004:60). Painful as this kind of ethnography may be to actually carry out, it has to be done if anthropology is going to have anything of real relevance to say in a world that seems increasingly to be structured by hate and fear. To accomplish this anthropology, we need to move beyond Walter Williams's well-meaning invocation of Boasian cultural uplift, and we need to engage, purposefully and actively, with the processes and forces that promote hate. We also need close analyses of demographic distribution of hate, where it is located, how it acts politically. This is why historically engaged analyses are important—we need to grasp the history of homophobic values, how they have come to emerge, spread, and signify. Moments or periods of transition are also crucial. When Cohen suggests that a shift in the portrayal and meaning of violence against people who engage in same-sex activity may be underway, when Boellstorff pinpoints such a shift and links it to changing ways through which the gendered self and the nation articulate, and when Murray discusses how globalization impacts on local economies in ways that allow corrupt politicians to portray male homosexuals as an internal "Other," we understand how homophobia becomes intelligible and salient, and how it comes to move people.

It is crucial to understand the language through which hate gets articulated. Hence the importance of interview studies like Sullivan-Blum's, in which the purveyors of hatred are allowed to talk and explain themselves. In addition, we also need an understanding of how homophobia circulates not just about queers but also among queers. This topic is one of the main subjects of Puar's *Terrorist Assemblages*, in which she discusses at length how "some homosexual subjects are complicit with heterosexual national formations rather than inherently or automatically excluded from or opposed to them" (2007:4). What the chapters in this volume contribute to that discussion are mundane but crucial ethnographic examples. So when a white gay man, using the Tagalog term that means "man with a female heart," dismisses Filipino forms of same-sex sexuality to the anthropologist Manalansan with a tart "That *bakla* thing—it is so homophobic"; or when a lesbian in Athens kicks two men out of her bar because they were kissing and is subsequently accused of homophobia, what exactly does "homophobia" mean? Can it possibly mean the same thing in those two different cases, given the racial, gendered, and classed positions of the different people who invoke the term? Who *can* invoke the term in the first place, and who is discouraged or prevented from doing so? With what right? To what effect? Finally and crucially, we need to engage in work that suggests ways of combating hatred and violence against queers. LaFont's warning that the language of human rights might not always be the most efficacious way to do this is both a solid anthropological caution about imposing Western values on non-Western cultures and an example of acute activist sensibility.

With all these studies in mind, we can reiterate the question asked by this book, "Can there be an anthropology of homophobia?," and we can answer it affirmatively. Indeed, on the strength of the chapters collected here, one could argue that there *should* be an anthropology of homophobia, an anthropology that documents hatred and violence against people associated with same-sex sexuality, that contextualizes it, dissects it, and seeks ways of combating it, even as it continually reopens the issue of what homophobia is, how it appears, what positions, subjectivities, and powers it anchors or challenges, how it circulates, signifies, moves, and works.

Notes

1 Accessed on January 3, 2005. The Westboro Baptist Church has about sixty members, most of whom are relatives of Fred Phelps, the man who founded the church. The church appears in the mass media much more frequently than its tiny size would seem to warrant because of the remarkable viciousness of its hateful messages and the spectacular ways in which it broadcasts them. For example, church members frequently picket the funerals of soldiers killed in Iraq and Afghanistan because they insist that their deaths are God's punishment for America's tolerance of homosexuality. In November 2007, Phelps and two of his daughters were ordered by a U.S. district court to pay $11 million in compensation to a father who sued the church for having picketed the funeral of his son, an American soldier who had been killed in Iraq. During the funeral, members of the Westboro Baptist church stood in view of the mourners, holding signs that

said "God Hates You" and "Thank God for Dead Soldiers" (*New York Times* October 26, 2007; November 1, 2007).

2   This conviction was later overturned by the Swedish Supreme Court, whose decision can be read at http://www.domstol.se/Domstolar/hogstadomstolen/ Avgoranden/2005/Dom—pa—engelska—B—1050–05.pdf.

3   Boellstorff also suggests that it is possible to have homophobia without heterosexism, and he offers Latin America as an example. It is difficult to imagine how Boellstorff can think that Latin America is somehow not heterosexist—even by the terms of his own definition of the concept. My own experience working in Brazil (Kulick 1998; Kulick and Klein 2003), and with the writings of anthropologists like Lancaster (1992), Melhuus and Stølen (1996), S. O. Murray (1995), Prieur (1998), and Weismantel (2001) leads me to strongly disagree with Boellstorff's conclusion and to wonder whether homophobia without heterosexism could ever actually exist in fact.

2

Homophobia at New York's Gay Central

Martin F. Manalansan IV

RECENTLY, a Euro-American gay friend returned home to New York City from a vacation to Morocco and regaled us with his escapades in bars and beaches over there.[1] After half an hour of giddy exuberant stories, his mood changed when he suddenly remembered what he considered to be an unfortunate incident. He visited a market where tourist souvenirs were sold. He was merrily shopping when he realized that people were looking at him but not in what he considered to be "typical native curiosity." Rather, he said, he felt uncomfortable when he saw some of them giggling. We were puzzled and asked if he was being paranoid in a foreign country. He adamantly said, "No way. It was homophobia pure and simple." When we asked how he could be so sure. He said matter-of-factly, "I know it when I feel it."

Homophobia has become part of the common everyday arsenal of categories among gays, lesbians, bisexuals, transgendered people, and other queers,[2] and yet it has a mercurial quality that becomes apparent depending on who is talking about or "feeling" the homophobia. Homophobia is seen as the enemy to be conquered. It is perceived as the "weapon" used by sexist and conservative quarters to further oppress gays and lesbians.[3] Therefore, homophobia is something to be eliminated or overcome. This is the reason why homophobia and its dismantling has become part of the queer empowerment agenda of queer activist groups and nonprofit organizations and is a ubiquitous item in workshop curricula as well as everyday conversations. In its typical usage, *homophobia* is an accusative term typically hurled at a person or an institution to signify the receiver as being inimical to queer interests.

Clearly, the easy deployment of the term *homophobia* has created a rather murky pool of meanings that blur if not merge into one another. Indeed, the term's seemingly fluid character has less to do with its intrinsic nature than with the undisciplined practices of wielding it. My concern in this chapter is not merely to illuminate the situation but to break down the turgid semantics. I aim to dislodge *homophobia* from its naturalized position in queer discourse by looking at its utility in transcultural situations. By *transcultural*, I mean situations or encounters that involve multiple cultures and racialized, gendered, sexualized, and classed subjectivities. I do not intend to provide a transnational framework of analysis. Rather, I am interested in the traffic of asymmetrical identities and practices in discourses on homophobia.

I argue that the term *homophobia* obfuscates racial, class, and other social hierarchies which maintain and prop up particular privileged and hegemonic groups. This is because homophobia is founded on the liberal enlightenment notion of the universal human subject who remains constant or unchanged despite shifts in sociohistorical contexts or moments (see Wickberg 2000). At the same time, this liberal conception hinges on the idea that practices around class, gender, race, and sexuality operate independently of each other.

Therefore, I submit that popular discourses surrounding homophobia fail to recognize the "intersectionality" of practices and ideas. Here, I follow the political theorist Cathy Cohen, who, in echoing feminists of the seventies and eighties, underscored the interconnections between the predicaments of marginalized figures such as the welfare queen and the lesbian bulldyke and advocated for a "broadened understanding of queerness . . . based on an intersectional analysis that recognizes how numerous systems of oppression interact to regulate . . . the lives of most people" (1997: 41; see also Hammonds 1994; Khayatt 2002).

But how does one know that one is encountering homophobia? Is it, as my tourist friend said, that one knows by the emotions that are stirred and the visceral reactions evoked? To engage with these questions, this chapter presents a critical cultural reading of persons, encounters, events, images, and ideas that are often categorized as homophobic or perceived as being imbued with homophobia. I am not primarily concerned with defining this phenomenon or even providing antidotes to it. Rather, I focus on examining homophobia as a mobile category located at the intersection of the traffic and travel of race, class, gender, and sexual identities and practices. The primary question that propels my examination is how the term's bounded and unbounded dimensions enable both its political and cognitive utility as well as showcase its limits and its dangers. I argue for not only a cultural particularist reading but a critical understanding of the crisscrossing of categories and subject positions.

Finally, I aim to depathologize homophobia and to conceive of it as a cultural product that oftentimes obscures if not veils other complex issues and problems. The pathological underpinning of homophobia has created situations and encounters where deviations from particular acceptable attitudes and narratives are labeled homophobic. I present four cases in order to critically dismantle homophobia as a master queer narrative or as pathology. These encounters are the results of my fieldwork with Filipino and other queers of color in the early to late nineties in New York City. Each case illustrates particular ways in which race, gender, class, and ethnicity complicate the easy concatenation of homophobia within that encounter. In each case, I propose to show how the inconsistencies prevalent in discourses around and about homophobia reveal their political and cultural inadequacies.

Sex or Else? Sexophobia is the Evil Sister of Homophobia

The first case involves the queer response during the closures of public-sex spaces in New York City in the early to mid-nineties. During my fieldwork, Rudolph Giuliani, then mayor of New York City, mounted a series of programs aimed at "cleaning up" and gentrifying the various neighborhoods. Samuel Delaney (1999) movingly records and critically analyzes the onslaught of neoliberal capitalist forces into the former renegade spaces of 42nd Street. Delaney convincingly shows how the various sexual spaces have given way to corporatized entertainment from Disney to the television network ABC. A queer activist group called Sex Panic, which was well aware of the detrimental process of Giuliani's "quality of life" campaign, mounted various efforts to combat this intrusion into the lives and spaces of queers.[4]

It was at this time that queer activists were clamoring for a way to express their dissatisfaction and create a rallying cry for all community members to unite around a single issue. Some activists posited the right to public sex as a foundational freedom that queers should not be denied and that all queers should fight for. As part of the politicization process, the term *homophobic* was used as an accusation against queers who questioned, disagreed, and/or hesitated in agreeing with the public-sex issue.

Most importantly, these recalcitrant queers were seen as not only homophobic but sexophobic, abnormally fearful of public sex, which in turn made them inimical to the "cause." What is clear is that this was a political move to get everyone on the public-sex bandwagon as well as a stage for labeling and locating groups and individuals within the political spectrum (for example, conservative vs. progressive). Therefore, public adherence to the issue of public sex became the defining element, at least for this encounter, of homophobia and, by implication, sexophobia.

The equation between sexophobia and homophobia is not altogether new. Martin Kantor (1998:13), in his study of homophobia's pathology, declared: "Many homophobes are basically 'sexophobes,' who have a negative feeling about all sex, gay or straight. Sex makes them anxious, or they find it revolting. To a degree, sexophobia is not abnormal. Many people seem to find some aspects of sex inherently anxiety-provoking, or even 'disgusting,' especially after their sexual excitement is over, taking with it the alchemy that turns physical dross into emotional gold. . . . But some individuals, straights and gays alike, are abnormally sexophobic. They find all forms of sex much more frightening/revolting than they actually are." This statement contradicts an earlier statement Kantor makes in his book about the pathological nature of all homophobes. If indeed homophobia is always and already pathological, and by implication all homophobes are sexophobes, who gets to decide normality? Where is the dividing line between the "normal" and the "abnormal"? How much fear is too much? Yet these questions seem irrelevant in the face of how accusations of homophobia and sexophobia create conflicting and ambivalent dilemmas in the lives of queers. For the gay public-sex political movement, the dividing line was based on one's political conviction concerning public sex without regard to other complicating situations. An African American gay man I interviewed during this time said: "Okay, I know that Zone DK [a gay sex club in Manhattan] and other sex clubs are being closed. I used to go to Zone once in a while, but I am not all that convinced that fighting these closures is the way to go. There are other battles we need to fight—being able to suck dick outside my house is not biggest issue for me. But why should I be accused of being homophobic? So, I disagreed with other gay guys over this—and all of a sudden I'm afraid of sex? And I'm homophobic? Where are we—Stalinist Russia?" This man's rather strong allusion to Stalinist dictatorship illustrates to a certain degree the one-sided and ironically oppressive nature of homophobic discourse within the queer community. The fact that one sector of vocal members of the community can accuse and label the rest as "abnormally" phobic creates a contradictory situation. Why are some queers in the business of pathologizing the rest of their community? More importantly, what does this process of pathologizing people and ideas, as practiced by the vocal and loud few, disregard and distort?

Power inequality in the queer community is always a volatile issue and is usually hidden from public discussion. However, in this specific case, the discourses of homophobia and sexophobia unraveled the structural elements at work. This power asymmetry is evident in terms of who gets to hurl accusations of homophobia at specific sectors of the queer community. For example, I observed several instances when queers of color objected to this particular agenda. For many of them, the agenda was presented without thinking about who gets to prioritize and even set up such issues. As one queer of color observed:

> This public-sex debate is really just one part, a small part of the really big issues. Why can't we discuss about which of these issues is more important? I am so afraid to speak up being one of a few people of color in the meetings. And the mere fact that you question the issue and not swallow it hook, line and sinker make you public enemy number one. Actually, it is either you are with us or you are homophobic. And sex-phobic. Me? I am about as positive about sex as the next guy but who the hell made these queens the voice of the community? Who got to crown them? Not me! And finally, what makes them think that by getting those sex clubs back we can solve many of our problems? People of color have tons of problems and why should having sex in the street be the one we fight for? What about the poor? What about immigration? And what about rac-

ism? Yeah, let's think about that for a minute and stop being the horny queens that we are . . . and think, what about all these other things?

At one public debate at the New York Lesbian and Gay Community Center organized by Sex Panic and held during the mid-nineties, one white activist actually harangued the queers of color in the audience that they should support the public-sex issue because it was a "fact" that the New York City police arrest more people of color than other groups. While this activist was supposedly making a case for the connection between racism and homophobia on the part of police and other authorities, he was unable to listen to views demurring from what he thought was a rational (if not moral) cause. What was left unexplained was why getting back the public-sex venues would benefit queers of color and alleviate racism. There is nothing on record indicating that more people of color frequent public-sex spaces or are arrested for being in these spaces. People of color are arrested for a wider array of criminal charges beyond being in public-sex spaces. While I discuss the problems of intersectionality between race and homo-phobia more extensively in the third case below, it is clear that the use of race in this situation was fairly facile and uncritical. Many of the queers of color I interviewed about this topic saw the public-sex debate as divided across racial and class lines with white gay middle-class activists leading the cause and people of color standing on the sidelines.

This situation raises the pivotal question of the gaze or the I/eye that is able to see or "feel" the homophobia. This question also arises in the next two cases. Often, homophobia is seen as a condition of a person or a thing, but what is seldom analyzed is that homophobia is part of a discursive formation with not only an object but a subject who sees, hears, and feels. In this specific situation, then, the subject is situated in a particularly privi-leged social and economic location though projecting an oppressed predic-ament. By virtue of this combined privilege and performed oppression, the male white middle-class subject is able to fix homophobia as a static politi-cal tool by anchoring it to a discourse on normality. In other words, those in the most vocal sector who hurl the accusations of homophobia are in a position to portray their specific sexual practices, rituals, and spaces as the norm. By situating themselves in a gay political mainstream, white middle-class activists are able to force those who disagree and/or hesitate to con-form or be pushed to the queer political and cultural fringe.

"Coming Out" to/of Homophobia

Whereas the public-sex debate signaled the dangers and limits of discourses about homophobia in the public political arena in the queer community, I now shift the discussion to a more intimate, if not what is stereotypically considered as private, realm, the coming-out narrative and its relationship to discourses about homophobia. Stories of coming out are narratives of unveiling, fleeing, and discarding homophobia. Indeed, the closet is constructed from the timber of homophobia-tainted temporal and spatialized emotions, ideas, and situations.

Coming-out stories are often couched in terms of their narrators' emergence from the dismal condition of homophobia—their own and that of the people around them. This process of emergence entails having to face and engage the dangers of hostility and hatred from mainstream society. Homophobia exists on both sides of the closet, but homophobia in this case is bifurcated into two unequal instances: the internalized homophobia among queers and the homophobia of the nonqueer "others" or the straight heteronormative population are popularly conceptualized as related but separate forms. The queers' internalized homophobia is seen as a consequence of the latter. However, in practice, these homophobic formations are not always clear-cut.

At the same time, the process of coming out is seen as a movement toward some form of authenticity, a higher level of awareness, and most importantly an attainment of social and cultural legibility. In other words, coming out is often seen both as a process and a state of awareness of the particular order of things. A person who comes out usually narrates this process as a shedding of one's own homophobic tendencies, at the same time becoming more cognizant of the dangers of homophobia that proliferate in the world.

The construction of the coming-out narrative, its cultural specificities, and its problematic relationship with discourses on homophobia were highlighted in one specific fieldwork incident. In the 1990s, I participated in a group discussion in Kambal sa Lusog, a Filipino queer group located in New York City. Composed of immigrant and second-generation Filipino American lesbians and gay men, Kambal sa Lusog was formed as a social and political group. Typically, disagreements during the discussion were often seen in terms of immigrant versus U.S. born. But a specific discussion about homophobia and coming out that became rather heated actually brought the two camps together.

One Filipino gay man who was born and raised in the United States started complaining about his mother. He said that while she has taken his coming out as a gay man rather calmly, she never asked him about his social life or about the man he was seeing. He also recounted that even after meeting his boyfriend, his mother has not really made it a habit to inquire about what is going on with his relationship. Toward the end of his story he sighed and said he was "resigned" to his mother's homophobia and blames it on the fact that she is an immigrant and would never assimilate into a Western or American way of life.

The group members looked at one another. One articulate Filipina lesbian who was also born and raised in the United States started to chide this young gay man. She said, "What makes you think that her silence is homophobic? Just because she has not asked you about your boyfriend does not make her any less or any more caring. Besides, what makes you think that by assimilating into 'American' habits, she will be a better person—or even a less homophobic person?"

Through nodding and softly whispered words, a good number of people showed their agreement with the lesbian's counterargument. A Filipino immigrant gay man said that the lesbian was right about the idea of silence. He asked the young man, "What were you expecting her to do? How did you want her to behave?" He went on to say that this young man could not see beyond the more overt signs of acceptance and he further suggested how short-sighted it is to take silence as a sign of hostility or even homophobia.

Elsewhere I have analyzed the meanings and the discursive dimensions of silence in Filipino culture.[5] However, I did not really consider how in another way silence itself signals homophobia apart from overt violence or visible hatred. But it was apparent to many immigrant and second-generation members of Kambal sa Lusog that silence could also signal the absence of homophobia and may be a strategy for communicating with one's children about sensitive topics such as sexuality or even for expressing emotions. Therefore, silence, which has popularly been imbued with overdetermined and excessive homophobic underpinnings in the mainstream, may also signify more positive meanings in transcultural encounters.

However, I would argue that this is not a simple case of cultural misreading or miscommunication. The Filipino young man not only deemed his mother's silence as homophobic nonacceptance; more importantly, he applied a popular American interpretation for the correct public performance of both coming out and of acceptable nonhomophobic behavior. The crucial lesson here is how the meanings behind coming out and homophobia have calcified to such an extent that any deviation from the script is suspect or, worse, homophobic.

A parallel case involves cross-dressing Filipino queer immigrants, who, in many sites and spaces in the queer communities, are often seen as embodiments of Orientalist exoticism and anachronism. One of the Filipino queer cross-dressers noted: "I know that when I go out in drag, people see me as this little Miss Saigon. Not just a gay man in a dress, but an Asian man who is 'of course' effeminate. The [mostly white and privileged] Chelsea boys have fun staring at me yet do they think I am one of them?[6] I would not think so."

In the same way that the next case I discuss here focuses on the construction of cross-dressing queers of color as premodern, these queers are branded as homophobic and sexist. These cross-dressing queers are seen by other members of the LGBT community as self-loathing since their gender-crossing appearance conforms to mainstream society's negative stereotype of all gay men. However, gender-crossing behavior, including drag, is often considered tasteless and an anachronous practice by many gay men. Cross-dressing queers are also often accused of being misogynists because they are seen to exaggerate and/or parody female attire and behavior. While I have extensively discussed the complexities of this dilemma in my book *Global Divas* (Manalansan 2003), for this chapter's purposes I am arguing that these Filipino cross-dressers are victims of the reification of a particular combination of behaviors and ideas that middle-class queers term as homophobic. Filipino queers in these instances can be seen as being guilty of not conforming to a mainstream script or normalized performance of gayness.

These events from my New York fieldwork mirrored in a different way a particular event in my recent field trip to Manila, where I met a white American gay expatriate. When I asked him about how he felt about gay life in Manila, he shrugged and said it was okay but there was something that irritated him. He admitted that the nightlife was quite colorful but that there was a persistent attitude toward gayness that he found unsettling, one having to do with the idea of gayness as being gendered feminine. He was troubled by the fact that people expected him to act "nelly"; he acknowledged that he was a little "swishy," but that did not mean he was less of a "man." I explained to him that this can be seen in terms of the Tagalog term *bakla* as a "man with a female heart," which is sometimes erroneously translated as "gay." He said, "There's the problem right there. You [meaning Filipinos] need to divest yourselves of these old-fashioned ideas. It's the twenty-first century—get with the program. That *bakla* thing—it is so homophobic!"

As in the previous case with New York Filipino queers, this American gay expatriate rendered homophobia as a failure to conform to acceptable authentic queer or gay behavior (which sounds like an oxymoron). These transcultural encounters that I have discussed reiterate this hegemonic arrangement whether in public political realms or in private intimate ones.

Don't Rain on My Parade!

The two cases about Filipino queers are analogous to another situation I encountered in teaching gay and lesbian history and culture to members of the gay and lesbian community as part of the Center for Lesbian and Gay Studies community outreach program. I coordinated a gay and lesbian reading group in a now defunct gay and lesbian bookstore in the Chelsea neighborhood. The topic for that evening was George Chauncey's book *Gay New York*, which chronicles the development of community among gay men in the city before Stonewall. The discussion was especially lively as there were older members of the group who could still remember the time that Chauncey was writing about. One older woman in her seventies reminisced how it was a major feat for her to walk the streets of the Upper West Side wearing pants.

The discussion took another turn when we were discussing the chapter on fairies. Fairies, according to Chauncey, were men who occupied an "intermediate sex" and who presented a feminine or feminized persona. One of the younger white men in the group said something to the effect that these people "do not represent me." I then asked him what he meant by "these people." He replied that he meant transvestites, transgendered people, drag queens, and cross-dressers. He said, "I work in Wall Street. I live a relatively quiet life but you know what most people think when they think gay? They think of a drag queen skipping down the street." He said that this image is widely disseminated in every Gay Pride Parade when all the newspapers print photos of cross-dressing, scandalously behaving queens instead of the "typical" and masculine-looking men in other parts of the parade.

Other people joined in the discussion, mostly to agree with him. However, I was struck by the fact that in this group of mostly white queers the only nonwhite person other than me was a black woman. It was this woman who, early on in the discussion, had tried to clarify whether the gay Wall Streeter was talking only about gender-crossing behavior. Most people did not pick up on this. Unfortunately, the discussion was cut short as the meeting was ending.

To my mind, the black woman was pointing to an issue that is often relegated to the background, that of race and gender. Indeed, the newspaper pictures that the Wall Streeter mentioned were not merely of drag queens but primarily of drag queens of color. What the black woman was pointing out is that we do not often see gender in isolation from other identities. Even more provocative is the idea that gender-crossing behavior (like that of the Filipino queers), when performed on colored bodies, provokes other forms of hostility and anxieties that cannot be contained merely as homophobia or even "trans-phobia."

In talking to the woman after the discussion, we both agreed that in the minds of these gay men and women, drag queens of color are, like the chapters in Chauncey's book, located in pre-Stonewall temporality. That is, drag queens of color are embodied history as well as anachronistic relics of premodernity. What do we make of this kind of hostility? Can it just be racist attitudes filtered through gendered lenses? Or is this another case of internalized homophobia?

I would argue that accusing the Wall Streeter of internalized homophobia is too easy and, in fact, extremely egregious. What this kind of accusation does is to cleanly pigeonhole this gay man's behavior as being antagonistic to gender nonconformity alone. At the same time, this typical practice repeats the damaging habit of separating identities and behavior as if they exist independently of each other, thereby seeing problems and solutions in narrowly discrete and artificially segregated terms. Consider the following passage by Byrne Fone in his historical analysis of male homophobia in the West: "Indeed, homophobia remains nearly untouched by other battles fought against social and religious hostilities, against racism, against sexism, against prejudice itself. It is contested, but it is still unconquered" (2000:184). While Fone's study contains useful information about violence against women and queer people of color, race and gender are not pivotal nodes in his analysis. Rather Fone suggests they are epiphenomenal and subject to other more important forces of history. Fone is not alone in this matter, as so many studies of homophobia treat this phenomenon as a discrete *thing* in itself and not a product of crisscrossing gendered, racialized, sexualized, and classed interests, forces, and subjectivities.[7] It is this key theme that fuels my final and rather polemical thoughts on homophobia.

Beyond Pathology: Homophobia
through Cultural Lenses

I must reiterate that the four cases I present in this chapter do not in any way suggest that hatred and violence against queers do not exist in the world. I do not deny the existence of these negative and horrible acts and ideas and I am equally vigilant in proposing the eradication or creating a vigilant stand against them. However, I offer more than a word of caution. I propose that we move away from the casual pathologizing of people and groups under the sign of homophobia. It is indeed paradoxical that queers—as part of the 1990s intellectual and political movement against the insidious process of societal normalization—should unwittingly reproduce this same process in their activism and everyday discourses. Pathology has been used against queers for a very long time, but we need not reify it in order to escape its chains.

The four cases have illustrated what I believe are persistent themes and issues around discourses on homophobia. First, it is clear that there are huge limitations in the deployment of homophobia as a label in political maneuvers within the queer community. Indeed, there is no "pure and simple" homophobia. Second, we need to recognize power inequities in the deployment of the label and the use of the discourses around homophobia. Who is the knowing eye that sees and feels? Third, we need to recognize that these transcultural moments or situations that I have used as cases are not rare idiosyncratic episodes, rather, as we live in an increasingly globalizing world, we will encounter how identities and subjectivities move and cross boundaries. Apart from cultural miscommunications, the other more pressing issue is how specific liberal political terms and labels that queers use to authenticate and verify a sense of belonging can no longer hold. Moreover, issues of authenticity and belonging under the aegis of homophobia forces us to ask questions about who is able to access particular cultural and economic resources. As I have suggested above, in the case of queers of color this kind of authenticity can signal, if not reinforce other forms of difference and marginality.

Daniel Wickberg (2000:57) in his trenchant analysis of the cultural history of the idea of homophobia suggests that it was established on the grounds of a liberal dream of a prejudice-free world and on a "model of normal personhood based on notions of personal growth, capacity for self-objectification, cosmopolitan tolerance for any beliefs that are not 'dogmatic,' and a refusal of authority and tradition." Clearly, "other natives" and queers of color that I have alluded to in this chapter are unable to reap the benefits of this enlightened idea and fall short of becoming the non-homophobic liberal subject.

In the face of all these conditions, I strongly urge the dismantling of the constellation of meanings around homophobia. Instead, queer cultural and political activists need to construct alternative discourses that dislodge and displace homophobia from its hegemonic position as an umbrella term for everything that is distasteful to queer speakers. In other words, we need to find a better language, a new set of semantics to adequately capture the intricate politics around queer lives. However, it may not be possible to find the ultimate silver bullet and this language of future may not totally escape the traps of the present one, but we must remain vigilant in mapping out the complex intersections that characterize discourses about homophobia to combat violence and injustice by pointing to possible discursive limitations as well as potentials for broad based change and transformation.

Notes

I thank David Murray for being a patient and rigorous editor. The Comparative Queer Studies reading group at the University of Illinois, Urbana-Champaign has been a haven, a "safe space," and an oasis for the discussion of ideas and for social camaraderie. Special thanks to Ricky Rodriguez, Siobhan Somerville, and the fabulous faculty in the Asian American Studies Program. This work is dedicated to my father.

1   My terminology involves using *gay* for those who identify as such and to signal the hegemonic role of gay in LGBT communities. I use *queer* sometimes as a rubric for LGBT as well as to signal the inadequacies of other identity categories and to carry on the work of queer theory against normalization.

2 Again, my use of *queer* here is to expand the limitations set by *gay, lesbian*. or *homosexual.*

3 See Pharr 1988 for use of this kind of metaphor. See DeCecco 1985 for a sensitive and broadly based schema for investigating homophobia. See Tully 2000 for an empowerment perspective.

4 I want to make it clear that I am not offering a definitive historical account of this moment but rather a mediated construction and understanding of it as seen through the eyes of my queer of color informants.

5 See Manalansan 1994.

6 Chelsea is the neighborhood in Manhattan that was and still is "gay central" for a particular and popular kind of white gay mainstream culture.

7 Roderick Ferguson (2004) calls this phenomenon where identities are parsed out into independent stable units as the "ideology of discreteness." It enables liberal activists to focus on specific issues such as gender or sexuality without regard to other intersecting identities.

3

"It's Adam and Eve, not Adam and Steve"

What's at Stake in the Construction of
Contemporary American Christian Homophobia

Constance R. Sullivan-Blum

THE DEVASTATION following Hurricane Katrina, according to some Protestant voices in the United States, was punishment for New Orleans' famous tolerance of homosexuality.[1] This type of antihomosexual rhetoric is the dominant media representation of some powerful branches of American Protestantism. Accepting this as an inevitable aspect of Christianity, however, does an injustice to the variety of discourses present in American Protestantism. Homophobia is not an essential facet of Christianity but a carefully structured web of social control based on a specific epistemology. It is imperative to critique the production of antihomosexual rhetoric in order to make visible the contradictions and power struggles among American Protestants over this issue. By understanding antihomosexual discourse this way, it is possible to imagine its end.[2]

Nowhere are the contradictory discourses about homosexuality more evident than in the mainline Protestant debate over same-sex marriage. Mainline Protestant denominations are important sites in which to explore American constructions of sexuality because their adherents represent a broad range of theological perspectives, from biblical literalists to theological liberals. The mainline denominations are large, powerful institutions that historically have represented American "civil religion." As such, they have acted as arbiters of social values in the United States. Mainline churches have built their credibility on an educated clergy and are marked by an ecumenical stance toward other denominations and faiths. They include the United Methodist Church (UMC), the Episcopal Church, the United Church of Christ (UCC), and the Presbyterian Church among others (May 1983; Roof 1982; Roof and McKinney 1987). Mainline Protestant churches are in contrast to fundamentalist denominations that reject ecumenism, adhere to a literalist reading of the Bible, and intentionally distinguish themselves from the mainline. Examples include the Southern Baptist Convention and myriad independent Baptist congregations.[3]

Until the emergence of the women's movement and the lesbian, gay, bisexual, and transgendered (LGBT) equal rights movement in the 1970s, mainline American Protestant theology had consistently imagined a rigid gender dichotomy, with heterosexual marriage arising from the natural order as revealed in the Bible. Research that examines the formation and meaning of right wing movements in the United States, such as Ginsburg's *Contested Lives* (1989), amply demonstrates the ways in which the transformation of gender expectations were identified by some Christians as the principal conflict inherent in the social values and economic trends of late modernity. For instance, Ginsburg argues that the battle over reproductive choice emerged in response to the substantially different ways of constructing "female gender identity" that became available at that historical moment (1989:110).

This insight can be generalized to the current contest over same-sex marriage. Claiming moral equivalency for same-sex couples displaced the naturalized heterosexuality which mainline Protestant groups had formerly held to be central to human relations. In response, antihomosexual rhetoric among some mainline Protestants, like anti-abortion activism, intensified in the late twentieth century. In this chapter, I examine the ways that same-sex marriage has come to represent the epistemological challenge of modernity to the concept of the unique revelation of scripture in mainline Protestant churches.

This research is based on participant-observation in churches located in upstate New York from 1995 to 2000. During that time, I attended church services in three congregations: United Church of Christ, Episcopal, and United Methodist. I also went to Bible studies, adult education sessions, and discussion groups that centered on the controversy of the LGBT movement in their churches. I read church memos and newsletters and newspaper articles; I subscribed to religious magazines; and I listened to Christian radio programs like *Focus on the Family* and *The Gospel Hour*. Finally, during the year 2000, I interviewed sixty-four people, forty-one of whom were ministers of local mainline denominations in and around a small, postindustrial city in upstate New York.[4]

A total of eighteen research participants, including both lay people and ministers, actively opposed the equal rights movement of LGBT Christians in their churches. This group referred to themselves as "evangelicals." Frequently, the term *evangelical* is used to describe autonomous denominations which, like fundamentalist churches, ascribe to biblical literalism. Evangelicals are distinct from fundamentalists in that they explicitly adopt strategies based on contemporary cultural trends to proselytize nonbelievers. For example, national evangelical ministries have famously developed TV variety and news shows and local evangelical churches frequently host Christian rock concerts, while many fundamentalists consider these activities evil. Like fundamentalists, evangelicals insist on a "plain reading" of biblical texts that they think are obviously intended as teachings or as historical accounts. In contrast to fundamentalists, however, some evangelical groups value rigorous biblical scholarship of disputed texts yielding a more historically contextualized interpretation of scripture. Their hermeneutic, therefore, can be subtle, and controversial texts are often informed by an appreciation of ancient literary styles and cultural practices (Jorstad 1993).[5] Many theological distinctions between the two groups, however, are less distinct. Ultimately, most evangelicals and fundamentalists agree that homosexuality is sinful and that same-sex marriage would be detrimental, even catastrophic, to American society.

But the term *evangelical* is not applied just to denominations. Individuals also call themselves "evangelicals" and are found in a variety of church settings including the mainline Protestant denominations. The eighteen evangelicals I interviewed were members of mainline denominations.[6]

In contrast to the evangelical participants, I interviewed twenty-three people who actively promoted the inclusion of LGBT Protestants in their churches. Unlike the evangelicals, they did not utilize a specific label to represent their theological and social positions. Because the progressive connotations of liberalism in terms of privileging rationality, individualism, and democratic principles were consistent with the character of the group (as were the failures of liberalism, including a tendency to ignore and depoliticize difference) I have labeled this group "liberals." Despite the fact that the liberal mainline Protestants had a less cohesive identity than the evangelicals, there was tremendous uniformity in their theology and epistemology.[7]

It became clear to me over the course of my research that both evangelical and liberal participants in the mainline denominations agreed that the debate over same-sex marriage was a pivotal moment for the future of mainline Protestant theology and practice. With its claim to rationality and an empirically based knowledge system, modernity threatens the epistemological underpinnings of biblical literalism in Protestant doctrine (Ammerman 1991; Marty and Appleby 1992; Armstrong 2000). For reasons discussed throughout this chapter, homosexuality has become the icon of this epistemological threat.

"Homophobia" as an Analytic Concept

The use of the term *homophobia* to represent the attitudes of my study group is problematic. The participants in my research referred to "homophobia" consistently, either by denying that they were homophobic or by accusing others of being homophobic. As outlined by Kulick in this volume, the concept of "homophobia" was introduced into the psychological literature in the early 1970s. It characterized the "homophobe" as mentally ill rather than the "homosexual." This reversal sparked a new, medicalized discourse around antihomosexuality that normalized same-sex erotic desire. However, it also served to depoliticize and individualize antihomosexual behavior and obscured heteronormative structures rather than challenging them (Kitzinger 1987; Wickberg 2000).

An additional problem with the term *homophobia* is the implication that homophobes harbor an irrational fear of homosexuals. Most evangelical Protestants I spoke to are not afraid of homosexuals; rather they believe that homosexuality is sinful and must be rejected as morally wrong. In extreme instances, some may be so fixated on the threat of same-sex eroticism to their ontological and epistemological frames that they in fact fear homosexuals. Once again, however, the psychological roots of this fear are less salient for this discussion than the social structures and discursive fields from which they emerge. Furthermore, privileging the rhetoric and practices of evangelical Protestants who are labeled homophobic renders invisible heterosexual Protestants who advocate for the inclusion of LGBT Protestants in their denominations as well as LGBT Protestants themselves who are acting as agents in their churches.

The term is nonetheless the most frequent descriptor of antihomosexual language, behavior, and theology used by the individuals and groups I spoke with, and thus it is unavoidable. LGBT Protestants employ it to describe their experiences of rejection in their denominations. Liberal Protestants employ it to describe evangelicals in their denominations and nationally. Evangelicals use it when distinguishing their opposition to homosexuality from a hatred of homosexual people. As it is, then, the backdrop against which all discussions about homosexuality in American Protestantism occurs, I will continue to use it (with the above caveats in mind) throughout this chapter.

Historical Context

Antihomosexual rhetoric, behavior, and doctrine among contemporary American evangelical Protestants are not essential features of Protestant theology. Rather, they are a response to the epistemological challenges of the social upheavals of late modernity. In American Protestantism, the epistemological danger was first heralded not by gender and sexuality but by the debate over evolution, which precipitated the establishment of early-twentieth-century fundamentalism (Lawrence 1989; Ammerman 1991; Armstrong 2000).[8] Anti-evolution fervor culminated in the Scopes trial of 1925, which epitomized the struggle between science and scripture (Lawrence 1989; Armstrong 2000). Despite the fact that Scopes was convicted, the trial was a public embarrassment to the fundamentalists, who retreated from public activism for the next fifty years (Lawrence 1989; Ammerman 1991; Armstrong 2000; Harding 2000).

After World War II, the epistemological struggle in American Protestantism began to reemerge. The war had deepened the despair over the dream of human progress and sharpened the edge of criticisms against the optimism of modernity. Beginning in the 1950s, a movement which came to be known as the "new evangelicalism" used popular television programs and dynamic preachers like Billy Graham to bring biblical literalism back into the mainline churches (Roof and McKinney 1987; Ammerman 1991; Jorstad 1993; Lienesch 1993).

During the 1960s and 1970s, the mainline denominations became increasingly polarized. Liberal Protestants became vocal and active in social justice issues such as the antiwar movement. At the same time, evangelicals sought to take the message of personal salvation to the world, beginning at home. In the mid-twentieth century, conflicts between liberals and evangelicals in the mainline centered on the ordination of women, reproductive choices, and the regulation of sexuality, including premarital sex, divorce, and homosexuality (Roof and McKinney 1987; Hunter 1991; Lienesch 1993).

As Ginsburg (1989) points out, contests over abortion, and by implication all these social issues, have as much to do with a critique of modernism as they do with preserving a conservative social order. In the same-sex marriage debate, evangelicals are resisting, albeit inchoately and inconsistently, the extension of scientific discourses into the domain of Christian morality. Liberals, on the other hand, see themselves as leading the culture into expanding definitions of inclusion based in part on what they understand as the scientific revelation of human nature. The historical shift described by Foucault (1978), in which discursive power over the meanings assigned to the body moved from the church to the domain of scientific discourses, has been incomplete and uneven. At the time of my fieldwork, same-sex marriage had become the primary locus of debate in American Protestantism, thus leading to threats of permanent schism within various denominations (Roof and McKinney 1987; Hunter 1991; Lienesch 1993).

The Stakes for Evangelical Mainline Christians

Repeatedly, those participants opposed to same-sex marriage claimed that their objection was not primarily about any cultural repulsion toward homosexuality but about the authority of the scripture and its ramifications for the construction of knowledge. A United Methodist pastor stated, "The battles are not just over homosexuality. The key issue is epistemology. How is one's belief structure derived? This is about one's view of the source of revelation. Does the Bible have continuing authority or not?"

Despite denials by some of the participants, evangelicals obviously do contribute to and generate antihomosexual rhetoric. Several evangelical

Protestants gave me books by fundamentalist authors like Tim LaHaye that explicitly describe homosexuality as sinful and pathological. This discourse is generated to mark a clearly defined epistemological and ontological boundary that, according to writers like LaHaye, is threatened by the relentless march of modernity and its attendant values (or lack thereof).

If liberals in mainline denominations are able to advance the argument that LGBT couples can be legitimately joined in marriage, evangelicals argue that the authority of the scripture is undermined. If scriptural authority is undermined then there will be no way to establish a claim on "timeless truth" (Lawrence 1989; Ammerman 1991; Marty and Appleby 1992; Armstrong 2000). The evangelical insistence on a "timeless" epistemology based on divine revelation through scripture resists the modernist discourse of scientific logic. This is not to say that evangelicals subscribe to a premodern epistemology that disregards science, but rather that they refuse to accept scientific discourses as having ultimate authority over meanings and values assigned to the body and its practices.

If the shift away from biblical truth claims is completed, evangelicals fear the loss of an epistemological stability that comes from knowing how to map their relationship with God. In the words of one minister, "Secular society gave up the cultural idea that we are a created people responsible to transcendent norms. Now everything is a matter of opinion. Everything is relative. There is no arbiter of morality." Knowing that "we are a created people," according to some of the Protestants I spoke with, means knowing that God designed men and women in complementary opposition (Nugent and Gramick 1990; Lienesch 1993; Gavanas 2001). In this way, the evangelical epistemological mooring is directly connected to the ontological realities of gender established in the creation narrative. One participant told me that it is not homophobia that makes evangelicals resist same-sex marriage but the scriptural revelation of the order of creation. She said, "I'm not denying homophobia [exists] in the mainline though it is not visceral. I know people who are gay or lesbian. But theologically and according to my worldview, [heterosexual] marriage is central to my faith. From Genesis to Revelations marriage is an icon of God and God's people. It is not peripheral. It is an image of God's relationship with humans as 'The Other.' Representing this is the otherness of male and female. This otherness is rooted in nature. It is the physical reality of male and female bodies doing what they are meant to do including having the potential for procreation."

The evangelicals argue that sexual responsiveness and desire are structured through and determined by gender (Lienesch 1993; Gavanas 2001). In this regard, they are not unlike many liberal and LGBT Christians. But they construct a much more rigid gender dichotomy and employ it as the basis for a discourse which posits heterosexuality as the only natural and morally acceptable sexual expression. Male and female attributes are imagined by evangelicals as natural, biological characteristics, constructed in complementary opposition to each other.[9] This not only provides the underpinnings for obligatory heterosexuality; it also provides the logic for monogamous, heterosexual marriage (Rich 1980; Lienesch 1993). Men are understood to be sexually aggressive and naturally promiscuous. Women are, on the contrary, understood to be sexually passive and biologically programmed to be nurturing (Rubin 1984; Ginsburg 1989; Lienesch 1993; Gavanas 2001). Sex in marriage, therefore, is imagined as the glue that keeps men and women together (Ellison 1993; Graf 1999). It creates a stable family unit. As one evangelical Episcopalian woman told me,

> There are enormous differences between men and women's sexuality. Feminists have spent thirty years ignoring those to the detriment of women. Women are emotionally relational. This accounts for the differences between homosexual men and lesbians. Lesbians are relational and are not prone to compulsive, anonymous sex like homosexual men. I am dealing in stereotypes here, but men have a powerful, enormous desire to have sex. Women want that and they desire a long-term relationship. Women have a powerful impulse for marriage and family. Men need a powerful motivation to make a lifelong commitment to women. When marriage is the only legitimate place for sexual expression men are motivated to stick around and raise the kids together.

As evident from her words, heterosexual intercourse in marriage is understood as the root of family stability.[10] Arguably, in American culture, sexual intercourse symbolizes the "enduring, diffuse solidarity" believed to be embedded at the heart of the nuclear family (Schneider 1980:52). The complementarity of gender as it is expressed in sexual intercourse is endowed with multivalent meanings. Heterosexual intercourse in this discourse is the bringing together of two halves to make a whole (Nugent and Gramick 1990; Gavanas 2001). For many of the evangelical Protestants with whom I spoke, the complementarity of gender reflects the wholeness of the image of God. They argue that God created male and female in His image and that heterosexual intercourse in its proper context (marriage) recreates that wholeness (Gavanas 2001).[11]

The theologian M. Hellwig characterizes this as the "classical myth of sexuality" which proposed that "God has created people according to a blueprint which is written in their bodies, in their anatomy; they are made to operate in a certain way, and when they operate in that way, their mission and purpose is fulfilled" (Nugent and Gramick 1990:34). According to this view, the inherent naturalness of heterosexuality was written on the body; it was evident in the fact that men and women fit together and are able to reproduce (Rubin 1984; Lienesch 1993; Gavanas 2001). In this logic, maleness and femaleness are ontological realities and heterosexuality is God's design for wholeness, a wholeness that reflects the nature of God. As one UCC minister said, "The proscription of homosexuality is not just mores or taboos. It is an accurate portrayal of God's design. Gender was created with complementarity. This is self-evidently obvious. It's how things work. Like electrical equipment, you don't put two male ends and two female ends together."

Same-sex erotic relationships, according to this discourse, cannot produce wholeness because the two halves are the same. Since there is no difference to generate meaning, the relationship lacks the power to create a "greater totality" both between the lovers and in terms of procreation (Weston 1991:137). As one evangelical participant said, "How can two men and two women together be whole?" Same-sex unions merely replicate the partners and result in narcissistic sexual behavior not unlike masturbation (Rubin 1984; Weston 1991).

In summary, for the evangelical Protestants I interviewed, the stakes over same-sex marriage could not be higher. Reconfiguring marriage to legitimate same-sex couples disrupts the authority of scripture. It threatens the centering of heterosexual marriage in the interwoven epistemology and ontology of the doctrinal Protestant worldview as expressed in the United States.

Liberal Counterdiscourses

As noted above, antihomosexual rhetoric is not the only discourse present in American mainline denominations. There are numerous individuals and groups arguing for the acceptance of LGBT people and same-sex marriage.

Liberal mainline Protestants evoke scientific discourses that naturalize and essentialize homosexuality in order to claim that God ordained it as well as heterosexuality. These discourses represent an epistemological stance that is central in the battle for the control over leadership of mainline Protestantism in the United States.

In liberal mainline traditions, scripture is considered "co-equal" with reason and tradition and is not privileged above them (Roof 1982; Lawrence 1989; Spong 1996; Crew 1997; Armstrong 2000). The epistemological stance of liberal Christians is based on the Enlightenment principles of reason, science, and the progressive, cumulative nature of knowledge. All the liberal Protestants I interviewed expect that secular, scientific knowledge will inform their Christianity rather than threaten their faith (Roof 1982; Spong 1996). While they revere scripture, they also believe that one must synthesize biblical knowledge with Church tradition, personal experience, and reason (Shepard 1987;, Spong 1994; Spong 1996). Being free of scriptural literalism permits liberal Christians to claim a more fluid, responsive relationship with the Divine because they are not bound to preserve the special epistemological status of scripture. They explicitly reject the notion that the canonical scriptures contain the complete and final revelation of God's nature and His relationship with humanity.

The majority of the liberal participants, both lay people and ministers, argued that the Bible was "the primary Word of God but not the only Word of God" or that it was "important but not inerrant" since it was a culturally and socially situated text. Many research participants argued that the word of God was not fixed with the canon of scripture because "the Holy Spirit continues to reveal Truth today." Or, as another participant put it, "I try to see the Bible in terms of what it meant to the culture in which it was written . . . and apply them to our culture . . . the Bible is the Word of God, but I see the Word of God as many things. I see the Word of God as Jesus. I see the Word of God as that part of God in you that speaks to me and that part of God in me that speaks to you. I see the Word of God as a quiet voice that no one can hear. [The Bible is] the Word of God, but it's not something to be applied literally and it's not the only Word of God."

Many of the research participants referred to the theological notion of Jesus as the Living Word of God to describe the continuing revelation of God in their daily lives. One woman said, "I follow the Word of God. Jesus is the Word of God and He never said anything about homosexuality." Jesus, they claim, is a living presence in their lives and their daily interactions continue to provide new insights into Divine will. As one Episcopal priest said, "Jesus is the revelation of God for me . . . [and] revelation is an ongoing process."

The liberals privileged the sayings of Jesus in the gospel over other scriptural texts. Frequently, I was told that since Jesus didn't think sexual orientation was important enough to comment upon in the gospels, there was no Christian basis for the condemnation of homosexuality. As one UMC minister put it, "My position is that whatever Jesus said goes double for me," implying that since Jesus said nothing about homosexuality, His silence is doubly meaningful as well.[12] A similar point was made when I was handed a brochure at a rally with printing on the front cover that said, "Turn the page to see what Jesus said about homosexuality." The inside of the brochure was blank. Homosexuality, liberal participants argued, was only brought up in the New Testament by Paul in his epistles, the implication being that this says more about Paul's prudishness than it does about God's condemnation of homosexuality.

This epistemological shift away from privileging scripture other than the Gospels is represented by their rejection of anti-homosexual rhetoric. They resent what they see as the fundamentalist monopoly on the representation of Christian attitudes toward LGBT people. One research participant said, "I can just remember . . . seeing Jerry Falwell interviewed outside of the church when [Matthew Shepard's] funeral was going on and [saying] . . . that [homosexuality] was sin. I was just horrified that this person represents Christianity and gets a public hearing on that. It just makes me really upset. I just get really tired that we allow this to be the portrayal of Christianity." During my research it became clear that liberal Protestants see themselves as providing a spiritual and an epistemological alternative to fundamentalism.

Additionally, liberal Protestants claim that homosexuality is a state ordained by God. They employed naturalizing discourses about sexual orientation that claim that homosexuality is fixed at birth, immutable, and at least partially biologically determined. Discourses that construct aspects of human social life as natural render them beyond human agency and control (Douglas 1983; Tsing 1995; Yanagisako and Delaney 1995; Franklin 1997). They use the argument that homosexuality is biologically determined and a part of the natural order to claim that an individual cannot help being gay or lesbian and is not required to change.[13]

The liberal participants repeatedly claimed that science and their own personal experience indicated that homosexuality is, in the words of one participant, "part of the natural order of creation." As one minister put it, "My judgment is that [homosexuality] is innate—something we're born with . . . because we all know that in this society lesbians [and] gays . . . are ostracized. Why would somebody want to choose to be ostracized? A very strange choice especially when it's as much as 10 percent of the population, maybe more. Why would that large of a population be choosing to be ostracized?"

They state that God's design is progressively revealed by science and found in nature (Lawrence 1989). Naturalizing homosexuality, therefore, makes a claim on both scientific rationality and the divine purpose of God. Framed by scientific epistemology, homosexuality is rendered explainable, functional, and inalterable. Accordingly, the liberal mainline participants are able to argue that the homosexual is an acceptable human variation, part of God's plan for human sexuality (Thumma 1991). Following liberal theological principles of equality and justice, same-sex couples cannot properly be denied access to the rites of marriage (Coontz 1992; Tronto 1993; Fortune 1995; Robb 1995; Spong 1996).

The bottom line for the liberal participants was that because of His love for humanity, Jesus would accept homosexuals into the church. All Christians should behave like Jesus. This understanding of the centrality of love (as taught by Jesus) to the Christian ethic overrides all other considerations for liberal mainline Protestants. As one minister told me, "I'd like to see myself as a little bit like Jesus and stand up for those who don't have somebody to stand up for them."

Furthermore, they argued, Jesus befriended the pariahs of His culture. If homosexuals are the pariahs of American culture, then it is a Christian's duty to follow the example of Christ and befriend them. The mission of the contemporary church, according to liberal participants, should be to become "a church where there are not outcasts." In the words of one lay informant, "The conservatives think we're denying the scripture. . . . I'm not disregarding scripture. I'm not violating scripture. I'm taking a look at scripture in its context. Not in my context, in its context. I feel I'm more orthodox than a conservative [is] because orthodoxy is . . . the original truth. I'm going back to the original truth. Not the one that we have developed because of changes in society and inaccurate translations. I'm going back to the original truth."

Mainline liberals I interviewed claimed an authentic Christianity because they behave the way Christ would behave toward LGBT people and therefore have a greater claim on "the original truth" of the gospel. This "original truth" has less to do with the chapter-and-verse heuristics of evangelicals and fundamentalists than with a commitment to liberal principles, privileging science and rationality over tradition and scripture, which naturalizes homosexuality and allows liberals to claim that God ordains it. Liberals make these linkages in an intentional effort to provide an alternative to fundamentalism.

Given these views, liberal Protestants deemphasize the use of scripture as an ethical guide, as it is only one of several necessary considerations including reason, personal experience, and science. The appeal to science by itself, however, is not adequate in formulating Christian sexual ethics. Scientific discourses do not by themselves control the way liberal Christians assign meanings to the body. The power of God must still be evoked. By asserting that science reveals an essential, natural homosexuality which is created by God, it follows that liberal Protestants must provide access for LGBT Christians to rites such as marriage in the name of justice and mercy.

Conclusion

If homophobia in mainline Protestant churches in the United States is constructed as monolithic and inevitable, the forces at work within these churches to combat it are rendered invisible. It is necessary to examine the production of knowledge about gender and sexuality in mainline Protestant religion and to examine the participants involved in the production of this discourse. If antihomosexual discourses are simplified, individualized, and depoliticized, the discourses of dissent and change that are already present within Protestant churches are disempowered (Mason 2002). Attending to the diversity within Protestant religious communities allows us to see homophobia as a historically situated, culturally constructed, and contested phenomenon, which is therefore open to social change. Liberal mainline Protestants are among the agents of that change.

The apparent tenacity of American Protestant homophobia can be explained by how much is at stake for evangelical and fundamentalist Protestants in the religious debate over the affirmation of homosexuality. American Protestantism has been grappling with competing epistemological models that have shifted over time. It has debated the ramifications of a scientific worldview, focusing at times on human evolution, the ordination of women, human sexuality, and reproduction. Visceral antihomosexual rhetoric among evangelical Protestants is the current means of marking epistemological boundaries in the rapidly shifting (and, for them, threatening) social terrain that is modernity. Simultaneously, there are Protestants arguing for the acceptance of LGBT people who are employing discourses which attempt to integrate or navigate between what most would assume to be competing epistemologies of scripture and science. Homophobia therefore cannot be considered a timeless or inevitable feature of Christianity but rather a culturally specific response to power struggles over the role, place, and significance of American Protestantism in late modernity.

Notes

1   See http://www.jeremiahproject.com and http://www.repentamerica.com for examples of this sentiment.

2   It is necessary to briefly distinguish between the antihomosexuality rampant in some contemporary Christian discourse and the episodic persecution of sodomites in Church history. Both Roman Catholic and Protestant churches had historically persecuted sodomites. Sodomy, however, was a general term that at various historical junctures included heretics and idolaters as well as people who engaged in same-sex erotic acts (Greenberg 1988; Vance 1989; Keiser 1997). Furthermore, as it is legally constructed in the United States, sodomy is not exclusively defined in terms of same-sex sex acts but also includes oral sex (between heterosexuals) and possibly even heterosexual sex with a condom (which could be defined as "unnatural" sex). In contrast with the contemporary notion of a homosexual identity, the sin of sodomy did not require a specific category of person. Due to the human predilection to sin, anyone could be tempted to sodomize just as anyone could be tempted to lie or to steal. The distinction between sodomy and homosexuality indicates that sexuality was mediated by historical and cultural factors (Boswell 1980; Katz 1983; Greenberg 1988; Vance 1989; Davies 1997; Keiser 1997).

3   Fundamentalist denominations and congregations are diverse and it is beyond the scope of this chapter to explore the complexity of their positions. However, mainline and fundamentalist perspectives exist in opposition to each other. Each frequently makes derogatory references about the other and claims historical and spiritual authenticity for itself (Lawrence 1989; Ammerman 1991; Hunter 1991; Marty and Appleby 1992; Jorstad 1993; Lienesch 1993).

4   While I interviewed both lay people and ministers for this research, I did not find

any significant difference between the groups relative to these issues. The significant differences pertained to the participants' theological identification on the liberal-evangelical axis.

5   For instance, in the 1980s, when I first became involved with evangelical groups, the story of Sodom and Gomorrah was frequently used to condemn homosexuality. While I was doing this research, however, none of the evangelicals even mentioned it. In the ensuing twenty years, the biblical story of Sodom and Gomorrah had become controversial. Evangelicals took scholarship on the tale seriously and no longer consider it one of the proof texts prohibiting homosexuality; in fact, there are now numerous debates concerning what the sins of the populace of ancient Sodom actually were and/or what they represented. However, fundamentalists continue to evoke it as evidence that God "hates" homosexuality. Many evangelicals currently see the Genesis creation story as metaphorical rather than historical. This permits them to accept scientific explanations of human origins while simultaneously advocating the moral relevance of the creation of Adam and Eve in the Garden.

6   While all the evangelicals I interviewed opposed same-sex marriage, it is important to note that there is a diversity of opinions among evangelicals on LGBT rights in their denominations and on the emphasis on conformity regarding human sexuality in Protestant theology. For instance, Peggy Campolo, a prominent evangelical, famously supports same-sex marriage while her husband, the Rev. Tony Campolo, does not. He argues, however, that other issues such as the war in Iraq are much more relevant to Christian morality. (See htttp://www.bridges-across.org) Nonetheless, evangelical discourses such as these are in the minority.

7   The remaining twenty-three interviews were self-identified LGBT Protestants. Space limitations do not permit me to explore their contributions. Because the debate over the inclusion of LGBT people in the American Protestant movement is the site where liberal and evangelical Christians make competing claims for an epistemological model, LGBT Protestants have an especially unstable and highly charged relationship to religious discourse. For a more complete discussion, see Comstock 1996; Fulkerson 1997; Gorman 1997; Long 1997; Yip 1997; Rodriguez and Ouellette 2000; Constantine-Simms 2001; and Sullivan-Blum 2003.

8   Evolution continues to be debated in the United States. Some evangelical groups attempted to legislate teaching "intelligent design," which opponents argue is a thinly disguised form of creationism, in the public school science curricula.

9   Evangelicals very frequently refer to the dominant gender and sex binary as rooted in biology. By grounding their argument in biology, they are naturalizing normative roles and evoking the power of God in and over creation.

10 This quote highlights the similarities between evangelical discourses on homosexuality and those of the anti-abortion activists discussed in Ginsburg 1989. For instance, it is clear that the speaker believes that women's interests are served by harnessing the irresponsible and irrepressible promiscuity of male sexuality to

the family through marriage. Legitimizing same-sex relationships, therefore, is damaging to women and to the family because it unties sex from reproduction and men from women. Similarly, the anti-abortion activists Ginsburg worked with felt that legalizing abortion essentially gave men permission to be sexually promiscuous and left women with the consequences.

11   The capitalization of "Him" and "His" in reference to God and Jesus throughout this chapter is based on standard Christian textual convention but implies nothing further in terms of my own personal or scholarly stance toward divinity. The reference here is to the creation narrative in Genesis that reads, "And God created man in His own image, in the image of God He created him; male and female He created them" (Genesis 1:27, New American Standard Bible).

12   This is referred to as the "argument from silence" and is highly contested by evangelicals. As one evangelical minister told me, "Jesus didn't say anything about pedophilia either." For a discussion of the problems with the "argument from silence," see Greenberg 1988.

13   Not all the discourses in American Christianity that naturalize homosexuality are used to make the claim that one's sexual orientation is ordained by God. The Roman Catholic Church, for instance, takes the position that homosexuality may be an inborn trait while still being sinful. This position is taken by a small number of evangelicals as well.

4

The Homosexualization
of Pedophilia

The Case of Alison Thorne and the
Australian Pedophile Support Group

Steven Angelides

ON NOVEMBER 5, 1983, less than a year after the infamous raids and public furor in the United States surrounding child pornography and the pedophile group the North American Man/Boy Love Association (NAMBLA), the Delta Task Force of the Victoria Police raided the Australian Pedophile Support Group (PSG).[1] With a dedicated thirty-strong police contingent, Delta simultaneously stormed a house in Melbourne, arresting seven men, and apprehended one man at his place of work (also in Melbourne) and a ninth man at his home in Sydney. All nine men were gay, and police alleged that the group was part of an international child pornography ring and the largest group of child exploiters in Australia. The men were charged with "conspiring to corrupt public morals." Two of them were also charged with a number of other offenses, including the use of premises for the sexual penetration of a child, the actual sexual penetration of a child, the possession of prohibited imports, child stealing, the manufacturing of child pornography, and gross indecency (*Sydney Morning Herald* 1983:2; *The Advertiser* 1983:1).

In both Sydney and Melbourne, crisis talks among gay and lesbian rights campaigners were held. Wary of what they perceived at the time to be a familiar cultural and rhetorical association of homosexuality with child seduction and molestation, activists agreed that, in spite of competing views in the gay community regarding the issue of pedophilia, the groups would nonetheless denounce both the police tactics employed by Delta and the use of antiquated and draconian conspiracy charges (Carr 1983–1984:6).[2] The spokesperson for the Gay Legal Rights Coalition, Alison Thorne, gave an interview to Mike Edmonds of Melbourne's 3AW radio later that week. In the interview she condemned the arrests of the PSG members, foregrounding the fact that most of the men were charged not with actually organizing, photographing, or engaging in the sexual penetration of children but merely with talking about issues relating to pedophilia. Thorne argued that this was an infringement of an individual's civil liberties and right to freedom of speech. She also, in the course of the interview, expressed personal opinions regarding age-of-consent laws. Were it not for the palpable rise in cultural homophobia in all Western countries in the 1980s, the events that followed Thorne's interview would almost defy imagination. Shortly after her comments were made public she was persecuted on the front page of Melbourne's *Sun* newspaper and by radio talk show hosts, hounded by other national and state newspaper syndicates, sued by the radio personality Derryn Hinch, and removed from her position as secondary school teacher. By any estimation this was, as we will see, a homophobic trial by media.

This chapter situates the case of the PSG and Alison Thorne in the broader context of rather profound social and political changes occurring in Australian, and indeed Western, societies in the 1980s with regard to sexuality in general and homosexuality in particular. At the same time as a powerful child sexual abuse movement was emerging to challenge the problem of child molestation, a right-wing lobby had also begun mobilizing in an effort to challenge homosexual rights campaigns. These movements converged around not only the volatile issue of children and sexuality but also the perceived threat posed by the figure of the child molester or seducer. This chapter argues that the media, police, and antihomosexual right-wing groups successfully manipulated this political climate and in doing so cleverly homosexualized the emergent and salient figure of the child molester, transforming him into a heteronormative construction of the pedophile. This served, on the one hand, I will suggest, to deflect attention from the fact that child sexual abuse had been exposed as a problem endemic to forms of normative male heterosexuality and, on the other, to halt the advancing campaigns for homosexual equality.

Delta Probe: From Street Kids to Pedophiles

"All the hard work has paid off—it has worked out as well as we could have hoped for," the head of the Delta Task Force, Detective Senior Sergeant Neil Comrie, told a newspaper reporter from the *Sun* after arresting the nine Australian PSG members in November 1983 (Vadasz 1984:5). "Operation Delta" is said to have begun its campaign in October 1982. Comprising eleven members, the task force was reportedly set up after eight top-ranking members of the Victoria police force viewed the documentary *Street Kids* a month earlier. The documentary is a rather grim real-life portrait of alienated and homeless youth in the area of Fitzroy Street in the Melbourne suburb St. Kilda, a place notorious in the 1980s for drug addiction and prostitution. About the documentary, Rob Scott, one of the makers, said, "The intention was to look at real kids in real situations . . . and to get their perspective of the world around them, the sorts of things they had to go through to survive." The sorts of things Scott is referring to, and which are glaringly and depressingly depicted in the film, are drug taking, heroin addiction, child prostitution, youth alienation, and homelessness. Most who previewed the film, including the eight top-ranking police officials, responded with horror and disbelief: "Their response once they had absorbed the shock," recalls Scott, "was 'what can we do?'" Similarly, he recalls the horrified responses of two social workers who also previewed the film. "They just freaked out. One initially reacted by bursting into tears. The initial reaction was one of revelation. But the considered opinion was 'this film should not be screened.'"

The following year the operations of the Delta Task Force hit the headlines. On March 30, 1983, the *Sun* published a front-page report by police roundsman John Silvester. A full-page image of Senior Sergeant Comrie looking disturbed while checking files on child vice in St. Kilda accompanied an article titled "The Kids on Our Streets: 'Delta' Probe Shock" (Silvester 1983:1–2). The article went on to detail "widespread child prostitution and pornography rackets in St Kilda." Delta, it said, "has discovered sexual use of children by adults which has disgusted police": "Police believe as many as 150 boys and girls aged between nine and 16 are involved in prostitution in the area. . . . The head of the Delta task force . . . said police feared one of the boys might be murdered by a sexual deviant" (1). The *Sun* story "spread like wildfire" (Vadasz 1983:5). A string of articles appeared in local and interstate newspapers and the issue received extensive coverage on television news and radio programs. Even a public meeting attended by approximately 1,000 people was held at the St. Kilda town hall in order to confront the social problem. However, in a scathing critique in the gay magazine *Outrage*, Danny Vadasz argued that the "media, abetted by the police force" had insidiously "redefined the problem." They had effectively shifted the focus of attention away from the multiple issues of youth alienation, homelessness, poverty, drugs, and prostitution highlighted in the film *Street Kids* and redirected them primarily toward those of child prostitution and pornography. Vadasz went on to point out how *Outrage* had interviewed the *Street Kids* filmmakers who said that they had not come across anything suggesting the scale of the problem outlined in the *Sun* article. They had also conducted their own research with sex workers and self-identified pedophiles and found that the youths involved in prostitution were invariably aged between fifteen and twenty and, far from totaling around 150 workers, constituted roughly only a "floating population of about 30–40" (Vadasz 1983:5).

Notwithstanding the accuracy of either Comrie's or Vadasz's accounts regarding the extent of child prostitution in St. Kilda, the one thing that is clear is the front-page report and the police responses that followed did much more than raise alarm and incite widespread community and media concern. The whole campaign, culminating in Delta's raid on the PSG, ultimately laid the groundwork, as we will see, for the displacement of the broader problem of "street kids' in St. Kilda into a problem of predatory homosexuals and homosexual pedophiles.

The raid of the PSG, code named "rockspider," headlined in the media and was heralded as not only the "biggest of its type in Australia" (*Sydney Morning Herald* 1983:2; *The Age* 1983:1), but also "the most successful police offensive ever launched against the sexual exploitation of children" (*Sydney Morning Herald* 1983:2). In what was proclaimed as both a national and international coup, newspapers reported that PSG was the Australian satellite of the international organizations, the British Paedophile Information Exchange and the North American Man/Boy Love Association. This provided the Victorian police force, as one *Age* report noted in an article the following year, with "tremendous kudos" (Wright 1984:10). However, that same *Age* report was in fact an exposé of the operations of Delta leading up to the PSG raid. The raid was the culmination of a one-man Delta infiltration of the PSG, brought about after Delta observed an advertisement for PSG in the gay press. The advertisement read: "Australian Paedophile Support Group. A NSW-based organization set up to provide a supportive mechanism for gay men and women, throughout Australia, attracted to or in relations with children. More information, in confidence, from the Gayline" (Wright 1984:10). Delta apparently employed Stephen John Mayne, a South Melbourne public servant, to infiltrate the group as a pedophile named Greg Daniels. After writing and arranging to visit the Australian Gay Archives for information on pedophilia, Mayne was given the phone number of a PSG member in Sydney, whom he subsequently visited. He discussed the possibility of setting up a Melbourne support group and was put in touch with a Melbourne man who had already been planning to do this. Wired with a microphone and radio transmitter, Mayne attended the inaugural twelve-strong meeting of the Melbourne group, and four more meetings after that. According to the *Age* report it was clear from the transcripts that Mayne had been attempting to entrap the PSG members. During a discussion of age-of-consent laws, Mayne asked, "In Sydney, do you sort of introduce other peds to kids and this sort of thing, or is it strictly just a meeting type?" One member responded in no uncertain terms: "Introducing people to kids and so on, I personally think that that's out, as far as we're concerned. I think as far as people with like interests and so on, I think that's the whole purpose, but I think once we start to act as sort of a recruiting centre for kids, I think we would really be up shit creek." While one of the members did offer tips on how to acquire a boyfriend by "flashing," as he had done, that same member responded impatiently at the same meeting to another of Mayne's comments, "Look, let's get this quite straight. This organization, the PSG, does not supply boys." At the November 5 meeting Mayne opened the front door and some eighteen policemen entered. All men in the meeting were charged with "conspiring to support and actively encourage one another to participate in acts of sexual penetration with persons under the age of 16 with intent to debauch and corrupt public morals and create in their minds inordinate and lustful desires" (Wright 1984:10).

It was apparent that the police had very little in the way of evidence, and the charges of conspiracy to corrupt public morals were most likely invoked as a politically expedient means to legitimate Delta's actions and to further their own reputation and antipedophile agenda. The police and prosecution hoped to exploit mounting community intolerance of child sexual abuse and pedophilia in this time of enormous public concern about child sexual abuse across the entire Western world. The child protection lobby and child sexual abuse movements had become incredibly powerful and successful forces in bringing the problem of child sexual abuse to public and government attention (Olafson 2002). They had successfully reversed the twentieth-century tendency to blame victims of sexual assault and had challenged the view that children were capable of providing meaningful consent in intergenerational sexual encounters (Summit 1983; Angelides 2004).

During this period, feminist activism in Australia had also begun to challenge the expression of male power through sexuality. Campaigns against not only child sexual abuse but also rape, sexual harassment, and pornography had highlighted the unequal and oppressive relations of power structuring society and organizing the genders and generations. With the passing of affirmative action and equal opportunity legislation, a critique of forms of normative masculinity and male sexuality had been initiated (Mason and Chapman 2003).[3] Importantly, child sexual abuse was exposed as a problem endemic to the patriarchal nuclear family and to hegemonic rather than marginal or deviant forms of masculinity and male sexuality (Angelides 2004). The critical spotlight, in other words, was placed squarely on the roles, behaviors, and beliefs of men in general rather than those of isolated groups of aberrant male deviates, as it had been earlier in the century. Elsewhere I have argued that this transformation of gender relations triggered a "crisis" of normative masculinity, one masculinist response of which was to seek out negative models of manhood to attack and scapegoat for the problems of child sexual abuse (Angelides 2005). The PSG occupied this site of negative masculinity.[4]

In spite of this shift in cultural and community attitudes around questions of gender, sexuality, and sexual power, the case against the PSG never made it to trial; at a committal hearing it was thrown out of court for reason of insufficient evidence. A defense barrister himself later suggested that the police and prosecution had more than likely "banked on having the case committed for trial by jury" in order to exploit shifts in community attitudes: "If it had gone to trial, I think it would have been very hard to defend a charge of this nature, given current community attitudes towards child molestation and towards paedophilia" (Wright 1984:10). While the gay press reported this as "the first success in the Melbourne gay community's campaign to have the self-appointed morality squad, officially known as the Delta Task force, disbanded" (Vadasz 1984:5), the whole incident signaled a rather insidious and irrevocable development. Not only had the Delta probe aroused widespread public anxiety and tapped into international fears about pedophilia; it had also, far more problematically, linked homosexuality and pedophilia more closely, by highlighting cases of homosexual pedophilia and downplaying those of heterosexual pedophilia. The homosexual pedophile was being cast as a negative model of manhood. Gay groups had frequently bemoaned what they perceived to be a widespread historical and rhetorical association of homosexuality with child seduction or molestation. However, this was in significant ways different from the rhetorical association of homosexuality and pedophilia that was now emerging. The close relationship between the terms *homosexuality* and *pedophilia* is reflected in dominant psychomedical research of the period. The tendency of psychiatrists and psychologists at this time was one of grouping child sexual abuse offenders into two categories: "regressed" and "fixated" types (Groth and Birnbaum 1978; Howells 1981; Finkelhor 1984; McConaghy 1993).[5] In this schema, fixated offenders are those who profess an exclusive sexual preference for young boys, while regressed offenders are those with a supposedly "normal" sexual preference but who are "situationally induced" to have sex with children. The infamous psychiatrist Neil McConaghy, known in the late 1960s and 1970s as an expert in aversion therapy as a cure for homosexuality, summed up the general rule of thumb: "Men who have a history of offending against girl children could all be considered as regressed, and homosexual pedophiles and hebephiles are fixated" (McConaghy 1993:312; see also Howells 1981:78).[6] Thus it was the homosexual offender who was identified as the "real" pedophile.

It is certainly the case that the PSG did themselves no favors by closely aligning their pedophilia with their gayness. Indeed, we might say that they unwittingly contributed to the homosexualization of the pedophile, in spite of the efforts of gay groups and activists in the late 1970s and early 1980s to dispel the link between homosexuality and child molestation and to insist on subtle distinctions between incest, child sexual abuse, and homosexual pedophilia. "Incest and pedophilia are two totally different issues, and should be treated as such," argued Jody Emerson in the magazine *Gay Community News* (GCN) (Emerson 1982:30–31). At the same time, gay activists had been urging communities and governments to consider lowering the age of consent. Even Gareth Evans, then senior lecturer in law at the University of Melbourne, was reported in the *Australian* newspaper in 1976 to have called, somewhat uncontroversially, it seems, for a lowering of the age of consent to fourteen at a national convention of the Council for Civil Liberties.[7] Such calls were a familiar theme in liberationist discourses of the 1970s. Gay groups in particular had often framed such calls more radically as an extension of earlier gay liberationist critiques of the patriarchal nuclear family, which they argued oppressed not just women but children. As Graham Willett declared in GCN in 1981, "The nuclear family is inherently oppressive of the child with the power relations skewed irreversibly in favor of the parents and particularly the father" (Willett 1981:24). Or in an issue of GCN dedicated to gay and alternative parenting in early 1982, Bruce Sims proffers the not uncommon but more vociferous gay liberationist rejection of the nuclear family as an oppressive institution: "So the theory needs restating. Again and again. Couple relationships are a disaster area, marriages are catastrophic and raising children in a nuclear family is a hell hole" (Sims 1982:26). However, with the rapid rise of the child sexual abuse movement and critiques of male sexuality and power, it was increasingly difficult to sustain subtle distinctions both between children and adolescents and between concepts of pedophilia and child sexual abuse (Angelides 2004).

It seems to me that the Delta operations marked a significant turning point in Australian society regarding acceptable attitudes toward issues of child sexuality and intergenerational sex, in both mainstream and gay community discourses. When the PSG released a press statement on November 14, 1983, it was one thing for them to claim that the Delta "accusations have been based on a total non-understanding of . . . the function of the support group" (Carr 1983–1984:6). An argument about freedom of speech and organization outside a context of recruitment of children was at least palatable, as the judge's decision on their committal hearing showed the following year. However, when the group insisted on the possibility of childhood sexual agency and the relationship between gay and pedophile identity and then tried to claim for themselves the status of an oppressed minority, they were treading on very dangerous ground indeed: "These accusations have been based on a total non-understanding of what a pedophile is. . . . The press has assumed that there can be no consensual sexual activity between children and adults. . . . As with women and other oppressed people, consciousness-raising groups have been important for pedophiles. Their support has been instrumental in establishing a gay identity for pedophiles" (Carr 1983–1984:6). The issue of pedophilia, and its relationship to gay identity, had already become a hotly contested issue in gay and lesbian communities in the few years leading up to the PSG raid. While many supported consensual intergenerational sex, many took the now dominant line and rejected it outright. Members of Melbourne Women's Liberation were vociferous in their condemnation of any propedophilia position and rejected the liberationist claim that pedophilia is an important challenge to the oppressive institution of the nuclear family: "The nuclear family is the site of patriarchal power, i.e., the unquestionable domain of 'father-right' over sexual access to women and children. The demand for sexual freedom for 'paedophiles' does not represent a withering away of the nuclear family, but the extension of the right of the father to all men" (Alliance of Revolting Feminists 1984:12–13). The national homosexual conference at the University of Queensland in 1984 was also rocked by a debate over whether to allow the PSG to hold a workshop on pedophilia. Revealing how volatile the issue was becoming, the Queensland premier, Joh Bjelke-Peterson, who was supported by the outgoing opposition leader and other MPs, as well as the University Senate, tried to ban the conference. The conference organizing collective first voted against the workshop, as a minority of the members opposed it, and then reversed its decision due to objections from other gay groups interstate. Interestingly, the dissenting minority members themselves hinted at this shift in social and cultural attitudes, even in the gay community. They claimed that their decision was not based on an ideological position on pedophilia as such but on the present political climate. They argued that a publicly announced pedophile workshop in the current climate in Queensland would jeopardize both the conference and the Brisbane gay community (Outrage 1984:5). While the political climate in relation to homosexuality has often differed markedly in Queensland from that of other Australian states, it is clear that the issue of pedophilia and its relationship to homosexuality and homosexual politics was becoming a volatile political issue in ways that it had not been just a few years earlier. This can be explained in large part, as I have noted, by the rather profound shifts in cultural and community attitudes in Australian and indeed Western societies more generally with regard to the issues of intergenerational sex, normative masculinity and male sexuality, and child sexual abuse. In spite of the case being thrown out of court, the conflation of homosexuality and child molestation, a long-standing myth and concern for gay groups, had received extensive public circulation. As we are about to see, enter gay activist Alison Thorne, and the community debates about homosexuality and sex education and the homosexuality and pedophilia equation would be irrevocably imprinted on the public imagination.

Alison Thorne, Decriminalization, and the
Sex Education Debates

When Alison Thorne, spokesperson for the Gay Legal Rights Coalition, weighed in on the debate about the Delta raid of the PSG in her radio interview on 3AW, she became the subject of a media and government frenzy. Her comments had, perhaps somewhat inadvertently and dangerously, brought together within the same frame of reference a number of community anxieties that had been bubbling away since the late 1970s with regard to the decriminalization of homosexuality, the age of consent, and sex education for secondary school children. Beginning in the late 1970s, campaigns for decriminalizing homosexuality in Victoria and New South Wales were gaining momentum. With the passing of the bill to decriminalize homosexuality in Victoria in December 1980 and the debating of similar bills in NSW throughout the 1980s until decriminalization in 1984, the issue of homosexual equality with regard to age-of-consent provisions and the effect these might have on sex education programs had been controversially debated. Community and parliamentary concern was sparked by the fear that if homosexuality were to be treated as a valid, alternative lifestyle, impressionable youth might be exploited and recruited into that lifestyle by pedophiles and homosexual teachers at a critical time of adolescent ambivalence.[8] One petition to the NSW Parliament made the connection plain and simple: "Legalization or decriminalization . . . would imply community approval and acceptance of these unnatural acts, and would encourage public solicitation of adults and particularly children in leisure and recreationary areas as well as schools and other educational institutions" (Hansard 1982:2231). Many thus feared a slippery slope from decriminalization to homosexual sex education to the seduction of children. Responding to the publication of a controversial sex education booklet, *Young, Gay, and Proud*, in which the central message was that homosexuality is "an equally valid form of expression to heterosexuality" (Jaynes 1998:2), MP Jeff Kennett (later premier of Victoria) sounded a common community refrain: "I am not opposed to homosexuality between consenting adults in private. . . . I am certainly opposed to such people trying to convert others to their own lifestyles" (Jaynes 1998:4). By "others," Kennett was obviously referring to children, and the homosexual/pedophile equation was unquestioningly instated.

When Thorne spoke out against the arrests of the PSG, the media frenzy and parliamentary debate that ensued immediately dovetailed with this fear of predatory homosexual pedophiles. During the interview, Edmonds had asked Thorne, "Alison, can you understand the feelings of, I would suggest, the large majority in the community who have children, the feelings that they would bear towards pedophiles?" to which she attempted to hint at a distinction between sexual exploitation or harassment and pedophilia: "I can understand people's feelings from the point of view that they have a lot of misconceptions and I don't think that a lot of the things that the media are doing really helps terribly much. Because pedophiles really care for children. Pedophiles would absolutely abhor child . . . abuse of children, are really concerned about consent" (Fih and Bunbury 1983:3). On the issue of consent, Edmonds inquired, "Does a child know about consent?" "I believe children are in a position to consent and it depends on the definition of the child," responded Thorne. "What the media has been talking about is people aged between 10 and 16 and I believe that those people are capable of consenting." In response to a further question about whether she would like to see the age of consent lowered or dropped altogether, Thorne said, "I believe that age of consent laws in themselves are reactionary things" (Fih and Bunbury 1983:3). The interview ended when the recess bell went off at the school where Thorne was teaching. Thorne had been speaking from a public phone that teachers were instructed to use to make personal calls. Appalled by the fact that a secondary teacher could hold such views, and determined to incite community rage, a 3AW radio presenter, Derryn Hinch, edited and replayed parts of the original 3AW interview on his radio program the next day, saying: "I was appalled to hear yesterday just after I came off air, appalled to hear an interview with Mark Edmonds. . . . An interview with one Alison Thorne from the Gay Legal Rights Committee. She was blaming the media, can you believe it, for pedophiles' bad public image" (Fih and Bunbury 1983:3). At the end of his broadcast, Hinch declared, with amazement and disgust, "Well there, you heard the recess bell. The woman expressing those views about the rights of kids to have sex with adults, the woman expressing those views, Alison Thorne from the Gay Legal Rights Committee, is a school teacher. In fact she is a teacher at Glenroy Technical School and I tell you I would not want, I would not let that woman teach my child" (Fih and Bunbury 1983:3).[9]

The media pounced on Thorne's comments. A front-page *Sun* article featured the blaring headline "SEX-AT-10 TEACHER OUTRAGE" (Robinson and Wood 1983:1–2). Sufficiently distorting the content and intent of Thorne's discussion, the article began by saying that "parents and MPs yesterday reacted angrily to a woman teacher's call to lower the age of consent for sex to 10." The article went on to outline the appalled responses of the minister for education, Robert Fordham, opposition spokesperson for education Walter Jona, and parents. "No person who blatantly advocates that it is acceptable for children to be the subjects of sexual acts with adults should be entrusted with the legal responsibility of educating children," Jona lampooned in Parliament. The education minister himself found the comments "tactless and repugnant," as did a concerned parent who was quoted as saying they were "revolting" and that "all the parents feel the same" (Robinson and Wood 1983:1). Outside Parliament, Jona told reporters he would be shocked if the government refused or was unable to guarantee moral protection for schoolchildren or safeguard them from unacceptable sexual influences such as Thorne's: "If departmental regulations do not empower the minister to act as the community would expect him to act, the minister should change the regulations" (Robinson and Wood 1983:2). Whether or not the minister of education had legal sanction to act in the manner implicitly suggested by Jona was, at this stage in the controversy at least, not a matter of concern. On November 12, 1983, the director-general of education, Dr. Normal Currey, in collaboration with Fordham, removed Thorne from her teaching position and transferred her to an administrative position. *The Age* ran another high-profile article, "Sex Talk Teacher Taken from Class," in which Fordham defended the move on the grounds of parental reaction to media reports. "This step is necessary," he said, "because of the importance of maintaining the trust and confidence that are such vital elements of the parent-teacher-student relationship. Ms Thorne's *reported* public statements, her use of a school telephone number as a contact point for statements and the subsequent strong reaction from parents at the school have all placed her in an extremely difficult position" (Fih 1983:3; emphasis added).

What ensued was an extremely lengthy battle for Thorne in an attempt to get reinstated. Despite a favorable decision by the Education Department's Committee of Classifiers to post her to Tottenham Technical School for the 1985 school year, Thorne again found herself at the mercy of an intractable education minister. After the announcement of Thorne's appointment was reported in *The Sun*, Fordham himself announced that she would "not be taking up the appointment." He made the announcement with at least the tacit approval of Premier John Cain, who told a press conference that Thorne was "not an appropriate person to be put before a classroom" (Outrage 1985). Thorne then lodged a complaint with the Victorian Equal Opportunity Board (EOB). On November 6, 1986, the EOB ruled that Thorne had indeed been discriminated against and ordered that she be reinstated to a classroom in a technical school from a list of ten schools that Thorne herself would provide (Equal Opportunity Board 1987:7).[10]

Just when the matter seemed to have been resolved, an even more extraordinary turn of events occurred. The government vowed to do more than simply appeal the decision in the Supreme Court. Not satisfied with awaiting a decision on the appeal and unwavering in their belief that Thorne's views made her an unacceptable educational influence on children, Premier Cain declared that he was prepared to legislate to keep her and others with views like hers out of the classroom. A government spokesperson told the press that the wording of the legislation would refer to "public disquiet on sexual matters relating to children" (*Melbourne's Star Observer* 1986b:1). All the major political parties backed the government's proposed legislation. The Liberal Party spokesperson on education summed up the almost uniformly held position when he told the media that Thorne's views on the age of consent and pedophilia made her unacceptable for a direct teaching role with children (*The Advertiser* 1986). Underpinning the concerns of MPs and parents was the unmistakable homosexual/pedophile equation. This was a fear of potential homosexual pedophilic seduction or manipulation posed by gay sex educators, a form of recruitment of impressionable children to the homosexual "way of life" or worldview. It had been unequivocally articulated in the ongoing sex education debates that were animating many Australian states as a result of the various campaigns to decriminalize homosexuality. It also reflected a local instance of one of the many ways in which the signifier of child sexuality was being steadily erased in the early to mid-1980s. For the basis of the proposed legislation, the Teaching Service (Amendment) Bill, was to enable the forcible transfer of any teacher—in particular those responsible for sex education programs— espousing views on children and sexuality that could be deemed unacceptable to community standards (Hansard 1986:3022–3028). In a community context where the hegemonic view held that no child of any age could consent to sex with an adult, what this meant was that one of the underlying functions of the legislation was to disavow the very conjunction "child sexuality." That the Melbourne Gay Teachers Group had been such an influential and controversial force in the Victorian Teachers Union in the late 1970s only added weight to the apparent necessity of the Teaching Service (Amendment) Bill.[11]

Only a matter of hours before the second reading of the Teaching Service (Amendment) Bill in the Victoria Parliament, a deal was struck between the Victorian government and Thorne. The government agreed to withdraw its appeal to the EOB ruling and remove the certification that prevented Thorne from teaching in exchange for the replacement of the clause requesting Thorne to provide a list of ten secondary schools from which the Education Department was to find one to accept her. While remaining a member of the secondary teaching service, Thorne was to be seconded to the tertiary Technical and Further Education (TAFE) sector. As well as being granted her choice of college and teaching area, there was an additional proviso that she could return to secondary teaching some time in the future; however, in order to do so she must first obtain the approval of the chief executive of the Education Department (Outrage 1987:8). While Thorne claimed that the agreement meant that "the government has conceded they discriminated against me," having "withdrawn their challenge to the EOB decision" and agreeing "to pay my $3,000 court costs," it is clear that the government was also successful in its homophobic goal of removing Thorne from the secondary teaching classroom (Outrage 1987:8). She never returned to secondary school teaching.

Conclusion

The PSG/Thorne controversy is instructive as a window onto broader cultural shifts with respect to practices and meanings of sexuality in Australia in the 1980s. It is also instructive as a local instance of some of the ways in which both pedophilia was homosexualized and any discussion of child sexual agency was erased at this time. Due in large measure to decriminalization campaigns in Victoria and New South Wales, issues pertaining to homosexuality were subject to an extraordinary amount of public and community attention. The effects of decriminalization campaigns in this volatile climate were, as the PSG/Thorne controversy reveals, double edged. Homosexuality may well have been decriminalized but it was also simultaneously pathologized in its relationship to children and to childhood. Homosexual equality was considered a potential threat to a child's sexual development and education. The homosexualization of pedophilia was irrevocably set in motion in spite, or perhaps because, of repeated reminders by feminist and gay activists that the majority of sexual abuses of children are of a heterosexual not homosexual nature and are committed largely by fathers, male relatives, and family friends. It scarcely mattered that many gay and pedophile support groups had earlier in the decade been clearly articulating distinctions between pedophilia, homosexuality, and child sexual abuse. Far from challenging such distinctions, it was the gay community's efforts in this regard, set against the backdrop of the PSG/Thorne controversy, that ultimately only lent weight to the conflation of homosexuality and pedophilia. Finally, neither did it seem to matter that, strictly speaking, pedophilia referred to sex with prepubescent children and not adolescents, yet all the high-profile cases of supposed homosexual pedophilia involved gay men and adolescents. In the public imagination and in dominant media representations it was frequently homosexual pedophiles who continued to be identified as the greatest threat to all children. This assumption was itself sustained, notwithstanding research data revealing that a much smaller proportion of homosexual men engaged in sex with prepubescent children than did heterosexual men. One widely cited study concluded that "the heterosexual adult constitutes a higher risk of sexual victimization to the underage child than does the homosexual adult" (Outrage 1986:7). The explanation for this was that homosexual men tend to be sexually attracted to pubertal and postpubertal masculine qualities and the prepubescent child is said generally not to exhibit these. Such widely circulating information about the overwhelming threat of male heterosexuality did nothing to deter the Delta squad from playing their part in the homosexualization of pedophilia.

As we have seen, even dominant theories of pedophilia in the late 1970s and 1980s, which on the surface seemed to "exonerate . . . gays" from the category of pedophile, as one community publication reported (Outrage 1986:7), nonetheless provided a theoretical justification with the regressed versus fixated schema for this kind of rhetorical and homophobic association of homosexuality and pedophilia. Never mind that research had indicated heterosexual men commit the overwhelming majority of sexual offenses against children: the "fixated" offender is usually associated with the pathological homosexual predator (or "true" pedophile), and the "regressed" offender is rendered the more harmless, somewhat normative, heterosexual male suffering from stressful life circumstances such as unemployment or marriage breakdown.[12] Unfortunately, the homophobic and heteronormative construction of the pedophile was reinforced by a sensationalist media focus on the least prevalent of these types of sex crime, that is, fixated homosexual pedophilia. Mainstream media representations continued to downplay research and crimes that highlighted the prevalence of intimate heterosexual danger and, instead, frequently exploited images of stranger danger and rendered them synonymous with predatory homosexual pedophiles, even when they were more accurately instances of homosexual hebephilia or consensual sex between adults and teenagers.[13]

The PSG/Thorne controversy constituted a significant moment in the emergence and homosexualization of the category of the pedophile in Australia. We might view this as a defensive projection of a hegemonic masculinist and homophobic discourse that served, on the one hand, to deflect attention away from the fact that child sexual abuse had been exposed as a problem endemic to normative heterosexual masculinities and, on the other, to halt the advancing campaigns for homosexual equality. Alison Thorne—and to a much lesser extent the PSG—was an extremely unfortunate political casualty—or to use Thorne's own characterization, "a political football" (Levy and Thorne 1985:66)—in a broader transitional process whereby cultural and epistemological concepts of childhood, sexuality, sexual abuse, and homosexuality were in a state of radical contestation and transformation.[14]

Notes

1 On the NAMBLA controversy, see Cozijn 1983:12–13.

2 "Conspiracy to corrupt public morals" was a common law charge inherited from Britain. In Australia at this time the perception of a mainstream conflation of homosexuality and child seduction/molestation was widely articulated by gay groups. It was also a conflation that right-wing Christian groups were constantly exploiting in their antihomosexual rhetoric. For instance, Christian publications such as *New Life: Australia's Weekly Evangelical Newspaper* were awash with articles about the likely burgeoning of child recruitment and seduction to the homosexual way of life that the social legitimation of homosexuality would unleash.

3 I am aware that feminism is not a unified and homogeneous movement but rather comprises a wide range of perspectives and political and theoretical positions. However, I am simply suggesting that the loose ensemble of feminisms in the 1980s together effected a widespread interrogation and critique of male sexualities and masculinities.

4 In framing the notion of negative models of manhood, I have drawn from the work of Kimmel (1996).

5 I should point out that in the early 1960s John McGeorge (1964:245) argued that there is "a large homosexual component in his [the 'true' pedophile's] behavior." However, this seems not to have been a common feature of dominant theories until the late 1970s and 1980s.

6 McConaghy received a grant from the National Health and Medical Research Council of Australia and was widely considered a foremost proponent of aversion therapy. He was reviled by the gay community in Australia and became the focus of its antipsychiatry campaign. On one occasion while McConaghy was speaking at a conference on psychiatry and liberation, gay activists began chanting and hurling abuse and eggs at him. See Willett 2000:105. "Hebephile" usually refers to someone with an erotic preference for adolescents between the ages of thirteen and sixteen.

7 This article was reprinted in *Campaign* (1986:4).

8 For a more detailed discussion of the conflation of pedophilia and homosexuality in decriminalization and sex education debates in Australia, see Angelides 2005.

9 Even when Hinch was accused by the Victoria Equal Opportunity Board of sensational reporting, he said he was guilty and proud to be guilty: "All I did was try and keep a warped teacher away from impressionable kids" (*Melbourne's Star Observer* 1986a:3).

10 The Equal Opportunity Board (1987:99) noted in its report: "One of the most unfortunate aspects of this case is the media reporting of Ms Thorne's views and the Board has found that the acts in respect of which Ms Thorne has lodged complaints would be highly unlikely to have taken place if the press and radio

reports of the Gay Legal Rights Coalition's Press Release and Ms Thorne's interview with Mike Edmonds had been full and accurate. Some member of the press and certain radio 'personalities' appear to have seen the press release and interview as an appropriate occasion for indulging in sensationalist reporting of the worst kind."

11   On the Melbourne Gay Teachers Group, see Jaynes 1998 and Willett 1999. Alison Thorne's profile as a socialist lesbian feminist activist raises the question of whether this status fed into the controversy in any significant way. On the surface, at least, it appears from the media coverage and parliamentary debates that, surprisingly, right-wing groups opposed to Thorne did not in fact exploit this profile in their rhetoric. Nor was gender a particularly salient feature of the Thorne controversy, except insofar as parliamentarians, journalists, and politicians expressed their shock that a woman could hold such views about pedophilia and the age of consent. The most that might be speculated is that Thorne's gender may have enabled the whole campaign to achieve greater shock value. Or, even more speculatively, as I have suggested elsewhere (Angelides 2005), there was perhaps some kind of unconscious reaction, even backlash, against feminism at this time because of feminist attempts to expose child sexual abuse as a problem associated with normative masculinity. Perhaps Thorne became something of a scapegoat in this backlash. Of course, this is highly speculative, and it is a notoriously difficult proposition to attempt to find empirical evidence that might link Thorne's lesbian feminism to the campaign against her. It is also worth noting that, although many lesbian feminists were opposed to the pro-pedophilia position and the lowering of the age of consent, feminist groups did not attack Thorne, publicly at least, for expressing her views.

12   Summarizing Groth and Birnbaum's account of the causal factors involved in regressed offender behavior, Howells (1981:78) notes "the precipitating events as physical, social, sexual, marital, financial and vocational crises to which the offender fails to adapt." See also Freund et al. 1972.

13   In Angelides 2005, I argue that this sensationalist media focus is tied to a broader cultural recuperation of hegemonic masculinity.

14   It is worth pointing out that the whole PSG and Thorne controversy did not appear to hold back gay rights movements in Australia. See Willett 2000. However, it would appear that, in the interests of obtaining widespread political and community acceptance for gay rights, many gay groups attempted to distance themselves from the issue of pedophilia and avoided taking propedophilia positions. As a result, discussion of pedophilia and child sexuality in mainstream gay publications began to wane in the late 1980s and 1990s.

5

Stolen Kisses

Homophobia as "Racism" in Contemporary Urban Greece

Brian Riedel

IN THE FALL OF 2002, the story traveled quickly around Athens, from friend to friend. The owner of a cafe in Thissio, a neighborhood of central Athens, had kicked out two men for kissing. Many versions of the story circulated, and people continued to talk about the event for several years afterward. The story's survival hung on the wealth of contradictions it offered. Many suspected or knew the owner of the cafe to be a lesbian. At the time of the expulsion, many lesbians and gays saw the cafe as a "gay and lesbian cafe" or at least argued that the majority of the clientele was lesbian and gay. Since the expulsion, despite a conscientious boycott by many lesbians and gays, the cafe has continued to have a steady stream of lesbian and gay customers. Then there are the wildly varying stories of just what the two men were doing. In one version, they kissed each other on the lips at one of the sidewalk tables. The most salacious retelling held that hands were underneath clothes, but in the somewhat more discrete location of a couch inside the cafe near the back. Another version held that the two men were not expelled at all but left in a huff because they were asked to be more modest. In many of these versions, discussion eventually turned to whether or not the incident displayed elements of *ratsismós* and *omofovía* (usually translated as "racism" and "homophobia," respectively).

At this point, the exact details of the event are well beyond reach, both overembroidered through recycling and possibly dampened by both the owner of the cafe and the two men involved, all of whom may well be tired of entertaining the topic. Regardless, the "truth" of the event seems to matter less now than its social recycling and the effective truths it has taken on through its assumption to collective memory. Through the contradictions and discussions that kept the story alive, the expulsion also raises a variety of ethnographic questions about the ways that "homophobia" might be said to work in Greece. Why might a lesbian risk alienating her core customer base by expelling two men for kissing? Was the event "homophobic" or not? Moreover, what might any of this have to do with "racism"?

This chapter aims to explore the parallel language of racism and homophobia in Greece by presenting several ethnographic vignettes from fieldwork with Athenian lesbian, gay, bisexual, and transgender social activists.[1] Through these vignettes, I argue that homophobia in Greece must be understood within three contextual frames: the history of the Greek language, a recent and ongoing shift in conceptions of same-sex sexual behaviors in Greece, and the cultural impact of Greece's transition from a sender of emigrants to a receiver of immigrants. Beginning in the 1970s, Greece began a slow shift toward the articulation of same-sex sexual practices as social identities, as opposed to practices in which anyone might engage.[2] Beginning in the late 1980s, immigration facilitated by European Union (EU) membership generated a societal focus on race as a central metaphor for social difference. Analyzing these transitions together reveals complications in applying "homophobia" as an unproblematic analytical category in Greece.

Omofovía and *Ratsismós*: Preliminary Linguistic Notes

Rather than positioning racism and homophobia as overlapping concepts, North American public discourse holds the object of homophobia to be clearly distinct from that of racism or from other forms of prejudice. For example, Daniel Wickberg observes that the object of "homophobia" is determined rather more specifically than that of "racism" or "sexism." Wickberg also notes that sexism and racism are seen as "social ideologies" (2000:45), while homophobia is often seen as a psychological condition inhering in an individual.[3] Byrne Fone (2000) follows a similar argument, where homophobia is related to but distinguished from other categories of prejudice. He writes that "homophobia has links with sexism as well as with anti-Semitism and with prejudice against people of color" (2000:5). However, Fone adheres to the logic that "the term 'homophobia' is now popularly construed to mean fear and dislike of homosexuality and those who practice it" (5).

In Greek public discourse, by contrast, *ratsismós* and *omofovía* do not demonstrate such clear demarcations. Returning to the cafe episode, both *ratsismós* and *omofovía* were used to describe precisely the same behavior. And yet, there are no cues of racial or ethnic *difference* among the agents of the cafe scene. In all versions of the story, the two men and the cafe owner are each clearly and unproblematically marked as Greek, a case in which the straightforward application of the category "racism" might seem to be inappropriate, at least if understood from the North American perspective outlined above. And yet, many Greek speakers apply the term *ratsismós* with no apparent dissonance.

One of the factors structuring this discursive overlap of *ratsismós* and *omofovía* is the evolution of the Modern Greek language itself, specifically the paths through which these words have gained meaning and currency. In the nineteenth century, as the emerging Greek state worked to distinguish itself from its Ottoman past, the Greek spoken by the people contained a liberal admixture of Turkish, Latin, and Italian elements. This form of Greek became known as *dimotikí* or "demotic" (literally, of the people). Some of the intellectuals leading the formation of the new Greek state saw this amalgam as unfit to serve as a language of governance or education, particularly for a nation-state aspiring to base its authority on the achievements of ancient Greek and Byzantine civilizations. Although the debate on language reform was divisive, the formulation espoused by the physician and classicist Adamantios Koraïs eventually supplanted the rest. Known as *katharévousa*, this form of Greek aimed, as the name implies, to "cleanse" both written and spoken language of non-Greek influence. It purposefully restructured both grammar and vocabulary, avoiding the impurities of demotic Greek by incorporating elements of classical Greek. Although *katharévousa* became the official language of the state, demotic continued on as common speech and the language of most creative writing. During the succeeding century, debate continued over which language form best served the people and the state. It was only in 1976, several years after the fall of the military junta, that demotic Greek was adopted as the language of state and education. The dominance of *katharévousa* has since faded. However, its influence continues as a marker of high-status language.

In this historical linguistic context, *ratsismós* and *omofovía* both entered postjunta Greece as loan words, marking both already as clearly not *katharévousa*. This is not to say, however, that both are therefore clearly demotic.

Orthographically and etymologically, *ratsismós* is linked to the significantly older demotic Greek word *rátsa*, variously translatable as "race," "breed," "stock," or "pedigree." Despite the precedence of *rátsa* in demotic, however, *ratsismós* is not derived from it. Rather, both *ratsismós* and *rátsa* are borrowed directly from the Italian *razzismo* and *razza*, respectively.[4] While most commonly used now to denote types of people and animals, *rátsa* may also be used idiomatically to describe a person as exceptionally witty or astute. For its part, the demotic Greek *ratsismós* is defined as "the theory that claims the superiority of one race that strives to maintain its 'purity' and its dominance over the others."[5] Even in this standard demotic definition, the term utilized for "race" is not *rátsa*, but *filí*,[6] which can refer to race, nation, or tribe; by contrast, the *katharévousa* words for "racial discrimination" or "racism" would be *filetikés diakríseis*, and not *ratsismós*. Thus, the standard demotic definition of *ratsismós* has an expansive capacity beyond the North American conceptualization of "race" in that it is not necessarily or only restricted to a form of discrimination based on perception of phenotype.

The emergence of the Greek word *omofovía* differs significantly from that of *ratsismós*. Orthographically and etymologically, it contains "good" Greek elements—*omo-* meaning "same" and *fovía* "fear." However, rather than indexing their literal Greek meaning, a clearly misleading "fear of the same," these elements correspond directly to the phonetics and denotation of the English "homophobia." Moreover, *omofovía* contends not only with *ratsismós* but also with two cognates, *omofilofovía* (literally, fear of the same sex) and *omofilofilofovía* (literally, fear of the homosexual). Significantly, however, debate over the distinctions between these three cognates seems to matter only to three groups of people: non-Greek academics, Greek academics who have studied abroad, and a relatively small group of Greek activists who focus on the rights of sexual minorities.

With this rarified background, *omofovía* is neither *katharévousa* nor demotic but occupies the liminal space of jargon and has yet to gain wide currency. As the vignettes below will illustrate, most people in Greece settle on *ratsismós* to describe what organizations like the International Gay and Lesbian Association would without hesitation determine "homophobia." The telling detail is that even among the Greek activists, the language of *ratsismós* is heard just as often as *omofovía* or any of its cognates. On a strictly linguistic level, the relatively wider recognition that *ratsismós* enjoys through its connection to the demotic *rátsa* may only further reinforce this tendency.

Defining the Object of *Ratsismós* and *Omofovía*

Given their distinct connotations of *omofovía* and *ratsismós*, how then can gay and lesbian activists deploy both in the context of sexual orientation? To explain that use, it is necessary first to articulate some of the assumptions animating the terms, specifically, how activists envision the *object of prejudice*, regardless of whether they call that prejudice *ratsismós* or *omofovía*.

In thinking about that object, Fone's definition of homophobia provides a particularly useful turn of phrase: "the fear and dislike of homosexuality *and of those who practice it*" (2000:5; my emphasis). The utility of his phrasing is that it guides our understanding of homophobia toward practices in which anyone might engage, shifting us away from the trap of thinking only with socially specifiable sexual identities that appear to inhere in the individual. Fone's formulation allows us to speak of the ways that homophobia might work in the lives of a self-identified bisexual woman who is married to a man, of black and Latino American men "on the down low," and, coincidentally, of a good many contemporary Greeks. At the same time, that utility does not come about because Fone had contemporary Greece in mind. In his work, as in most surveys of homosexuality that adopt a globalizing or transhistorical point of view, discussion of Greece is mostly limited to the ancient Greeks; Fone does not once mention the modern Greek state.[7] One could argue that "nearly every age reinvents Greece in its own image" (Fone 2000:17) and that Western homosexualities depend upon the idealization of the Greek past for their own narrative authenticity.[8]

In locating the object of *ratsismós* or *omofovía* in the Greek case, however, such unmediated recourse to the classical Greek past leads to a dangerous presumption of timelessness and continuity: thus the crucial project of tracking how contemporary Greeks, living in a place whose ancient forms are claimed by so many others, might go about relating to and deploying their own pasts.[9] For their parts, Greek gay and lesbian activists both avoid and embrace classical referents. For example, James Faubion is careful to note that when he asked one of the more prominent Greek activists, Gregory Vallianatos, "what meaning he gave to 'being gay' [. . .] he did not appeal to classical exemplars" (Faubion 1993:240). Vallianatos found them no longer relevant, not just for himself but for other Greeks as well. At the same time, not all Greek gays and lesbians dismiss the classical past as willingly as does Vallianatos. A long-standing electronic mailing list targeting lesbian women is named "Sapphides," drawing on the name of the famous poet Sappho; analogously, annual summer gatherings of Greek and non-Greek lesbians take place on Mytilene (also known as Lesvos).[10] In much the same way that Herzfeld or Faubion might argue about the various symbolic uses to which any point in the historical record of Greece might be put, the classical past does remain as a resource, yet it is a deeply freighted one and by no means stands as a required touchstone for the present day articulation or legitimation of same-sex desire in Greece.

In that spirit, an examination of the ethnographic record of contemporary same-sex sexuality in Greece reveals two significant trends.[11] On the one hand, remarkable importance continues to be attributed to social and cultural expectations of gendered behavior, in accord with the broader ethnographic literature of Greece.[12] On the other hand, a historical moment occurred in which understandings of same-sex sexual behavior began to shift from a sexual economy based primarily on gender roles to one where sexual identities as such began to proliferate.

In the 1970s and earlier—how much earlier, we may never be able to say, but clearly *not* in an unaltered stretch back to the time of Plato—one could describe the predominant Greek understandings of same-sex sexual practices as based primarily on strong gender roles and the pervasive social strength of kinship obligations. Gender was mapped both onto sexual positions and onto conceptions of full personhood in ways that situated gender nonconformity as outside the properly social or human. Here, the relationship of gender behavior to sexual practice was suggestive rather than determinative. Nonconforming gender behaviors indicated the possibility of nonconforming sexual practices; however, for a man to submit himself of his own free will to penetration by another man was of itself effeminizing. As James Faubion argues, "The effeminate man in Greece, traditionally and still today, is among the most scorned of social subversives. He is not always, and of course should not be confused with the 'homosexual' " (1993:222). The notion of a *sexual identity* as such lies outside this gendered system. To underscore this point, Faubion writes, "Until about a decade ago, *omofilofilía* [homosexuality] had no demotic currency whatever. Until about a decade ago, it seems to have had no actual referent, either" (1993:217).[13]

Beyond the ethnographic record, the celebrated author Kostas Taktsis (1989) provides rich accounts of the social outcomes of this understanding of same-sex sexual practices. He describes a sexual economy where the couplings of bodies were not determined by a socially available sexual identity but by a code of gender behavior; social connections between men were not bound by the idea that sexual contact between them was illicit in and of itself. Further, though we can suppose that there were men whose sexual lives revolved exclusively around other men, we can be certain that exclusivity was by no means a prerequisite for participation in that sexual economy. The only prerequisite was that the workings of that economy, pervasive though they might be, remained in the realm of the unarticulated common secret. Same-sex sexual contacts were the stuff not of social identities but of private and concealed pleasures.[14]

In the context of this sexual economy, in 1977, the first public homosexual movements in Greece were organized on a growing wave of leftist social agitation fueled by the experiences of intellectuals who had been abroad during Greece's military dictatorship, fallen only three years earlier. The "Greek Homosexuals' Liberatory Movement" (AKOE, by its Greek acronym) reached a peak of organizational strength in the early 1980s. It still exists as of this writing, although in a much altered form, and is now accompanied by a host of other organizations.

Faubion (1993) and Kostas Yiannakopoulos (1998) argue that around the time AKOE was founded, a new perception of sexual identities was beginning to take root in Greece (at least among those urbanites who might see themselves as homosexuals) which eventually would coexist and compete with the preexisting sexual economy based on gender roles. Faubion refers to this new perception in his discussion of the displeasure Gregory Vallianatos felt with the term *homosexual* and his preference for the term *gay* (Faubion 1993:237). For his part, Yiannakopoulos describes the new perception as a recognizable and visible "gay homosexuality" (gay *omofilofilía*) in contradistinction to what he terms a "masculine homosexuality" (*arrenopí omofilofilía*), which designates same-sex "sexual practices which do not entail a homosexual identity" (Yiannakopoulos 1998:82) and which apparently leaves intact the masculine gender of the practitioners.

Parallel Models of Sexuality

Regardless of its precise provenance, it would be wrong to suggest that this new discourse of sexual identity overtook the preexisting sexual economy entirely. These two ways of seeing same-sex sexuality continue to coexist, if in tension. That coexistence forms part of the foundation for any understanding of homophobia as an analytic category in contemporary Greece.

The parallel models suggest first that, in the context of socially proliferating sexual identities, some individuals who engage in same-sex practices will tend to distance themselves from those who take up sexual identities in a socially visible way. Elisabeth Kirtsoglou (2003, 2004) has documented similar dynamics in a group of women who, though they do have erotic relations between them, refuse lesbian identity. Further, it is not as if Greek activists have ignored such refusals and organized around the notion of a sexual identity anyway. Indeed, the subtitle of AKOE's journal, AMFI, underwent a significant change in the early years of the organization. In 1978, it read "for the liberation of homosexuals," ostensibly directing the liberatory project to a class of people, the species "homosexual"; by 1979, it had changed to "for the liberation of homosexual desire." Clearly implying that same-sex sexual desires could be present in anyone, that subtitle would remain through the last issue of AMFI, published in 1994.

This coexistence suggests something of a hypothesis about why *ratsismós* and *omofovía* continue to circulate in parallel, aside from the relative youth of *omofovía* as a term and the recognition *ratsismós* enjoys with its more inclusive definition. Those whose lives are not patterned after a politicized "sexual identity" are less likely to participate in social circles where prejudice against homosexual practices and identities is spoken of as *omofovía*, a term they may find doubly foreign (linguistically and sexually). It seems reasonable to suppose that "homophobia" as an analytic category will not overtake "racism" until sociosexual identities significantly displace gender roles as the hegemonic organizing trope of the same-sex sexual economy.

The salience of understandings of same-sex sexual practices based on gender roles is also sustained by the continued use of gender-inflected words that predate the emergence of sexual identity politics in Greece. For example, the most common slang terms used for lesbians include *ntalíka*, *plakomoúna*, and *trivádes*. Literally connoting a "truck driver," *ntalíka* is employed primarily to indicate its object's lack of proper femininity. Indexing an occupational stereotype of a gruff and unpolished laborer, it implies a domineering personality, suggesting that this relation of power extends into sexual affairs in much the same way that the term *diesel dyke* might do. While *ntalíka* does not explicitly refer to sexual positions, however, both *plakomoúna* and *trivádes* do: they describe the act of two women rubbing and pressing their genitals together. Linguistically, *plakomoúna* is the more vulgar and explicit of the two, translating literally as "press-pussy"; *trivádes* maintains a more euphemistic relation to the position, referring only to an act of "rubbing" between women. As with *ntalíka*, however, the weight of the insult for both terms stems from a failure of full womanhood. With the male absent from the sexual scene, the reproductive rationale of sex is vitiated, and the act is reframed as purely about selfish pleasure. The ethical implication is that such women have ceased to nurture and care about others in a properly feminine way (despite the fact that *plakomoúna* and *trivádes* both open the possibility of women actually nurturing and caring about *each other*).

Consider also the terms used for men: *poústis*, roughly translatable as "faggot," indicates not only sexual passivity but also femininity and conniving. The majority of the term's derogatory power comes from the assertion that its subject lacks proper manhood; the *poústis* allows his abuse, accepts being penetrated, has no sense of shame, will be duplicitous, and surrenders his humanity without a fight.[15] While *poústis* refers to sexual positions, its scope of reference pushes beyond sex itself, pointing most strongly to the quality of the person's moral character.[16] Thus, although *poústis* is often used to describe the *character* of some gay men, it does not denote a homosexual identity per se; the two categories should not be conflated. Similarly, the term *malákas* also slides between the description of sexual behavior and that of personal character. Sexually, it denotes the masturbator, but it also denotes a moral character not properly human. Socially, the *malákas* is both rude and stupid, the jerk who is not man enough to do things the right way. Even if used ironically and playfully (and then, only between friends), both

Brian Riedel

poústis and *malákas* simultaneously engage three levels of social discourse: an insult to full humanity, a slur on the masculinity of the subject in question, and an insinuation of failure to fulfill a properly male and insertive sexual role.

Omofovía at the Anti-Racist Festival

In this cultural context, where same-sex desire is linked to sexual depravity and a lack of full or proper humanity (primarily defined in terms of masculine/feminine qualities), some lesbian and gay activists see the need for large-scale conversations on the subject. To that end, several activist organizations assembled a panel discussion on discrimination among sexual minorities in June 2003, at the 8th Anti-Racist Festival held in Illision Park in Athens. The annual festival has over time come to host some 140 organizations, the vast majority of which support immigrants and ethnic minorities in Greece with a broad range of antidiscrimination, antiglobalization, and anticapitalist messages. For several years, this festival was also the largest regular public display of lesbian and gay organizations in Athens.[17]

At the panel itself, prejudice toward homosexuals, transsexuals, and *travestí* was spoken of in several terms: *omofovía*, *omofilofovía*, and *ratsismós*.[18] Still, most speakers employed the language of *ratsismós*. That tendency was also visible in the preparations for the festival made by the Gay Citizens' Initiative (Protovoulía Omofilófilon Politón, or POP). While debating the language to use in their presentation, they continued to speak in terms of *ratsismós*, even though they noted that they found the term unsatisfactory. No one argued that *ratsismós* was an ideal term; they all understood it to refer specifically to race rather than to sexuality. At the same time, the author of POP's draft statement for the festival found *omofovía* both insufficiently Greek and too vague. He argued that as a direct borrowing of *homophobia* from established non-Greek activist and academic discourses, it read literally in Greek as "fear of the same" and thus failed to accurately communicate the object of fear. Another contender was *omofilofilofovía*. While it very clearly denoted the object of fear (the homosexual) and had the virtue of being good Greek, it was considered too awkward to use. In the end, the group settled for *omofilofovía*, which, though still somewhat cumbersome, denoted more clearly its object, the "same-sex." Although no activist ever voiced the argument in this way, *omofilofovía* advertised the fact that it was *not* a loan word; it instigated a level of reflection and debate among the activists that the quick adaptation of the foreign term *homophobia* never could.[19] Despite the care put into the debate over the draft statement, POP's choice of language did not catch on at the panel discussion. Everyone, including on occasion POP activists themselves, deployed the language of *ratsismós*.

The gay and lesbian presence at the Anti-Racist Festival provided a platform for public discussion of sexuality that might otherwise not exist. Other speakers at the panel discussion repeatedly argued for the naturalness of common interests between POP and the Greek left, anticapitalist movements, and organizations working for the rights of immigrants. Drawing on these connections, one might argue that *ratsismós* presents certain advantages to lesbian and gay activists in Greece. Given that *ratsismós* functions somewhat flexibly as prejudice against a "natural condition"—a group similarity that subjects do not choose but into which they are born—the term seems to allow some evasion of arguments that assign moral blame to those who "choose" nonconforming practices. Further, the umbrella term *ratsismós* could also be construed to provide greater social leverage than a more specific term might. Unlike *omofovía* or its cognates, it might operate to unite homosexuals, transsexuals, and *travestí* in a coalition with other, more "established minorities."[20] If POP's dissatisfaction with *ratsismós* can be taken as any indication, however, no momentum currently exists to support such positions.

Parsing *Ratsismós*

Regardless of what hypothetical value *ratsismós* might have for the activists, the events around the Anti-Racist Festival illustrated how *ratsismós* persists as a descriptor of discrimination toward same-sex sexual desires and those who practice them, even in the face of deliberate conversation about terminology. Further explanation of this persistence lies in the social context supporting the quotidian use of *ratsismós*, a context produced through Greece's recent transition from a nation of emigrants to a nation of immigrants.[21]

Popular histories of this transition unfailingly summon the national myth of ethnic homogeneity that Greece harbored for much of the twentieth century. This perception of former homogeneity is historically grounded in the Great Catastrophe, a forced population exchange required under the Treaty of Lausanne, signed after the Greek army was routed from Asia Minor by the Turks in 1922. While the cross-migration of over one and a half million people between present-day Turkey and Greece by no means made the Greek nation-state racially or ethnically homogenous, it did play into a sense of collective national identity that was to remain relatively unshaken for generations, until 1981, when membership in the European Community brought about a loosening of Greece's borders and an economy that demanded cheap labor. Within the decade, the demographics of Greece seemed all too suddenly changed.[22] Although Albanian migrant laborers were not the only newcomers, they became and remained a focal point for all problems with immigration. For example, one of the more frequently televised issues in 2004 was the case of an exemplary high school student who, because he was of Albanian descent, was denied the honor usually accorded to the top scholar of holding the Greek flag at the lead of his school's parade on a national holiday.

By the end of the 1990s, increased immigration from Central and Southeast Asia had displaced Albanians in the national consciousness, though not completely. *Ratsismós* had become a staple of public discourse, and by 1996, during the buildup to the 2004 Olympic Games, the government was announcing that Greece was "multicultural." All the same, Greece's international relationships continue to demonstrate that the myth of an ethnically pure nation retains a powerful symbolic hold. Greece remains embroiled in a bitter dispute with Turkey over Cyprus, a conflict rooted historically in many Greeks' and Greek-Cypriots' desire for the union of Cyprus with Greece, despite both the long-standing residence of ethnic Turks in Cyprus and the failure of the Greek irredentist project signaled by the Treaty of Lausanne in 1922. On other fronts, a new power struggle has developed with the Former Yugoslav Republic of Macedonia, to which Greece refuses to grant the use of the name "Macedonia," claiming that name to be exclusively Greek.

Through its rise in public discourse, *ratsismós* has also come to be an object of inquiry in the Greek academy, particularly in the work of Georgios Tsiakalos, dean of the faculty of education at Aristotle University of Thessaloniki. Faced with seeming contradictions between documented attacks against immigrants and claims that "there is no racism" in Greece,[23] Tsiakalos argues (through a socioeconomic analysis) that racism appears in

Greece as institutionalized self-interest on the part of the state and upper economic classes. He concludes that, despite values upholding "traditional Greek hospitality" (*filoxenía*) and specific condemnation of racism by the Greek Orthodox Church,[24] the systematic exploitation of immigrant labor by the upper strata fosters a fear-based climate of xenophobia among the lower economic classes of the Greek citizenry, a climate that he argues may "turn into racism in state-provided conditions" (2006:205). While his argument is focused primarily on immigration, Tsiakalos provides additional analysis of the broader public discourse of racism in general. Distinguishing it from xenophobia, he writes that racism "is exclusively associated with negative facts that happened abroad" (195), specifically institutionalized systems such as Nazi Germany, apartheid South Africa, and the American South. "In all cases," he continues, "the concept is associated with unfair, aggressive behavior exclusively originating from victimizers." For Tsiakalos, then, although racism is claimed to be somehow "not Greek," it is a systemic problem, structured by the relationships among immigrant labor, the apparatus of the state, and different socioeconomic classes of Greek citizenry.

Where Tsiakalos applies a Marxist reading to challenge the claim that there is no racism in Greece, the work of the social psychologists Lia Figgou and Susan Condor (2006) utilizes discourse analysis. Although it is not their intention, their work also provides additional evidence that *ratsismós* functions in an expansive metaphoric range. Figgou interviewed a range of Thessalonikans about Albanian immigrants and noted their use of the terms *ratsismós* and *prokatálipsi*. Condor and Figgou argue that among lay observers "there is a significant difference between defining racism and prejudice in general abstract terms and explaining particular discriminatory actions in practice" (2006:239). They found that their interviewees explained concrete examples of racist behavior through rhetorics of fear or danger, rather than any abstract theory of racism. Most suggestively, however, Figgou and Condor also document how "respondents tended to use the terms [*ratsismós*] and [*prokatálipsi*] as functional synonyms" (224). Beyond linguistic interchangeability, their analysis finds that both terms could be used equally to refer to "an ungrounded belief in the existence of categorical differences between peoples," "intolerance of existing differences between groups," "attribution of out-group 'difference' to nature rather than to social forces," and as "feelings of antipathy towards members of low status groups on the part of the high status groups" (225). These two observations—the practical interchangeability of both terms and the broad semantic range given to each—are strong indications of the expansiveness of *ratsismós* as a category in public discourse.

Why Do the "Muscle Men" Kiss on Elia?

There are many examples from my fieldwork that, like the cafe example with which this essay began, demonstrate not only a broad range of potential objects of *ratsismós* but also a variety of subjects who deploy the language of *ratsismós* in cases where all social agents are unproblematically Greek. One such example comes from an editorial column in 2002 titled with the question "Why do the 'Muscle Men' Kiss on Elia?" The column appeared in NITRO, an Athens-based, glossy lifestyle magazine aimed at a broad male audience throughout Greece. Although few praise its journalism, the magazine maintains a solid market share and regularly features satirical editorials and interviews with well-known Greek and international celebrities. NITRO is an example of what is seen as possible, acceptable, and marketable in present-day Greek media.

Concerning this particular column, the editorial staff at NITRO certainly found it marketable enough; they placed the title on the cover page of the magazine. On the magazine's contents page, that teaser title changes slightly, as if to clarify just what the column is about: "Why Do Gays Kiss on Elia?"[25] The article itself is headed by a half-page color drawing by a freelance illustrator (see figure 1). Two men are featured in their bathing suits on a beach with mountains in the background. The scene presumably takes place at Elia, one of the most famous beaches on Mykonos, an island most Greeks immediately equate with decadence and gay men. The two men's bodies are tanned and muscled, with a conspicuous lack of body hair. They are leaning into each other with pursed lips and bent wrists, seemingly oblivious to the young boy in the foreground staring up at them with an expression of confusion and horror. Visible in the background between the two men, another man looks on the scene, his hands on either side of his protruding and slightly furry belly and his jaw set in firm disapproval. A woman is also watching, only her head visible in the background, with her eyebrow arched.

The article beneath the image presents a familiar argument: the author objects to public displays of affection among gay men, not only because he

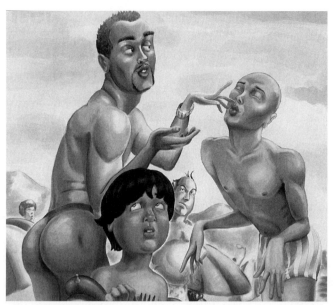

Figure 1. Illustration from the Greek periodical *Nitro*, no. 84 (October 2002). Reprinted with permission.

finds them disturbing but also because he feels he is prevented from expressing his opinion by a double standard that gays have created by designating themselves as oppressed. The author thus observes that, although he could simply yell out to any straight couple to behave properly, he would be considered a *ratsistís* to chastise a gay couple. Immediately after stating this complaint, however, he hastens to clarify: "I believe in the right of each person to choose whatever sexual life he desires and that this choice is no one else's business. ok?" His target is clearly not gays themselves, just their proper public behavior. He concludes: "The point is, if you do it publicly, no one will believe that you did it because you had to. And no rule can forbid someone from showing you that they don't approve of what you do (and not of what you are) or from jeering at you, not because you're gay, but because you're a *malákas*." Presumably, the author would not want anyone behaving like a *malákas*, regardless of the genders involved; if this is the case, many a lesbian and gay Athenian might observe that there is no shortage of heterosexual couples eligible for social control. Indeed, the author imagines three possible scenarios should that eligible couple be a man and a woman (curiously, he never mentions two women doing the same): "Either you act like you don't see them, or you yell at them, or you whip it out and play with it, encouraging them with your participation." "But in the case of gays," the author continues, "you act like a *malákas* yourself not to be seen as a *ratsistís*."

Not once in the *NITRO* article does the word *omofovía* or any of its cognates appear. The language is entirely of *ratsismós*, clearly deployed as the appropriate frame for speaking about discrimination toward gay men. Moreover, the only remarkable aspect of these men, for both the author and the illustrator, is their sexual identity; no cues of non-Greekness are given in either the article or the illustration. In parsing the meaning of *ratsismós*, the column thus forms an important supplement to the expulsion from the cafe. Given only the cafe example, it might have been possible to argue that gays and lesbians simply appropriated the language of *ratsismós* to function as a kind of internal argot. *NITRO*, however, is a broad-circulation magazine targeting mainstream Greek men. The column indicates that *ratsismós* enjoys broad social currency in Greece as a term capable of embracing what North American analysts would call homophobia.

Ratsismós as Transphobia

The referential scope of *ratsismós* also extends to another area, where even *omofovía* might fall short: discrimination based on gender affect and gender identity.[26] One example of this use of *ratsismós* comes from the activists themselves. Spurred by a police raid in 2003 on a gay bar in Athens that resulted in one of the arrested committing suicide while in jail, activists began a series of mass meetings that eventually found a home at the Politechneío, a university complex in central Athens still strongly associated with the student rebellions that precipitated the fall of the dictatorship in 1974. At one such meeting, the activists were discussing the inclusion of transsexuals and *travestí* in those meetings and the general level of cooperation between activist groups. Several *travestí* observed that most activists tend to exclude transsexuals and *travestí*. When Vangelis Yiannelos, then president of the Greek Homosexual Community (whose name in Greek gives the acronym EOK), rose to defend both his record and that of EOK on that point, Paola, then president of the Organization for the Solidarity of Transsexuals and *Travestí* of Greece (SATTE), shouted over him and directly accused him of being a *ratsistís*, clearly meaning prejudiced against transsexuals and *travestí*.[27] While the standoff eventually calmed down and the meeting continued, the intensity of the drama lingered and subsequent speakers were careful to be inclusive in their language.

Yiannelos's protests aside, Paola's accusations accurately describe a large number of Greek gay men. While speaking with nonactivist gay men about how Greek society sees homosexuality and what can be done to improve that relationship, many professed they would distance themselves from excessively effeminate gay men, and specifically from *travestí*. This distancing is also reflected in their professed criteria for erotic partners, the most pervasive of which is that they want their partner to be *sovarós* ("serious," a cue for masculinity); many are reluctant to date anyone *trelós* (crazy) or *grafikós* (usually "graphic," but in this case, someone who draws undue attention or makes a scene). As if to emphasize the rectitude of these convictions, some of these young men further qualify themselves, somewhat defiantly, as *ratsistés* (plural of *ratsistís*). They do not see themselves as *omofovikoí*.[28] They feel that effeminate gay men, and *travestí* in particular, give homosexuals a bad name by extravagantly exceeding the boundaries of acceptable behavior, and that their excess impedes the acceptance of homosexuality in Greek society. They imagine that the only jobs *travestí* can hold include singing at an Athenian drag club called "Koukles," or sex work on Syngrou Avenue, or more likely some combination of the two. They imagine that *travestí* and transsexuals are mentally unbalanced, either genetically, or from the hormones involved in gender reassignment.

Ratsismós Redux?

As these vignettes demonstrate, the language of *ratsismós* functions in a variety of settings, including mass media, formal meetings, and casual conversation. For a wide range of speakers, regardless of their sexual identities or desires, *ratsismós* is the word of choice to describe discrimination against not only those marked as "non-Greek" but also those who are seen as gay, lesbian, bisexual, transgender, or *travestí*.

Despite a number of alternative words aimed at addressing homophobia as distinct from *ratsismós—omofovía* and its cognates—various factors act to reinforce this expansive meaning of *ratsismós*. Until notions of sexual identity overtake a sexual economy based on a particular and relatively rigid model of gender roles, those whose lives are not patterned after politicized sexual identities will likely continue to avoid social circles where prejudice against same-sex practices is spoken of as *omofovía*. Social circles made distinct through differing models of same-sex desire thus inhibit the spread of a coherent discourse among the groups that activists would seek to unify. Linguistically, *ratsismós* sounds more familiar; it is related to the demotic *rátsa*, whereas *omofovía* is presently limited to academic and activist jargon. That familiarity gives *ratsismós* an advantage against which proponents of *omofovía* must work to gain traction. Moreover, as the NITRO article indicates, the use of *ratsismós* to describe homophobia is sufficiently widespread that, even if all lesbian, gay, bisexual, and transgender activists were to agree upon *omofovía* or one of its cognates as the proper term, it would still take some time to displace *ratsismós*.

Given the discursive dominance of *ratsismós* over *omofovía* and its cognates, one alternate path for the activists might be to embrace *ratsismós*, rather than promote some other term. Such a move might allow greater leverage to tap into other networks for social change; the activists' regular participation at the Anti-Racist Festival indicates their recognition of the benefits of an alliance at the very least. The embrace of *ratsismós* might also provide an umbrella term for a range of Greeks in the same way that *queer* did for the United States and elsewhere. However, judging by POP's internal debate, their dissatisfaction with *ratsismós* is strong enough that they desire something more specific. What that more specific term will be remains to be seen. Again, if POP's internal debates (and those of other activists) are any indication, the alternate term of choice may well be *omofilofovía* rather than *omofovía*.[29]

For both Greek and non-Greek analysts, these parallel languages of *ratsismós* and *omofovía* color the ways that "homophobia" may be said to work in contemporary Greece. At a basic level, caution should be exercised in understanding what people mean when they use the language of *ratsismós*. To which social agents do they refer? How do speakers position themselves with respect to those agents? In some contexts, it is also important for English-speaking analysts to adjust their translation of *ratsismós* to account for its expansive possibilities, perhaps toward the concept of "discrimination" and its related parts of speech. Most importantly, however, one cannot conclude that there is no developed or sustained critique of discrimination against homosexuality in Greece, simply because a language specific to antihomophobic inquiry has yet to be broadly established. On the contrary, public discourse around *ratsismós* and *omofovía* shows that this critique is very much in motion, and the routes that critique will take in the future will likely have to do both with broader social changes and shifting notions of same-sex desire.

Notes

My thanks go to Anna Apostolidou, Marios Eliakis, James Faubion, Dave Fleischer, David Genac, Andrea Gilbert, Argyris Kavidas, Anna Mihopoulou, David Murray, Valantis Papathanasiou, Aimee Placas, Michael Powell, Angela Rivas, and Ayla Samli for their insights on previous drafts. Thanks are also due David Valentine, who suggested that I write this essay. I am also grateful for the careful attention and helpful comments from the anonymous reviewers at Duke University Press. All translations are my own; transliterations follow the system preferred by the *Journal of Modern Greek Studies*.

1   That fieldwork took place over twenty-six months, from the summer of 2001 through the summer of 2004, and was made possible by the support of the Research Institute for the Study of Man and the Rice University Center for the Study of Institutions and Values.

2   Greece is by no means unique in this respect; similar dynamics are evident in many locales across the globe, in cultural settings as divergent as Bolivia (Wright 2000), the Middle East (Massad 2002), and the Philippines (Manalansan 2002).

3   See Martin Manalansan's chapter in this volume for a crucial analysis of how homophobia is always already produced in the interstices of social categories and subject positions.

4   See Institute for Modern Greek Studies 2006.

5   The Greek here translated reads "theoría pou ipostirízei tin anoterótita mias filís kai apovlépei sti diatírisi tis 'katharótitás' tis kai stin kiriarhía tis epí ton állon" (Tegopoulos-Fitrakis 1997).

6   See Institute for Modern Greek Studies 2006.

7   See Foucault 1990a, 1990b; Miller 1995; Murray 2000; see also Tin 2003 for a refreshing exception that proves the rule.

8   See also Dover 1978; Winkler 1990; and Halperin 1990.

9   See Herzfeld 1985, 1987, 1991 and Faubion 1993.

10   Venetia Kantsa (2002) provides a detailed account of these gatherings.

11   See Sioubouras 1980; Patsalidou 1982; Theodorakopoulos 1982; Herzfeld 1985; Loizos and Papataxiarchis 1991; Faubion 1993; Yiannakopoulos 1998; Karayianni and Tolis 1998; Vasilikou 1998; Kantsa 2002; Phellas 2002; Boukli and Kappas 2004; Kirtsoglou 2003, 2004; Apostolidou 2004.

12 Among others, see Peristiany 1966; Gilmore 1982; Vermeulen 1983; Herzfeld 1985; Dubisch 1986; Cowan 1990; Seremetakis 1993; Moore 1995.

13 It should be noted that while Herzfeld's extensive work on Greek masculinity is foundational for much of Faubion's analysis of same-sex relations, Herzfeld himself extends his analyses only fleetingly to the topic of same-sex relations (see 1985:77,158).

14 Taktsis wrote only about the same-sex contacts of men. For insight into those of women, see Kantsa 2002 and Kirtsoglou 2003, 2004. Also, much as in other locations, the need to maintain the common secret spurred the development of a specific argot in Greece, known as *kaliarndá*. The documentation of the argot (Petropoulos 1993) is worth comparing to Gayle (Cage 1999) and Polari (Baker 2002). Elements of it have been incorporated into demotic, but it remains a sign among gay men not only of depth of knowledge of gay life in Greece but also of femininity; some men disavow knowledge of *kaliarndá* in order to mark their own masculinity, despite the words they actually employ. On a separate note, an arrangement of gender and sexuality among men like that described by Taktsis and Faubion is by no means unique to Greece; see Deniz Kandiyoti's work on masculinity and travesti in Turkey (e.g., Kandiyoti 2002).

15 For an extended analysis of gender and language, see Faubion 1993.

16 Herzfeld has also documented this sense of insult to moral character (1985:77, 158).

17 Since the time of fieldwork, Athens Pride has displaced the Anti-Racist Festival as the largest regular public display. Begun in 2005, the 2007 incarnation brought nearly two thousand people to march through the central streets of Athens for lesbian, gay, bisexual, and transgender rights, including representatives of twenty-eight organizations and political parties. One of those organizations has also explicitly embraced the rhetoric of *omofilofovía* by incorporating it into its name: Símpraxi katá tis Omofilofovías—Thessaloníki (Cooperation against Homophobia—Thessaloniki).

18 *Travestí* is a self-descriptive term used by Greek men who dress and behave as women and who often engage in sex work. Although they may have taken hormones or undertaken breast construction surgery, they have retained their male genitalia. While there are significant parallels to *travestí* discussed by Don Kulick (1998), there are significant differences, too, which are further complicated by the shifting fortunes of *travestí* as a social category in Greece over the last three decades. Further, within the organization SATTE (Greek Organization of Support for *Travestí* and Transsexuals), there is considerable discussion as to whether they are "still" gay, or whether being gay men was a stage they passed through on their way to becoming women, or whether they are something else entirely. For a more detailed discussion, see Apostolidou 2004. Another perspective is available in an autobiography from the postoperative celebrity Tzeni Heiloudaki (2002).

19 Significantly, Valantis Papathanasiou, a Greek sociologist who trained in Paris, Brussels, and Toulouse, argues that the similarity of *omofovía* to *homophobia* is instead an advantage. For him, it facilitates understanding across disciplinary and national boundaries and properly marks the theoretical development of *homophobia* beyond the Greek academic and activist traditions.

20 As this hypothetical umbrella term, *ratsismós* may itself be subject to the same tensions as *queer*, a term that has never enjoyed a level of success in Greece comparable to that which it had achieved in the United States. The quotation marks around the couplet "established minorities"—and not just around one or the other term—are meant to signal the lack of recognition of minority groups in Greece at the political level, despite the degree of social fascination and concern with the demographics reflected in discussions of *ratsismós*.

21 Again, Greece is hardly unique in this respect. Similar transformations have occurred in Italy and Spain (Triandafyllidou 2000).

22 This perception of ethnic diversity as somehow "new" to Greece took root in the 1980s despite the long-standing presence of Roma (Messing 1981; Alexandrakis 2003), Jewish, Vlach, Slavic, Arvanite, and Macedonian populations (Danforth 1995; Cowan 2000), to name but a few. Loring Danforth in particular provides an enlightening analysis of Greek national policy and popular response toward ethnicity and race over the twentieth century.

23 Tsiakalos 2006:195. Unfortunately, Tsiakalos's essay provides the term *racism* only in the English, without reference to the actual Greek words; see, however, Figgou and Condor 2006.

24 *Filoxenía*: literally, "love of strangers." Cornélia Zarkia (1996) presents a cogent discussion of Greek ideas of hospitality in the context of the economic pressures of mass tourism. Although racism itself remains outside her focus, her analysis of how Greek hosts behave toward foreign tourists versus Greek tourists is salient.

25 Rather than *omofilófilos*, the term used in the table of contents title and for the majority of the column itself is *géi*, the Greek transliteration of the English *gay*; see Halkias 2002.

26 The recent development of a rhetoric of "sissyphobia" in the United States and elsewhere (Bergling 2001) also suggests that gender nonconformity may be a primary target of phobic reactions, rather than sexual practices per se.

27 Sadly, Yianellos passed away in 2006.

28 All the same, many Athenian activists see such thinking as indicative of *esoteri-kevméni omofovía* (internalized homophobia), another of the subjects brought up for discussion at the Anti-Racist Festival.

29 See note 18 above, concerning Cooperation against Homophobia—Thessaloniki.

2 Transnational Homophobias

6

Not Quite Redemption Song

LGBT-Hate in Jamaica

Suzanne LaFont

SEVERAL YEARS AGO while I was living in Jamaica conducting research, an American friend who is gay came to
visit me. We were dancing the night away at the Roof Club
in Port Antonio when Buju Banton's hit song from 1992,
"Boom Bye Bye," blasted from the sound system.

> Boom bye, bye inna batty bwoy head[1]
> Rude bwoy nah promote them nastiness,
> Them haffi dead.

> *Bang, bang into gay man's head*
> *Homeboys will not tolerate their nastiness*
> *They must be killed*

"Boom Bye Bye" received a great deal of media attention for
its gay-hate message. In fact, the song, its popularity, and the
backlash against its gay-bashing lyrics seem to have internationally "outed" Jamaica's hatred of LGBT people.

That night at the Roof Club, I was grateful that my friend
did not understand Jamaican patois. I did not translate and
felt ashamed by the deception of my silence. I had been living
in Jamaica for three years and pretty much loved everything
about the country except for what seemed to be a national
preoccupation with policing nonconformational sexual and
gender behavior.

I began to wonder how we, as anthropologists, should cope with the aspects of our research cultures that are at odds with our own values. Many anthropologists face this problem when they do participant observation in settings where their beliefs about gender, race and ethnicity, spirituality, class, and politics are challenged. Some of us worry that we are not practicing cultural relativity if we find certain cultural practices and beliefs intolerable. Others conflate cultural relativity with the acceptance of any or all "different" cultural practices and beliefs. As Don Kulick observes in this volume, anthropologists have a tradition of defending the people we study rather than exposing negative practices and beliefs. However, we must also speak, without apology, about all aspects of culture, "negative" and "positive" (however these are defined) in order to understand them, even while accepting that the "understanding" is subjective and problematic.

Queering Homophobia

As I began to research the hatred of LGBT people in Jamaica, it became clear to me that it was problematic to refer to it as homophobia. As Kulick says, it is time to problematize the term *homophobia* and analyze how it has shaped our understanding of the hatred of LGBT people. It is important to critically examine the term with the intent of unsettling its meaning, deconstructing the assumptions behind its usage, and dethroning it as a concept that best defines LGBT-hate.

For years researchers and scholars have been critiquing the use of the term *homophobia* (Chodorow 1999; Sedgwick 1990; Young-Bruehl 1996). Despite criticism, the usage persists, and *homophobia* is the word most frequently used to describe and explain sexual intolerance in Jamaica and elsewhere (Fone 2000). There are, however, several problems with use of the term. When the psychologist George Weinberg coined the term in the 1960s, he used it to describe heterosexuals' fear of being in close quarters with homosexuals. He also applied it to homosexual self-loathing (Herek 2003). Since its introduction, the definition and usage of the term have changed dramatically. *Homophobia* began as a specialized psychological term and later, as a psychological concept, it became part of popular culture.[2] *Homophobia* is increasingly used by social scientists to describe culturally constructed beliefs, attitudes, and behaviors that are antihomosexual. Thus we see how some societies and regions of the world, on the basis of their treatment of "homosexuality," are considered "homophobic." As Kulick points out, "[Homophobia] . . . has been naturalized as a set of understandable psychological structures that everyone has . . . but that reasonable people resist and try to come to terms with."

The idea that homophobia is prompted by an individually psychologically based *fear*—a phobia—does not necessarily hold true. It has been argued that homophobes are afraid of homosexuals because (1) the latter stir up their own latent homosexuality; or (2) homosexuals are a threat to the patriarchal social order. Popular belief holds that phobias are personal psychological afflictions that cannot always be completely controlled, cured, or understood. For example, no one would argue that claustrophobics or acrophobics should be held fully responsible for their fears. But such thinking does not work when applied to homophobia. It is problematic to believe that the intolerance of gays and lesbians, in its many forms, can be reduced to an individual psychological or "fear-based" disorder.

Thus the current usage of the word *homophobia* obscures more than it clarifies. The perception of homophobia as a personal, private, or individual prejudice is not only incorrect; it clouds our understanding of the issue. Blaming individuals for discrimination and violence that result from the hatred of LGBT people obscures the social, economic, and political dynamics behind that hatred (Kinsman 1996). When a hate crime is identified as the result of an individual's psychological problems, it is considered a tragedy rather than a call for political and social change (Jakobsen and Pellegrini 2003). It lets society off the hook for tolerating or promoting bigotry.

The definition of *homophobia* as a term to describe "fear of or contempt for lesbians and gay men" is also too narrow in its scope. Hate crimes are often directed at gays, lesbians, bisexuals, transsexuals, the transgendered, cross-dressers, and everyone else who does not fit into a rigid model of female and male heterosexuality.

The hatred of LGBT people in Jamaica serves as an example to illustrate the problems with this popularly held understanding of homophobia. With regard to the idea that homophobia is about fear of homosexuals, Alexis Petridis (2004) recounts what one Jamaican told him: "We can't be homophobic because phobia means fear and we aren't afraid of them." In addition, intolerance of gender and sexual diversity is much more than individualized aggression and is not necessarily a personal affair in Jamaica. Hate crimes against LGBT people often involve groups and sometimes mobs. Furthermore, there exists almost universal acceptance of discrimination against gays and lesbians. A poll conducted by the *Jamaica Gleaner* on September 20, 2001, found that 96 percent of those asked responded no to the question "Do you feel that homosexuality should be legalized?"[3]

LGBT-Hate: Not Just Idle Talk

When Buju Banton's "Boom Bye Bye" created an international outcry, some Jamaicans were quick to defend it and claimed that Westerners misunderstood the metaphoric meanings of such lyrics. Carolyn Cooper of the University of the West Indies said, "What New Yorkers might see as DJ's homophobia could just as well be understood as an Africanist affirmation of complementary opposites: earth and sky, male and female" (Christgau 1993). Metaphorical meanings aside, several songs with similar messages followed in the footsteps of "Boom Bye Bye" and became widely popular.

In 2002, Grammy winner Beenie Man's hit song "Damn" included the lyrics "I'm dreaming of a new Jamaica, come to execute all the gays" (Stephens 2002). These lyrics relay the tone but not the prevalence of these songs. It has been estimated that in any given week, at least three of the top-twenty hits capitalize on antigay sentiment (Daily 2002).

Such lyrics are not empty threats. In January 2006, a young gay man drowned after he jumped in the Kingston harbor to escape a gay-hating mob that chased him to the water's edge (Jamaican News Reports 2005–2006). He had good reason to fear for his life. In December 2005, gunmen broke into the home of the AIDS activist Steve Harvey and in the course of the robbery accused Harvey and his two roommates of being gay. According to the roommates, they denied being gay, but when Harvey made no such denial he was abducted and later found shot to death (Younge 2005). When Brian Williamson, the cofounder of J-FLAG (Jamaican Forum of Lesbians, All-Sexuals, and Gays), the only Jamaican LGBT rights organization, was murdered in June 2004, a crowd gathered outside his home, celebrating his death and shouting, "Let's get them one at a time" and "Let's kill them all" (Human Rights Watch 2004).[4] Earlier that year a mob in Montego Bay, urged on by the police, chopped, stabbed, and stoned a gay man to death (HRW 2004).

In fact, hate crimes against LGBT people have been perpetrated for years.

In 1997, in St. Catherine District Prison and Kingston's General Penitentiary, sixteen men, presumed to be gays, were killed in a prison riot after it was announced that condoms would be distributed to prisoners to curb the spread of HIV/AIDS. The prison guards left their posts to protest the suggestion that they were having sex with prisoners and in the ensuing riots "straight" inmates murdered men who were gay or suspected of being gay (Amnesty International 2000).

For various reasons, not all hate crimes are listed as such, yet it has been estimated that between 1997 and 2002, more than thirty gay men were murdered while many others have been beaten, threatened, harassed, fired from their jobs, and evicted from their homes (HRW 2004; Thompson 2002). An analysis of these and other hate crimes in Jamaica reveals commonalities: Violence against LGBT people is exceedingly vicious, it is often carried out by groups, it is usually unprovoked, the police are sometimes complicit, and on occasion, these crimes are premeditated.

I used to think that the image of Jamaica as a sexually charged, sex-positive culture was an enigmatic contradiction to the sex-negative messages directed at LGBT people. Heterosexual sexuality is flaunted everywhere in the public domain. The country is replete with sexually explicit advertisements, announcements for Bare-as-You-Dare fetes, and radios blasting dancehall lyrics that boast of the singer's heterosexual capabilities—sometimes in great detail. I have, however, come to understand that in-your-face heterosexuality is not at all inconsistent with the hatred of LGBT people. In fact, proclamations of heterosexuality are just as important as the denouncement of homosexuality in defining appropriate sexual and gender behavior (Lancaster 1995). They are two sides of the same coin. It is not enough to vehemently deny homosexuality; it is also necessary to establish one's heterosexual prowess. Of course hegemonic heterosexuality is not unique to Jamaica, nor is the aggressive public stance against homosexuality, as other chapters in this volume demonstrate. But my research findings challenge some popularly held notions regarding the hatred of LGBT people. According to my data, women endorse LGBT-hatred as vehemently as men—although, to my knowledge, it is men who commit most of the violent crimes about LGBT people. And young Jamaicans tend to be the most adamant LGBT-haters—a reversal of the usual assumptions of young-liberal, mature-conservative generational difference. These are significant findings as it has often been assumed that rural, elderly men were the most conservative. Although this may be true in the United States, the Jamaican data suggest that young urban Jamaicans are more conservative than their rural counterparts and may, in fact, be getting more, rather than less, conservative (Goldstein 2003).

These observations raise questions: How and when did Jamaica evolve to its present state of sexual intolerance? And why does LGBT-hate seem to be increasing at a time when tolerance of diversity is the current transnational mantra? In what follows, I will outline how, in Jamaica, the hatred of LGBT people is the result of a confluence of political, historical, cultural, and ideological factors.

Discourses on LGBT-Hate

My original research objective was to trace the political economy of Jamaican sexualities through time, keeping in mind that sexualities are mediated by social forces, which in turn are shaped by political economies.[5] However, the historical records on sexualities,[6] desire, and sexual behavior are scant, and I found it difficult to reconstruct the historical "sexual terrain" of Jamaica. Yet it was clear that sexualities in Jamaica have developed through the influence of multiple, intersecting African and British sexual meanings which have, in turn, been shaped by the interrelatedness of slavery, colonization, class, race, gender, and religion. Sexual morality in Jamaica has evolved through processes of syncretism, reaction, resistance, exploitation, and opportunism (LaFont 2001).

As my research progressed, I found that in the absence of concrete historical data detailing sexual history, Afro-Jamaicans have constructed a mythologized version of past sexual morality. Rather than attempting to reconstruct history, I analyzed Jamaican narratives for their "history." I investigate how current beliefs draw on this mythologized history to explain and legitimize today's hatred and intolerance of LGBT people.

When discussing the past, Jamaicans often refer to the "first time people" and the "ole days." These terms are vaguely used to refer to the days of their ancestors; however, there is no set definition of who the "first time people" were or when the "ole days" occurred. When inquiring, I received responses that ranged from the postslavery era to the generation of their grandparents. Importantly, there seems to be general consensus that life used to be much better in the days of the "first time people," when, it is believed, family values were strong, violence was rare, and people adhered to Christian sexual morality. It is generally believed that "first time people" married before having children, stayed married, and were monogamous, and that there was no rape, incest, or homosexuality during their era. The perception of the lives of the "first time people" is often used in contrast to current quality of life and sexual morality (LaFont 1996).

In contrast, Jamaicans claim, most children in Jamaica are now born out of wedlock (87 percent); teenage pregnancy rates are high (23 percent); absentee fatherhood is common; many people have children with multiple partners; "roots" reggae music has largely been replaced with sexually explicit dancehall music; and women wear *batty riders* and other revealing clothing to clubs where dance movements mimic sexual intercourse (United Nations 2000; LaFont 2000; Stolzoff, 2000).[7] In truth, many of these perceived social ills developed during the slave era and have been a part of Jamaican sociocultural life for centuries (Clarke 1957; Simey 1946). The point is that it is believed that these ills are increasing, and this, coupled with the perception of increased alcohol consumption and drug use, has fueled the public view that Jamaican society is in decline.

In order to understand the concepts of the "first time people" and the "ole days" it is instructive to look at the social, economic, and political factors involved in the development of Jamaican sexual morality.

Race, Class, and Respectability

Throughout Jamaica's history, most Afro-Jamaicans have had little access to wealth and power. The colonial legacy of racial discrimination and social and economic inequality continues today and is compounded today by Jamaica's debt crisis, high unemployment, violence, and corruption—a combination of circumstances that leaves most Jamaicans impoverished (Harrison 1997).

In this context, respectability became one way to achieve status (Braithwaite 1971; Smith 1962; Smith 1988). The importance of respectability permeates Jamaican society on many levels and has been well researched (Anderson 1986; Austin 1984; Foner 1973; Powell 1984).[8] Respectability is based on a combination of moral character and adherence to strict societal norms regarding gender and sexual behavior. It is a prerequisite for social mobility and strongly influences ideas and attitudes about gender and sexuality.

Class has played an important role in the construction of respectability. Wealth was and is not necessarily the decisive factor in determining respectable status; in fact, Afro-Jamaicans often cite the immorality of elites as a way to challenge wealth or race as the prerequisite to respectability. In lieu of having access to wealth and in face of racial discrimination, many poor Afro-Jamaicans have claimed and continue to claim moral superiority over the rich and the whites (LaFont 2001). An important component of the perceived moral upper hand over the whites and elites was and still is sexual moral superiority. For poor Afro-Jamaicans, taking the moral high road meant that appropriate gender and sexual behavior became narrowly defined, whereby reproductive heterosexual activity was seen as the only type of natural and moral sexual behavior. This has provided and continues to provide poor Afro-Jamaicans with a sense of respectability that has always been difficult to acquire in the face of a racial hierarchy and in the absence of wealth.

Class divisions are complex and sexual morality (or lack thereof) often works to reinforce class antagonisms. Many Jamaican elites blame the current poverty of their nation on poor Afro-Jamaicans' sexual behaviors such as male promiscuity, teenage pregnancy, the prevalence of children born out of wedlock, and the "slackness" of the dancehall lyrics popular among poor Afro-Jamaicans. At the same time, poor Afro-Jamaicans criticize white Jamaicans, wealthy Afro-Jamaicans, and/or foreigners for engaging in immoral sexual behavior such as oral, anal, and same-sex sexual activity. For example, Jamaican men who date tourist women are ostracized for ostensibly engaging in male to female and/or female to male oral sex, a sex act Western women are said to demand (Pruitt and LaFont 2004). A musician I know threw an American groupie out of his hotel room in the middle of the night after she tried to fellate him. He complained that if she was willing to do that, she had surely done it to other men. How could he kiss lips that had been on a penis? And Coco Tea, a famous dancehall artist, had to go on the record and deny rumors that he had oral sex with his wife, assuring the public that he thought "oral sex a nastiness" (*ExcesS Weekend* 2001). Indeed, there are many terms to describe oral sex and all of them are deprecating, such as "eating under the table" and "bowing." At dancehall shows, it is important for the performer to get a *forward* from the crowd.[9] Common ways to elicit *forwards* are calls to the crowd to express condemnation of unacceptable sexual behavior, such as oral sex or same-sex sexuality. Sure-fire *forwards* include "Hold up yuh hand if yuh nuh like *battyman*, hold up yuh hand if yuh nuh suck pussy, yuh nuh *bowcat*" (Petridis 2004).[10]

Despite condemnation of such behavior at all class levels, wealthy gays, lesbians, and bisexuals have a level of immunity which is often unavailable to their poorer counterparts. As long as gay-lesbian-bi sexualities remain undercover, in the closet, and "uptown," the illusion of respectability is maintained and allows for the continuation of an unspoken agreement between wealthy homosexual and heterosexual Jamaicans. One gay Jamaican man observed, "Gay Jamaica is divided along much the same line as the country in general. There are those who have and the have-nots . . . This has in effect created two gay societies: one which is less persecuted and more affluent and a more vulnerable poorer group" (Anonymous 2006).

I spent part of my initial fieldwork (1989–1992) living in Stony Hill, a suburb of Kingston featuring luxurious mansions in close proximity to shacks constructed out of corrugated iron. Two of my wealthy neighbors were gay. It was an open secret and they were not approved of by others living in the area, but during the time I lived there, they were not harassed. In 2005, one of my female informants, a domestic worker, commented on one of these same men, "When me live in Stony Hill there was a gay man living near us and he used to have these young-young guys. Young-young-young school guys them and he send them to school and buy them the most expensive shoes and clothes and food . . . That was very bad! Very bad!"

Speaking of her shantytown neighborhood in Kingston, one of my older female informants explained, "In Cassava Piece you don't have any lesbians —you won't find those girls. . . . You have girls who do those things but if you go to Half Way Tree or Cross Roads [lower-income areas] in the night-clubs there, you don't find lesbians. They know where to go—like by New Kingston [a wealthy area]."

Suspicion of homosexuality and/or refusal or inability to behave like a "real" man or woman puts poor Afro-Jamaicans at risk of public harassment or worse. This creates a double hardship for poor LGBT people; shantytown living does not allow for much privacy but if they come out or are found out, they risk ostracism or worse. In 2004, Human Rights Watch interviewed several gay men who had been fired from their jobs and/or chased away from their communities with "battyman mus' dead" threats. One interviewee explained that the ability to live in a wealthy neighborhood provides some protection. "Those that can afford, they can rent an apartment and will not be molested. But we cannot afford it. Some might attempt to rent a little house [shanty]. But within days, or it doesn't be a month, they have to run away, leave everything they have" (HRW 2004:52).

Gendered behavior is not necessarily the defining factor in LGBT-hate; effeminate men and masculine women are more frequently the target of hate crimes, but masculine gay men and feminine lesbians are also reviled (HRW 2004). All trans people are assumed to be gay or lesbian and are treated accordingly. The following is an account of an effeminate gay man living in Cassava Piece, as told to me in 2005 by one of the current female residents: "One used to live where me live. . . . I never really see him in a close relationship with a man but oh, you'd like to see him go on! Boy, everything that woman do, he do it. They *run* him out. They *run* him out from up there . . . And they beat him. They beat him up really bad but him never go to the police . . . Him leave. His mother was living there . . . And you know, when his mother died, him don't come for the funeral because him afraid. Everybody in the area know him a gay man."

Although most violence is directed at gay men, women suspected of being "sodomites" are sometimes targets of organized "correctional" gang rapes (Silvera 1996). The Jamaican poet Staceyann Chin describes her own rape in her poem "Unspeakable Things" (Walters 2001):

> I am there
> Dreaming of the paradisal home
> Where, if memory were my only reminder
> I would convince you
> That it isn't really illegal
> To be a lesbian in Jamaica
> In my dreams I would write
> That a dozen boys didn't drag me into a bathroom to show
> me what a real dick
> feels like . . .

The Importance of Christianity

Historically, British missionaries were crucially influential in shaping the definition of sexual respectability. Christianity claimed a higher moral ground, provided guidelines in an unstable world and a psychological sanctuary from the degradation of slavery. Many Afro-Jamaicans embraced Christianity but did so on their own terms. They did not simply worship the European God; they incorporated elements such as spirit contact from West African religions (Simpson 1978). They also stopped short of completely embracing all sex-negative Christian dogma. This Creolized sexual ideology approved of sexual activity as a natural part of human pleasure, but sexuality had to be expressed within the confines of respectability. As the Jamaican writer Makeda Silvera (1996:169) observes, "Our grandparents gained access to literacy through the Bible when they were being indoctrinated by missionaries. It provided powerful and ancient stories of strength, endurance, and hope which reflected their own fight against oppression. This book has been so powerful that it continues to bind our lives with its racism and misogyny."

The church continues to be a powerful institution in Jamaica and many people take the scriptures at face value, including the Genesis story of human creation. Concerning homosexuality, their attitudes are similar to those expressed in fundamentalist Christianity elsewhere. A common refrain is "Why would you need two men together and two women together, when God only made a man and a woman? I've never heard of him making Adam and Steve, or Eve and Louise, I know only Adam and Eve." The biblical story of Sodom and Gomorrah is also frequently and erroneously cited as God's condemnation of same-sex sexuality (Parrinder 1998).

When it comes to heterosexual behaviors, Christian Jamaicans are often more flexible in their morality, ignoring the biblical rulings on fornication and adultery. For example, dancehall artists, who are notorious for having "plenty gal," also use references from the Bible to justify their gay-hating lyrics. Sizzla, whose lyrics include "Sodomite and batty bwai mi seh a death fi dem [Lesbians and gays, I say death to them]," stated, "We won't tolerate homosexuals, we won't tolerate lesbians. . . . We must keep the covenant of the most [high] and give thanks and praise" (Burnett 2004). When the dancehall performer Spragga was asked why he wrote gay-hating lyrics, he answered, "I wanted to tell people that this [homosexuality] is wrong in the sight of the Lord" (Pitter 2001).

Popular clergy also frequently weigh in on the issue. In 1999, the Jamaican Council of Churches officially protested a proposed concert by the Village People, calling their music "repugnant"—the concert was eventually cancelled (Faul 1999). Bishop Jones, a renowned Jamaican (and brother of the actress Grace Jones), who currently preaches in the United States, announced during a visit to the island that Jamaicans should resist pressure from LGBT rights advocates: "If you have laws and legislation that ban certain things based on the principles of the Scriptures and based on your Christian background, then let it stand there. . . . If your laws are based on your Christian points of view, then you must stand your ground" (Dawes 2004).

The stance of most Christian denominations in Jamaica is articulated in an article in the *Jamaica Gleaner*: "In the Bible, homosexuality or same sex relations is consistently presented as an abomination and never as an orientation. Scriptural language is always strong and denunciatory, as well as plain. Whether in the Judaic Scriptures of the Old Testament, particularly the books of Leviticus and Deuteronomy, or the Christian New Testament, homosexuality is condemned as not only sin, but also perverse sin" (Hall 2003).

Given the historical and ongoing importance of religion in Jamaica, such interpretations of the Bible help perpetuate LGBT-hate. Reports of tolerance in other parts of the world often create backlashes, many of which are led by church officials. Reports of research on a gay gene, the ordainment of a gay Anglican minister, and the release of the movie *Brokeback Mountain* all prompted editorials written by clergy reminding Jamaicans what the Bible says about homosexuality (Boyne 2004). The general position can be characterized as "Who are we to question the word of God?"

LGBT-Hatred Is Legitimized by Institutions of the State

Heterosexism is institutionalized in Jamaica, and prejudice and discrimination against LGBT people are not only tolerated but supported in part by law, the police, and politicians. One particular law is used to criminalize male same-sex sexuality: the Offences against the Persons Act prohibits "acts of gross indecency" (generally interpreted as referring to any kind of physical intimacy) between men, in public or in private. The Offence of Buggery is specified in section 76 of this statute, and is defined as anal intercourse between a man and a woman or between two men (International Gay and Lesbian Human Rights Committee 2000). Convictions can carry a penalty of ten years hard labor in prison (Williams 2000). It should be noted that the Jamaican law criminalizes sodomy and "unnatural acts," not homosexuality per se, and is silent on lesbianism. Many Jamaicans, however, (mistakenly) interpret these laws to mean that homosexuality itself is illegal.

Police statistics on arrests, charges, and conviction rates for the Offences against the Persons Act and the Offence of Buggery are not published. Human Rights Watch (2004) found that the laws are more frequently used to intimidate and harass LGBT people rather than to put them in jail. A Jamaican lawyer reports, "In all my years as an attorney, I cannot recall seeing a man and a woman engaging in consensual anal sex ever prosecuted for buggery. . . . The buggery and gross indecency laws basically sanction discrimination against gay men" (*Jamaica Gleaner* 2001). Even when men are caught in "compromising" positions, prosecutions are rare, because blood or semen must be analyzed to prove penetration.

The police have broad latitude regarding the use of these laws and can and do detain and arrest persons suspected of gross indecency or buggery. There have been many reports of police beating, threatening, harassing, and arresting men and women simply because they appeared to be gay. Human Rights Watch (2004) interviewees reported events that included six cases of harassment and/or threats, eights cases of beating, and three arrests. Only one man was charged and the charges were subsequently dropped.

Despite such reports, when K. K. Knight, the senior superintendent of police, was interviewed, he stated, "We haven't had any reports about violence against homosexuals. *Most of the violence against homosexual is internal.* . . . I know that there is a sort of revulsion against homosexuals, lesbians, but evidence does not substantiate that there is any level of violence perpetrated against them" (HRW 2004; my emphasis).

The belief that jealousy is behind the murder of gays and lesbians is widespread. One of my female informants from Cassava Piece commented, "You have some of them get killed and sometimes they killed one another because of jealousy." The press helps perpetuate this belief. When Brian Williams, the cofounder of J-FLAG, was murdered, one newspaper columnist wrote, in a piece titled "Those Flaming Homosexuals," "Based on cursory investigations, all indications are that he was murdered by someone 'in-house.' The police report that he was chopped all over his body. This is fairly consistent with previous murders in Jamaica involving male homosexuals" (Wignall 2004). This is in direct conflict with what is known about hate crimes. Extreme brutality, multiple stab wounds or gunshots are characteristic of hate crimes based on gender identity, sexual orientation, and race (Gender Public Advocacy Coalition 2002).

Political leaders also help to legitimize LGBT-hate. In June 2001, P. J. Patterson, the prime minister, long believed to be gay (a fact many Jamaicans believe is responsible for their failing economy), publicly affirmed his sexual orientation with the statement "My credentials as a lifelong heterosexual are impeccable" (White 2001). He also reassured the public: "Under my watch . . . we have no intention whatsoever of changing those laws that make homosexuality illegal" (Davis and Roxborough 2000). Not to be outdone, the opposition leader, Edward Seaga, featured the dancehall band TOK's "Chi Chi Man" song—which carried the message "Rat tat tat, every chi chi man dem haffi get flat" [Every gay man must be shot dead]—in his election campaigns (Davis 2003).[11] The Peoples National Party responded by adopting the slogan "Log on to Progress." "Log On" was a hit song by the dancehall artist Elephant Man which included the lyrics "Log on, and step pon chi chi man" (*Jamaican Cave* n.d.).

The Ministry of Tourism has also stepped into the LGBT-hate ring. They have made it clear that gay cruise ships are not welcome but have stopped short of banning them from docking. Subsequently, some gay tour operators have issued warnings to their patrons about traveling to Jamaica (Davis and Roxborough 2000).

LGBT Activism in Jamaica Today

There are voices of dissent regarding the treatment of LGBT people in Jamaica, but they are few and far between. Dissent is so unpopular that when a University of the West Indies academic journal, *Small Axe*, published an article titled "Homophobia and Gay Rights Activism in Jamaica," the author felt the need to publish it under a pseudonym (Williams 2000). Opting for such anonymity is a common practice in Jamaica.

Formal LGBT activism did not come to Jamaica until 1998, when the LGBT organization J-FLAG was launched. There had been a gay community and gay bars prior to this time but they have always been underground, reviled but tolerated. Even as J-FLAG boasts a professional website, its locale remains unknown: "Due to the potential threat for violent retribution, we cannot publish the exact location of our office" (J-FLAG 2001). Furthermore, when it was rumored that members of this organization were going to rally and march through a major commercial area in Kingston, hundreds of citizens, women and men, young and old, armed themselves and lined the streets daring any *battyman* to show themselves. None did, but the nonevent inspired Spragge Benz to write a song titled "Nuh Inna Dat [Not into that]":

Why man waan wine man in front a I man
That caan gwaan inna my land . . .
Get ready and guns out
J-Flag dem a brag and a talk bout
Out a di closet dem a go walk out.
But man nuh inna det, dem betta
For if dem come out, they might be shot

*Why does a man want to dance close with another man
    in front of me (or us)*
That can't go on in my land
Get ready and guns out
J-Flag members brag and talk about
Out of the closet they are going to walk
But, man not into that, they better stay inside and hide
For if they come out, they might be shot.

HIV/AIDS seems to have been another contributing factor in an increase in hostility toward gays and has allowed for LGBT-hate to be more open. It is probably not a coincidence that the awareness of the disease and the problems associated with it occurred shortly before the gay-bashing "Boom Bye Bye" became a hit. In the early days, HIV/AIDS was believed to have been brought to the island by foreign gays, reinforcing the idea of the sexual immorality of whites and foreigners. HIV/AIDS is still considered by many to be a "gay disease" and homosexuality and HIV/AIDS are often conflated. This is believed in spite of the fact that in 2004, 68 percent of the new cases were attributed to heterosexual sex (Jamaican National HIV/AIDS Prevention and Control Program 2004). This conflation is so pervasive that HIV/AIDS educators are often assumed to be gay and are threatened, harassed, and arrested, thereby impeding HIV/AIDS education and intervention (HRW 2004). The island's chief medical official, Dr. Peter Figueroa, believes that fear of discrimination based on sexual orientation is detrimental to the fight against HIV/AIDS (Davis 2003). Due to the gay stigma, people suffering from HIV/AIDS have sometimes been denied medical treatment at public facilities. When it is provided they are usually secluded from other patients, and their confidentiality is often breached by health care professionals (HRW 2004).

Amnesty International and international gay rights movements, along with J-FLAG's efforts and pressure from LGBT Jamaicans living abroad, are currently advocating for legislative change. In fact, most of the support for gay rights comes from outside rather than inside the country. Recently the "Stop Murder Music" (SMM) campaign launched by the British-based gay rights organization Outrage! has been influential in having gay-bashing dancehall artists sanctioned. Some concerts by Beenie Man, Buju Banton, Bounty Killer, Sizzla, Capleton, and others have were cancelled in Europe and the United States as a result of public reaction and pressure. Outrage! has also mobilized a campaign to pressure music stores to pull the offending music from their shelves (Petridis 2004).

However, these efforts have created a backlash in Jamaica causing defiance among the dancehall performers who refuse to "bow" to foreign pressure. Two weeks after Virgin Records issued a weakly worded apology from Beenie Man, he was back on stage in Jamaica, denying that he had apologized and performing his gay-bashing favorites. Bounty Man and Sizzla have refused to apologize and Sizzla is quoted as saying, "They can't ask me to apologise. They've got to apologise to God because they break God's law" (Petridis 2004).

Ultimately, economics may be the driving force for change. It is estimated that the cancellations and reduced record sales have cost the Jamaican performers and artists millions of U.S. dollars. In 2005, a tentative agreement was reached between representatives of the reggae industry and SMM whereby SMM agreed to stop its campaign and performers have agreed to stop inciting violence toward lesbians and gays. It remains to be seen what impact, if any, this will have in Jamaica. If dancehall artists simply cut the gay-hating lyrics while performing abroad but continue to earn *forwards* for using forbidden lyrics, they will mostly likely be celebrated for standing up to *Babylon*.[12]

Criticism from international human rights organizations such as Human Rights Watch and Amnesty International regarding the treatment of homosexuality in the country has thus, generally speaking, had a negative impact on gay rights in Jamaica. By forcing the issue of gay rights out of the closet, such organizations generate publicity and public dialogue, resulting in mostly negative media coverage such as hateful editorials, political cartoons that stereotype gays, polls showing that most Jamaicans think homosexuality should be kept illegal, and news reports of politicians and celebrities boasting of their heterosexuality while having to refute accusations of being gay. Most media coverage strengthens the notion that LGBT-hate is part of the national culture and effectively silences or stifles dissenting viewpoints.

Conclusion

Throughout the world sexual intolerance has been shaped through complex historical interaction of racial, political, economic, and religious forces. In Jamaica intolerance of sexual and gender diversity is perpetuated by a mythologized version of the past, class divisions, the importance of respectability, the involvement of the church, and the support of those in authority and power.

Today, intolerance of gays is championed as evidence of Jamaica's moral superiority over Western liberal sexual ideology and is regarded as a virtue. Tolerance of gays is seen as morally reprehensible and un-Jamaican, tarnishing the national image. Many Jamaicans reject "foreign" sexual immorality defiantly and with pride and proudly claim to have a moral upper hand over Western societies. They view the international pressure to change their laws and views about gays as an example of postcolonial imperialism. They believe that upholding their sexual morals is an integral part of their cultural rights.

Jamaica has received international criticism for its institutionalized discrimination of gays. The country is in breach of the United Nations Human Rights Regulations, despite being a signatory and responsible for upholding the regulations. These actions illustrate the global dialogue between human rights and sexual rights (Chanock 2000). Sexual rights have not been widely accepted as a legitimate component of universal human rights. In fact, they constitute one of the most contested arenas of human rights and, as this volume demonstrates, these contestations are occurring in many other nations beyond Jamaica.

Engelke (1999:293) notes that morality and moral sentiment "constitute a serious obstacle to human rights activism" and "that there are problems with the practice and theory of such a universalising discourse." It is necessary to find a place for cultural difference within the framework of human rights and to recognize that human rights mean different things in different cultures. Yet it is unclear how this will be accomplished. One step in this direction is to better understand the cultural context and political economy of sexualities and to analyze gender and sexuality systems with all their "positive" and "negative" attributes as intrinsic, rather than marginal, to sociocultural life.

Notes

1   *Battyman* has been used to label gay men for several years—the word *batty* refers to the buttocks.
2   See Wickberg 2000 for an excellent discussion of the history of the use of the term *homophobia*.
3   The poll involved interviews with a thousand people in all fourteen parishes and had a margin of error of plus or minus 3.2 percent; www.jamaica-gleaner.com.
4   J-FLAG's mission is "to work towards a Jamaican society in which the Human Rights and Equality of Lesbians, All-Sexuals [all those included in the non-heterosexual continuum who defy labels], and Gays are guaranteed." The organization's homepage is available at http://www.jflag.org.
5   My research in Kingston began in 1989 when I spent three years in the country conducting ethnographic research on gender. I returned to Jamaica in 1993, 1994, 2001, and again in 2005 to collect data and conduct in-depth interviews about Jamaican sexualities.
6   I use the term *sexualities* rather than *sexuality* to highlight the existence of rural/urban, class, race, identity, orientation, and individual variations.
7   *Batty-riders* are shorts that do not cover the bottom part of the buttocks. One of the informants described women at the dancehalls: "Them always wear *batty-riders* and the whole of their bottom is out of doors."
8   For the most in-depth discussion on the importance of respectability in the English-speaking Caribbean, see Wilson 1973.
9   A *forward* is the crowd showing appreciation by waving their hands in the air and cheering.
10 In Jamaican patois, a *bowcat* is someone who performs oral sex, in particular, men who perform oral sex on women.
11 *Chi chi* is a termite and wood is a euphemism for penis, thus as the chi chi eats wood, the gay man "eats" penis.
12 Rastafarians have popularized the term *Babylon* as a way to describe the system, the white or foreign establishment, or the police.

The Emergence of Political
Homophobia in Indonesia
Masculinity and National Belonging

Tom Boellstorff

ON NOVEMBER 11, 2000, about 350 *gay* and male-to-female transvestite (*waria, banci, béncong*) Indonesians gathered in the resort town of Kaliurang in Central Java for an evening of artistic performances and comedy skits.[1] The event, in observance of National Health Day, was sponsored by several health organizations as well as the local France-Indonesia Institute: many heterosexual or *normal* Indonesians also attended. Events like this have been held across Indonesia since the early 1990s, and those present had no reason to suspect this night would be any different.

However, at around 9:30 p.m. about 150 men who later claimed to be members of the Gerakan Pemuda Ka'bah (Ka'bah Youth Movement) burst into the Wisma Hastorenggo hall where the celebration was underway.[2] Arriving in a mass of motorcycles and jeeps, many wore the white hats or robes associated with political Islam. Shouting "God is Great" and "Look at these men done up like women. Get out, *banci*!,"[3] they assaulted those present with knives, machetes, and clubs. Sounds of shattering glass filled the air as the attackers smashed windows and destroyed chairs, tables, and equipment. No one was killed but at least twenty-five were injured; witnesses spoke of persons "bathed in blood" from severe wounds. At least three persons were hospitalized, including the local director of the France-Indonesia

Institute, who among other injuries was struck in the head by a sword; another victim suffered injuries near his right eye after being hit with clubs and a chair; yet another was struck over the head with a bottle until the bottle broke.[4] Others were hurt while fleeing; one *gay* man was injured when leaping from a window to escape. The attackers also robbed and verbally abused their victims, vandalizing the vehicles used to transport participants to the site. These male attackers displayed a high state of emotion throughout the incident; one *gay* witness described them as filled with cruel anger (*bengis*), possessed by anger (*kalap*), hot-tempered and wild (*beringas*), and shouting sadistically (*bentakan-bentakan sadis*).[5] Fifty-seven men were arrested following the event but all were soon released without charges being filed.

This incident was foreshadowed by another one year earlier. For two decades in Indonesia a series of groups—ranging from formally structured entities to small clusters of persons in rural areas or even single correspondents—have worked to link together *gay* men and *lesbi* women in a national network.[6] Dédé Oetomo, an anthropologist and linguist based in Surabaya (East Java), has been a major figure in this movement and in the mid-1990s became involved with the Education and Propaganda division of the People's Democratic Party (Partai Rakyat Demokratik or PRD), which includes a call for *lesbi* and *gay* rights in its platform. In 1998 Oetomo even stood as a candidate for national parliament under the PRD banner.

Through the efforts of Oetomo and many others, plans were hatched in the early 1990s to hold a meeting that could strengthen the national network. In December 1993 the First National Gay and Lesbian Congress was held without any negative consequences at Kaliurang, the very location where the violence described above would take place seven years later. From this meeting was born the Indonesian Lesbi and Gay Network (Jaringan Lesbi dan Gay Indonesia or JLGI). The JLGI successfully staged a Second National Congress in Bandung (West Java) in 1995 and a third in Denpasar (Bali) in 1997. Like the first National Congress, these events attracted from fifty to one hundred participants from Java, Bali, and Sulawesi (persons from other islands rarely attended because there was no money for scholarships). At no time did these events draw unfavorable public attention. The Denpasar Congress, which I attended, was covered extensively by the local newspaper *Nusa* in a five-day series of feature articles (November 24–28,

Figure 1. Cartoon from *Gatra* magazine, September 18, 1999, commenting on the Solo incident. Note the angry men in the background, as well as the magazines held by the two men, arms linked in flight, that read "*Rakernas* [*RApat KERja NASional* or "national working meeting"] Lesbian & Gay Solo." The shirt of one man reads "JLGI."

1997); much of the coverage repeated stereotypes of *gay* men and *lesbi* women as obsessed with sex, but it also included statements by public figures calling for Indonesian society to "embrace" *lesbi* women and *gay* men.

In the wake of these successes, plans were soon underway for a fourth meeting in 1999—the first to follow Soeharto's fall.[7] That September, members of twenty-one organizations and groups came from Java and Bali to the city of Solo in Central Java to participate in the meeting, which was to take place at the Dana Hotel on the ninth and tenth, with a press conference to follow. Such a press conference had never taken place before and represented a substantial move to claim public recognition in a post-Soeharto civil society. By at least September 7, however, several Muslim organizations in Solo had learned of the meeting and, in sharp contrast to the indifference that greeted the previous congresses, declared that it should not take place. Moreover, this rejection took the form of threatened violence—specifically, to burn down the Dana Hotel and kill anyone found there.[8] The secretary of the local Indonesian Muslim clerics' council, Muhammad Amir, stated that the meeting would be "very embarrassing [*sangat memalukan*]. As if we are legalizing the practice of such sexual deviations."

Once these threats became known the meeting was cancelled, but the Muslim organizations soon learned of a backup plan to hold a press conference at the local PRD office; on September 10 a group of youths from these organizations surrounded the office and threatened to burn it down. Death threats were made against Oetomo and a mobilization took place across the city based on rumors that the meeting would be moved to an undisclosed location. H. Sadili, a member of the governing board for the Solo Muslim Youth Front, said that "if they become known, they'll definitely become the target of masses running *amok*."

Masculinity and the Nation

From one perspective, these incidents appear as further cases of the dreary efflorescence of violence following the fall in 1998 of Soeharto's "New Order," violence whose genealogy stretches back through the New Order (1967–98) to the colonial state. From another perspective, however, they are bluntly novel: historically, violence against nonnormative men in Indonesia has been rare to a degree unimaginable in many Euro-American societies, where assaults on homosexual and transgendered men are familiar elements of the social world.[9] What is in particular need of explanation is the cultural logic that makes this new genre of violence comprehensible to Indonesians (*gay* or not, Muslim or not) so that these two events could have a continuing, generalized impact.

In a review of anthropological writing on violence in Southeast Asia, Mary Steedly cautions against either essentializing violence (as an inevitable dimension of human sociality) or culturalizing it (as a necessary element of a particular social system). The third alternative Steedly proposes is to "localize" violence: "By this I mean exploring the full particularity of its multifarious occasions: how it is produced in certain circumstances; how it is deployed, represented, limited, imagined, ignored, or instigated; how it is identified, disciplined, interrogated, and, of course, punished" (Steedly 1999:445–446). My only quibble with this alternative is that when violence is framed in terms of localization, a presumption that culture is local in the first instance grounds the analysis in the last instance—no matter how emphatically the constitutive role of the state, the legacy of the colonial encounter, or other translocal forces such as "world religions" enter the interpretive frame. In the cases at hand here, both the "deviant" masculinities and the cultural logics of the attackers drew their structuring assumptions from national and global discourses. Given the long tradition of assuming that "deviant" masculinities as local in nature, this may seem unusual, but this translocality of *gay* subjectivity is, I argue, linked to why the violence occurred. Understanding these incidents can illuminate how the full particularity of violence's occasion can involve an imagined Indonesian community (Anderson 1983), rather than the ethnolocal categories (Javanese, Madurese, Buginese, and so on) that, however historicized and problematized, continue to dominate anthropological investigations of the archipelago (Boellstorff 2002). This chapter incorporates an attention to what was unique about these incidents (that they targeted nonnormative men), with attention to national topographies of culture, toward the goal of investigating intersections of emotion and violence.[10]

I wish to ask how emotion figures in violence understood as political. In the historical moment in which I write, emotion and political violence come together most starkly in the figure of the terrorist. The "terror-ist" is the limit function of the emotion/violence nexus, and the terrorist's terror is by definition political, else the person is solely a mass murderer. Against claims that emotion is a precultural, even acultural psychological response function, it is clear that the terror produced by political violence is a cultural phenomenon. This means its form is always historically and geographically specific. *Political homophobia* is the name I give to an emergent cultural logic linking emotion, sexuality, and political violence. It brings together the direct object of nonnormative Indonesian men with the indirect object of contemporary Indonesian public culture, making enraged violence against *gay* men intelligible and socially efficacious.

Through highlighting the role of national belonging in this violence, I suggest that norms for Indonesian national identity may be gaining a new masculinist cast. I also hope to foreclose reductive explanations in terms of Islam. While at present Islam may represent a necessary condition for these new forms of violence, it cannot explain their relationship to masculinity, emotion, and the public sphere. In reconfiguring official Islam's heterosexist rejection of male homosexuality and transgenderism into political homophobia, the perpetrators of this violence are not just expressing religious belief but reacting to a feeling of *malu*, a complex term that can be provisionally rendered as "shame." While informed by Islamic sexual norms, the context and timing of the Kaliurang and Solo incidents reveal a new problematic evoking these feelings. This is the sense that the potential for the nation to be represented by nonnormative men challenges a nationalized masculinity, enabling what has long been understood to be a normative male response to malu—namely, the masculine and often collective enraged violence known in Indonesian as *amok*. By definition, amok is always a public act. The attackers in Kaliurang and Solo, who claimed to represent a post-Soeharto vision of the national, may have sought to shore up a perceived shameful threat to the nation through public violence directed at the events themselves. That it is these events which are considered shameful, and that violence is seen as their proper counter, indicates that these attackers' vision of the nation is normatively male. Emotion here can be used to divine politics.[11]

Political homophobia highlights how postcolonial heterosexuality is shaped by the state, but in ways specific to particular colonial legacies and national visions, and which therefore vary over time as well as space. A substantial literature now documents the massive effort undertaken by the Indonesian state to inculcate gendered ideologies of the ideal citizen, a national masculinity and femininity. As I discuss later, historically a wide range of forms of kinship and gender could be found throughout the archipelago. However, at present the family principle (*azas kekeluargaan*), with its associated ideologies of "State Momism" (Suryakusuma 1996) and "State Fatherism," sets forth narrow visions of masculinity and femininity as the foundations of society.[12] Implicit is the heterosexist ideology linking these ideally gendered men and women into the citizen-family. As we see in nationalist literature going back to the 1920s, the idea of becoming a modern Indonesian is often framed in terms of a shift from arranged to "chosen" marriage (Alisjahbana 1966, Siegel 1997, Rodgers 1995). While there are still arranged marriages, and many that fall between arrangement and choice, the ideal of chosen marriage now dominates images of the proper Indonesian citizen. I have noted elsewhere (Boellstorff 2007a: chapter 1) that when marriage is arranged sexual orientation is secondary, but that when marriages are based on love and choice, sexual orientation becomes a new kind of problem. In contemporary Indonesia, choice, to be national, must be heterosexual choice, and while both man and woman choose, the dominant ideology is that men pursue while the "choice" of the woman is secondarily that of refusal.[13] It is through heterosexuality that gendered self and nation articulate. In the new Indonesia, men who publicly appear to make improper choices threaten this gendered and sexualized logic of national belonging.

I come to the topic of political homophobia from a larger project in which I explore how Indonesians occupying *gay* and *lesbi* subject-positions are shaped by national discourse (Boellstorff 1999, 2003). It bears noting that so-called traditional homosexual or transgender roles, primarily limited to ritual and performance contexts, can still be found in many parts of Indonesia. *Gay* Indonesians occasionally draw upon these "traditional" sexualities to claim legitimacy (they are almost exclusively for men). In reality, however, few *gay* Indonesians identify with or even know of these "traditions": they see themselves as (to employ the Indonesian term) *modern*, part of a national community (see Boellstorff 2005: chapters 2 and 3). These Indonesians are found across the archipelago, even in rural areas, and are more likely to be lower class than members of the jet-setting elite that stands so frequently as the trope of the "Third World" homosexual. It is in this sense, as persons whose sexualities are irreducible to locality or tradition, that *gay* Indonesians could be seen as a major, if unintended, success story of Soeharto's New Order—truly national subjectivities. *Gay* Indonesians are not marginal to the body politic but a kind of distillation of national discourse. For instance, they take the national ideology that the nation is an "archipelago" of cultural difference and rework it to think of themselves in terms of a "*gay* archipelago" that explains both their position in the Indonesian nation and their position in a global archipelago of globalizing homosexualities (Boellstorff 2005). This is not an Indonesian version of "Queer Nation"; the impact of state ideology on *gay* Indonesians is not primarily at the level of politicization. Few *gay* Indonesians are involved in the kinds of political work exemplified by the failed Solo national meeting. For a dominant ideology to impact subjectivities, it is not necessary for that ideology to be loved or even clearly understood, as we see in Euro-American homosexualities, so shaped by sexological legacies of which many lesbian and gay Euro-Americans are unaware (Foucault 1978). Thus, the mere fact that state ideology does not look favorably on *gay* subjectivities does not permit us to assume that its influence upon those subjectivities is purely repressive: that dominant ideology casts its shadow upon *gay* subjectivities (it is not coincidental, for instance, that *gay* Indonesians might think of themselves in terms of an archipelago).

Homophobia and Heterosexism

Like much of Southeast Asia, Indonesia is often characterized as tolerant of homosexuality, bisexuality, and transgenderism. Like most myths this is a false belief that contains a grain of truth, and to identify this grain of truth I develop a distinction between "homophobia" and "heterosexism." Most behavioral sciences use "homophobia" as if it transparently reflects a set of real-world conditions. Psychological correlational studies employ measurements like the "Lesbian Internalized Homophobia Scale" that assume, for instance, that a lack of desire to affiliate with other lesbians and gay men, or a pleasure at being perceived by others as heterosexual, are a priori indicators of "internalized homophobia" (Szymanski et al. 2001:34; see also Floyd 2000; Wright et al. 1999). In fact, the concept originated in the early 1970s. As Daniel Wickberg notes in his cultural history of the term, "Unpacking the idea of homophobia reveals liberal norms and assumptions about personhood and social order rather than just liberal attitudes toward homosexuality itself" (2000:43).

As Martin Manalansan notes in his contribution to this volume, a racial politics informs the very concept of homophobia. As I discuss elsewhere (Boellstorff 2005), the drawing of a line around a subset of human experience and terming that subset "sexuality" is a foundational moment permitting exclusions of ethnicity and race, as well as other domains, like class and gender. (Such acts of categorical exclusion are, of course, key to the articulation of most domains of social identification.) The idea of homophobia is predicated on a white middle-class male imaginary where homosexuality can stand as the sole axis of oppression. This unitary imaginary of "homophobia" is part and parcel of its interiorizing tendencies; that is, its assumption that oppression is located in individuated dispositions and practices, rather than socially situated discourses. For these reasons I am sympathetic to those who recommend dispensing with the term *homophobia* altogether.

Yet in alliance with a "new queer studies" that deploys a "queer of color critique" to reconfigure otherwise irreparably contaminated conceptual frameworks (Manalansan 2003; Ferguson 2004), here I argue for a redefinition of homophobia that sharpens the concept by tactically and heuristically setting it alongside the concept of "heterosexism." The distinction between homophobia and heterosexism can provide a powerful conceptual rubric to address questions of violence—particularly if we employ the binarism not as a gloss on precultural reality but as embodying assumptions about politics and the self. If homophobia employs a Freudian problematic to locate antipathy in the individuated psyche, heterosexism employs a Gramscian problematic to locate antipathy in hegemony. Heterosexism refers to the belief that heterosexuality is the only natural or moral sexuality. It does not imply the gut-level response that homophobia does; for instance, a bureaucratic structure may be heterosexist but it cannot be homophobic. It operates at the level of generalized belief and social sanction rather than on an emotive plane. In the Euro-American context, this gives heterosexism a cultural currency that homophobia lacks. While few Euro-Americans would admit to being homophobic, many—for instance, much of the Religious Right in the United States—would openly affirm they are heterosexist, often through terms like profamily. Homophobia and heterosexism form a binarism, building on distinctions between emotion/thought, personal/public, and ideational/material. While the binarism does not isomorphically diagnose a real-world division between two forms of oppression, it proves heuristically productive for understanding the imbrication of violence and emotion. Like all terms in English or any other language (from *marriage* to *city* to *desire*), *homophobia* and *heterosexism* must be qualified when used in non-Western contexts (as in Western contexts). Yet such qualification does not disqualify terms from critical use; it is in fact the basis for any project of critical analysis (Geertz 1990:77).

In many cases homophobia and heterosexism feed off each other; heterosexism creates a climate where fear and hatred of nonnormative sexualities and genders can take root, and homophobia creates a climate where heterosexuality is assumed to be superior. However, this is not necessarily the case in all times and places. Delinking homophobia and heterosexism gives us new perspectives on sexual inequality, not only in Indonesia but in other parts of Southeast Asia where there is a need for "a more refined model of cultural antipathy" toward homosexuality (Jackson 1999:229). It is possible to have homophobia with little or no heterosexism—cases (like some Latin American contexts) where many forms of sexuality are recognized to some degree as natural, yet emotional violence against homosexual persons exists (see, for instance, Kulick 1998). It is also possible to have heterosexism with little or no homophobia, where heterosexuality is presumed superior to other sexualities, yet this does not lead to violence against homosexual persons.

This latter state of affairs has predominated in Indonesia until recently: heterosexism over homophobia. Since violence against *gay* men qua *gay* men is almost unknown in Indonesia, and since in addition the Indonesian Civil Code (based on the Dutch Civil Code, which is in turn based on the Napoleonic Code) has little to say about homosexuality and transgenderism (and to my knowledge there have never been arrests for homosexuality in postcolonial Indonesia),[14] Euro-American visitors often misrecognize a "tolerant" culture. This is because for Euro-Americans the constant threat of violence is the disciplinary pedagogy marginalizing nonnormative sexualities and genders. (If in my home country of the United States I imagine walking down the street holding the hand of my male partner, what I fear is not that others will think me immoral, nor that they will enact laws against me, but that they will physically assault me.) In the absence of homophobia, heterosexism is assumed to be absent as well. However, despite the fact that there is little homophobia in contemporary Indonesia, heterosexism is pervasive. The expectation that everyone will marry heterosexually is voiced in many belief systems across the archipelago but gains added contemporary force from the state's portraying it as essential for becoming a modern citizen. The "tolerance" of homosexuality exists only because Indonesians keep these practices secret and do not publicly proclaim homosexual identities, a state of affairs strikingly different from the case for the transvestite identities of warias, as discussed below.

Homophobia as Thuggery?

The potential sea change in Indonesia is the masculinist drawing of a connection between homophobia and heterosexism, such that the former can stand as a condition of possibility for the latter—in a context where heterosexism has historically held a dominant cultural position without homophobia's aid. By exploring how changing masculine representations of the nation shape this shift from everyday heterosexism to political homophobia, I hope to avoid reducing political homophobia to either thuggery or Islam. While we yet have no concrete data, it is plausible that the attackers involved in the Kaliurang and Solo incidents were paid, as have been many of those involved in political violence in Indonesia since 1998. That persons were paid, however, does not mean that emotions were not involved (it appears that many men involved in the rape of ethnic Chinese women in Jakarta in 1998 were paid; yet their erections were no less real). I am particularly keen to avoid treating Islam as a source of political homophobia. The pivotal question of this chapter is not whether official Islam disapproves of homosexuality (as a heterosexist cosmology, it obviously does) but how and why Islamic (male) youth groups have, at a certain point in time and within the nation-state of Indonesia, transformed this heterosexism into homophobia. The homophobic reaction of these Islamic youth groups appears not as a specifically religious response (those attacked were not in mosques or demanding religious recognition) but as a reaction to feelings of malu associated with representations of the nation.

It is true that in the Kaliurang and Solo incidents the perpetrators represented themselves as belonging to fundamentalist Muslim groups, and that Central Java is a hotbed of these groups. These groups have also attacked other social groups or places they associate with immorality, such as brothels and discos.[15] On one level, then, political homophobia is linked to a wider cultural dynamic where Islam represents an avenue for political struggle that includes conceptions of an Islamic polity (Hefner 2000). However, while to date Islam may be a necessary condition for political homophobia, it is not a sufficient condition and these incidents cannot be "read off" political Islam. Such an analysis could not explain why antipathy toward *gay* men should be expressed in an emotional and violent manner, rather than, say, the passing of an Islamic legal judgment (*fatwa*) or some form of nonviolent social sanction. This linkage of Islam with violence is both an Orientalist stereotype (Lawrence 1998:4) and a self-Orientalizing stereotype taken up by some "fundamentalist" Islamic groups: Muslim intellectuals in Indonesia have cautioned against taking this representation at face value (Wahid 1999). There is a wide range of Muslim groups and belief systems in contemporary Indonesia, many of which tolerate sexual and gender minorities. Crucially, most *gay* Indonesians are themselves Muslim, and we lose sight of the rich cultural contexts in which they reconcile sexuality and faith if we treat Islam as a direct source of political homophobia rather than a contributing (but not determining) factor. Indeed, it is unclear to what degree Islam is a confounding variable, since it is also the normative, majority religion (approximately 90 percent of Indonesians follow the Islamic faith; Indonesia is thus home to more Muslims than any other nation). In contexts where other religions dominate, it is typically the fundamentalist variants of that religion (Hinduism in India, Christianity in the United States) that have the cultural capital to employ violence, and in these cases it is also linked to masculinity (Hansen 1996).

Engendering Violence

In the rich body of anthropological work on emotion in Southeast Asia, a central conceptual category has been the Malay/Indonesian term *malu* (and its analogues, for example, Javanese *isin*, Balinese *lek,* Bugis *siri'*, Tagolog *hiya*). *Malu* typically appears in dictionaries translated as "shame" or "embarrassment," but the anthropological literature is unanimous in concluding that this fails to represent the complexity of malu and its centrality to Southeast Asian conceptions of sociality. Long before Clifford Geertz construed Balinese polities as "theatre states" (Geertz 1980), he inaugurated the dramaturgical metaphor in an analysis of lek (the Balinese near-equivalent to malu). Phrasing lek as "stage fright," Geertz concluded: "What is feared— mildly in most cases, intensely in a few—is that the public performance that is etiquette will be botched, that the social distance etiquette maintains will consequently collapse, and that the personality of the individual will break through to dissolve his standardized public identity" (Geertz 1973:402).

It was from precisely this passage that Ward Keeler launched his critique of Geertz, based on his own study of isin (the Javanese near-equivalent to malu). For Keeler, the weakness of Geertz's metaphor was that it "implies a distance between actor and role, and so between self and social persona, which is misleading" (Keeler 1983:161). In a manner foreshadowing Butler's performative theory of the constitution of the Euro-American gendered subject (Butler 1990), Keeler argued, in effect, that the actor comes into being as a social persona only when on stage. He concluded that isin is neither shame nor stage fright, but *an awareness of vulnerability in interaction* (158). In my reading of the literature, and based upon my own ethnographic work, Keeler's analysis of Javanese isin is valid not only for Balinese lek but Indonesian malu and its other analogues. Indeed, there is general agreement that malu is nothing less than a key site at which Southeast Asians become social persons. In their review of the literature on malu, Collins and Behar conclude that it is "a highly productive concept that has effects in a wide array of personal and social realms," including the political domain (Collins and Behar 2000:35). They also emphasize the linkages between malu and sexuality: "As with the English concept of shame, malu is closely associated with sexuality. The Indonesian word for genitals (*kemaluan*) echoes the English expression 'private parts.' Furthermore, sexually provocative behavior by self or others should elicit malu. . . . Gender-inappropriate behavior causes both men and women to feel malu. A boy would feel malu if he behaved like a girl, for example by displaying tears in public" (42).

But while sexuality can elicit malu in both men and women, "the most obvious gender difference in the construct of malu is in the appropriate response to being made malu. While women made malu are expected to become withdrawn or avoidant, crying out of the sight of others, men are expected to react aggressively" (48). In the cases of political homophobia at issue here, we find not only a masculinist expression of malu but a masculinist and politicized trigger of malu. While rarely openly discussed, many Indonesian men have had experiences of being seduced by other men—at religious boarding schools (*pesantren*), at a friend's home, in a park, or elsewhere. While men who think of themselves as *normal* rarely discuss such incidents, *gay* men have described them to me during fieldwork, as illustrated by the excerpt below, from an informant recalling events near Kediri in East Java:

> Shall I tell the story? I used to live in the pesantren, from the last year of junior high school through until the end of high school. About four years . . . it was at that time that I started to understand same-sex relations [*awali mengerti hubungan sejenis*] because I was seduced by my Koranic recitation teacher. . . . I was eighteen or nineteen years old at the time and he was twenty-five years old. The first time we were together I didn't have any emotions [*belum rasa*]. . . . When we were sleeping together he liked to hold me and he'd ejaculate . . . at the beginning I felt very uncomfortable [*risih*]. I didn't like feeling the sperm in his sarung . . . but he started asking me to hold his penis . . . eventually I started to like it. . . . He had his own room, so we could do it easily. He was always very helpful to me in my studies; perhaps at the beginning he was only sympathetic [*simpatik*] and eventually there arose desire [*timbul suka-suka*].

Here, my informant uses a language of emotion to describe a landscape of desire in which a *normal* man desires another man sexually. At the point when these sexual relations occurred, my informant did not yet think of himself as *gay*; it was one *normal* man seducing another. What is typical here is that the emotional response is of discomfort, not rage; when *gay* men talk about *normal* men who spurn their advances the reaction is described as one of refusal not violence. It appears that what is interpreted as "sexually provocative" or "gender-inappropriate" male behavior leads to violence when it involves staking a claim to civil society. There is no evidence that the *normal* men who have engaged in the acts of violence described in this chapter are somehow a different kind of person from the *normal* men who in other contexts experience and even act upon a desire for other men: at issue is not an essentialized difference but a social context.

That the sense of malu is masculinized can be seen not only in that the perpetrators were male but that the response took the form of violent group attacks—of amok. This cultural logic that links malu to amok is of particular interest because if malu is a site of subject-formation, amok is typically understood to be its opposite: a gut reaction where the masculine self disappears into raw action (and often, into a crowd). The contrast is not interior versus exterior, since malu involves the public self, and amok is an intentional state, not just mindless physical action (it has been evoked, for instance, by resistance to colonialism). The distinction pivots not on interior versus exterior but self versus society. Amok is a gendered response to malu; it counters a sense of vulnerability in interaction with a sense of *invulnerability in action*. The question is: why, at this point in time, would acts by *gay* men to access civil society be perceived as initiating a chain of emotions beginning in malu and ending in amok? In these cases, the entry of male homosexuality into public discourse is framed as motivating a gut-level reaction of malu, as if one's own (male) social self is threatened. I am interested in this dynamic, in how political homophobia bridges malu and amok when a particular kind of nationalized masculinity is at stake. This may be because the nation is perceived to be in immanent danger of being represented by nonnormative men.

While there is a male-specific typical reaction to malu, and while gender-inappropriate behavior can elicit malu, the range of acceptable masculinities has been quite wide in many Indonesian contexts. For instance, in Java, where the Kaliurang and Solo incidents occurred, " 'pure' Javanese tradition does not condemn homosexuality and regards a very wide range of behavior, from he-man to rather (in [Euro-American] terms) 'effeminate,' as properly masculine" (Peacock 1968:204). This has even included the political realm: the most notable recent example of this was the incident in 1995 when Joop Ave, then minister for tourism, post, and communication under Soeharto, fled New Zealand after being accused of accosting a male staff member of the Carlton Hotel in Auckland. Despite widespread rumors that Ave was *gay*, he not only kept his post but the mass media dismissed the "homo rumors" even while openly pondering why Ave had never married.[16] This was not simply due to journalistic fear of state reprisal; it reflected a general belief that so long as Ave did not publicly proclaim *gay* status, his possible sexual activities with men, while perhaps leading to gossip, did not threaten his public position.

Until recently the fact that men engage in public male-male sexuality (for example, at a park, disco, or performance event) has not resulted in malu. For Indonesian men male-male sexuality has either been ignored, used contrastively to underscore one's own social propriety, greeted with curiosity and even titillation, or casually looked down upon. But it has not led to a personal feeling of malu that could justify violence. Historically, successful Indonesian masculinity has not hinged on a sole sexual attraction to women, so long as one eventually marries. Prior to marriage, same-sex encounters remain common (but almost never publicly acknowledged) in a wide range of contexts, from religious boarding schools to markets and shopping malls. Often these activities are construed not as "sex" but playing around (*main-main*), particularly if anal penetration does not take place. After marrying it is by no means unknown for men to continue to engage in homosex (or discover it for the first time); a lack of cultural salience for homosexuality and gender segregation make it possible to hide such activities.

In this context where it is assumed all men will marry women but also that they may have sex with other men and/or with warias, violence is almost never linked to homosexual erotics. Warias, while hardly celebrated, are an accepted part of the contemporary Indonesian social mosaic and can be found in a wide range of contexts, from salons to music videos (see Boellstorff 2007a:chapter 2). Acts of violence against *gay* men have been rare. When, for instance, an Indonesian man encounters another man expressing sexual interest in him—even in public—the man will typically either politely refuse or agree to the sexual encounter and keep quiet about it afterward.

I recall another incident from the Kediri region; I was in the company of a group of *gay* men from the area and two *gay* men from Surabaya. We were spending the evening in a part of the town plaza (*alun-alun*) where *gay* men meet for conversation and to find sexual partners. As often happens in such a place, other Indonesians could be found nearby—*normal* couples with children in strollers, groups of older men, and women running late-night errands. Closest to us, however, were a group of young men sitting on a low wall under a tree. As we walked by, Amir—one of the *gay* men from Surabaya—struck up a conversation. The men were aged from sixteen to twenty-one and had come to this part of the town square without realizing its significance. When they asked what we were doing in town, Amir explained that we had attended a meeting of the local *gay* group. In response to their blank stares, Amir calmly clarified what *gay* meant—and that he was *gay* himself and liked to have sex with men. The youths giggled but did not take offense; indeed, they remained all evening. One of them eventually pulled Amir aside to say that he was interested in having sex with men but did not want his friends to know about it. This story is not atypical: across Indonesia, street youths are a common feature of the public areas used by *gay* men, yet these youths typically do not accost them; they leave them alone, asking for cigarettes or pocket money at most, often having sexual relations with (or even becoming long-term partners of) *gay* men.

The pattern seems similar across the archipelago and across religious or local difference. On another occasion I was out on Saturday night with three *gay* men in the city of Singaraja in north Bali. We made our way to the park where *gay* men and warias often spend their evenings. I rode on the back of a motorcycle driven by one of the *gay* men; another motorcycle carried Made and Danny, two Balinese *gay* men very much in love. It was late but the park was still busy, with a mix of *gay* men, warias, and *normal* men, many sitting along the benches of a bus stop. I sat down on one bench with several warias and three *normal* men; at another bench two meters to my right, under a streetlight, Made sat with Danny in his lap, their caresses visible to all who drove or walked by.

After a few moments one of the *normal* men, with long hair and a stocky, athletic body, sat down beside me and introduced himself as Gus. A few pleasantries passed our lips; then, silence. After a few moments Gus gestured toward a waria standing nearby and said, "That one is pretty, like a *normal* woman [*perempuan biasa*]." I asked, "Do you like to have sex with warias?" Gus replied, "Yeah, sure, it's *normal*, because there is passion [*gairah*]." Then I pointed to Made, who was embracing Danny at the other bench, and asked, "Would you like a man like that, who isn't made up?" Gus shrugged and said, "No, no thank you! I couldn't do that, because there is no passion to have sex with someone like that." Gus's reaction, like that of the youth in Kediri, was not homophobic. His desire for warias was not paired with an emotional repugnance toward *gay* men; he was not offended by Made and Danny and did not find my question insulting. Examples like these are infinitely more representative of contemporary Indonesian society than the Kaliurang incident: for an Indonesian man to attack another man because that other man expresses sexual interest in him, or because effeminate men appear in public, has been rare indeed.

The emergence of political homophobia indicates how the public presentation of male homosexuality and transgenderism can now occasion malu even if one does not participate oneself, because in the post-Soeharto era, masculinity is nationalized in a new way. With the nation under perceived threats of disintegration, attempts by nonnormative men to access civil society can appear to threaten the nation itself. While both *gay* homosexuality and waria transvestitism figure in this calculus, recall that "waria" is a publicly recognized social category. As Peter Jackson notes in the case of Thailand, under such a discursive regime male homosexuality can represent more of a danger than transgenderism, since it is more difficult to fit within a heterosexist logic where those who desire men must be effeminate (1999:238). Male homosexuality is also more threatening than transvestitism due to the widespread Southeast Asian assumption that inner states should match exterior bodily presentations (Errington 1989:76). Warias, who identify themselves as men with women's souls, properly display this inner mismatch in their cross-dressing. In contrast, *gay* men have a different kind of desire from normative men (they "desire the same"), but this inner deviation is not exteriorized; some are effeminate, but most are indistinguishable from *normal* men. The cultural expectation that exterior presentation should match inner state or belief has been politicized before; during the Soeharto years one of the most successful ways to create fear of a by-then nonexistent communist movement was to describe it as an "organization without shape" (*organisasi tanpa bentuk*), that is, a collectivity whose exterior did not match its interior, just as it was supposed that individual communists were failing to exteriorize their political beliefs. With their difficult-to-read desires, *gay* men can be interpreted as a kind of masculinity tanpa bentuk—not when they make sexual propositions to other men in private, but when they appear to stake a public claim to civil society; that is, when they appear political. It may be for this reason that *gay* men have been the primary target of political homophobia, while warias and *lesbi* women have been attacked to date only by virtue of their association with *gay* men.

Conclusion: The Emergence of Political Homophobia

It is in the Indonesian context, where heterosexism has predominated over homophobia, that the recent attacks gain such significance. For the Muslim youths involved in these attacks, the public presence of nonnormative genders and sexualities became interpreted in phobic terms, as a psychic threat to proper masculinity. This made violence not only thinkable but sensible as an emotional "gut reaction" to what was now interpreted as an assault on the nation's manhood. We see a shift from an intellectual assumption, rarely voiced because taken for granted, that all Indonesians should marry heterosexually, to an emotional assumption, carried out with knives and clubs, that nonnormative men threaten the nation's future. I term this a shift from everyday heterosexism to political homophobia, and the character of this emotional rage shows us that the nation envisioned by these attackers is normatively male. While all homophobia has political effects, the notion of "political homophobia" is useful for highlighting violence deployed as a means of controlling who can make claims to belonging. The violence of the Kaliurang and Solo incidents was directed at demands for inclusion in a new public sphere and not at the mundane romances and seductions of everyday life.[17]

Alarmism is not the goal of this analysis, and I do not mean to suggest that political homophobia will become an everyday occurrence in Indonesia. At the time of this writing there have been no events like those of Kaliurang and Solo since November 2000. However, the linkage between emotion and violence that these events have set in motion does not hinge on repetition. A single incident can have sustained emotional consequences for its intended indirect object; we see this in the World Trade Center attacks and the destruction of the Babri Mosque in India in 1992. Indeed, the Kaliurang and Solo incidents continue to affect *gay* Indonesians. We see this most clearly in Yogyakarta (near Kaliurang), an important center of *gay* community and publishing since the early 1980s; since the Kaliurang incident all *gay* organizations in that city have ceased meeting and all *gay* publications have ceased production. A book launch held by Dédé Oetomo at a Muslim university in Yogyakarta in early November 2001 for a volume of his writings on homosexuality and Indonesian society took place without incident, but a second event to be held at a local bookstore was interrupted by the police, who prevented the event from taking place on the pretext that it would disturb public security.[18] More broadly, intermittent attacks on warias and *gay* men, including assaults on *gay* men in public places and incidents where warias are assaulted and their hair forcibly cut, have occurred in several parts of Indonesia, including Aceh, Bali, and Java.[19] However, there is little evidence that everyday homophobia is on the rise.

Perhaps the most urgent question is how political homophobia will shape struggles over Indonesia's emerging post-Soeharto civil society. Historically *gay* men and warias have appeared only rarely in the political sphere either as topic of discussion or trope. When the latter has occurred, it has usually been to speak metaphorically of persons who change their opinions (like warias change their gender presentation). For instance, in 1999, in a volume of essays concerned with demonstrating that Islam is incompatible with political violence (*kekerasan politik*), Abdurrahman Wahid—a noted Muslim intellectual and recently president of Indonesia—spoke metaphorically of intellectuals changing their opinions as changing their sex, jokingly admonishing them not to become warias (Wahid 1999:182).

Compare this with the situation two years later, when the populist and often anti-American newspaper *Rakyat Merdeka* (published from Jakarta) ran a front-page headline concerning U.S.–led attacks on the Taliban with the title "*Amerika Bencong!*"[20] (*Béncong* is a variant of *banci* [waria].) The headline was accompanied by a photograph of President George W. Bush doctored to include lipstick, earrings, and a leather jacket. Here nonnorma-

Figure 2. George W. Bush as emotional transvestite. Image from *Rakyat Merdeka* newspaper, October 7, 2001.

tive men stand not for shifting intellectual views but a compromised nation. The article claimed that the United States was a béncong because rather than challenging Osama bin Laden to a one-on-one duel, Bush had the audacity (*berani*) to invite its allies to attack Afghanistan en masse in the search for him. In other words, the United States had no malu, no sense of vulnerability in interaction, and thus felt a rage—a sense of invulnerability in action—that compelled it to enroll others to join in amok violence. The United States is presented as operating under a nationalized intersection of manhood and emotion. It is the dynamic of the Kaliurang and Solo incidents, displaced into the figure of the nonnormative male. Under a cultural logic of political homophobia, Bush-in-drag—representing a nation's failed masculinity—appears both violent and a proper target for violence.

My hypothesis is that it may be political homophobia that makes this image intelligible to the Indonesian public regardless of religion. In place of national masculinity as benevolent and paternal (however violent in actual practice), we find it embattled, in danger of losing its very manhood. It is thus called upon to deflect this shame in a properly masculine manner, by violently striking down any representation of itself by homosexual, effeminate, or transvestite men. As Indonesia continues to struggle through a period of tense uncertainty, anthropological attention to the public face of emotion and the heterosexist gendering of national belonging can contribute to a better understanding of how violence is not the "primordialist" suspension of culture but the working out of cultural logics of inequality and exclusion to their horrific but comprehensible conclusion.

Notes

Research in Indonesia was funded by the Social Science Research Council, the National Science Foundation, the Morrison Institute for Population Studies at Stanford University, and the Department of Cultural and Social Anthropology of Stanford University. This chapter was largely written under the auspices of a Postdoctoral Fellowship in Southeast Asian Studies in the Department of Anthropology, Research School of Pacific and Asian Studies, at the Australian National University. I thank these institutions for their support. Helpful comments were provided by Edward Aspinall, Lena Avonius, John Ballard, Shelly Errington, Byron Good, Karl Heider, Andrew Kipnis, Johan Lindquist, Francesca Merlan, Bill Maurer, David Murray, Dédé Oetomo, Wilhelm Östberg, Kathryn Robinson, and Rupert Stasch. A special thanks to Joshua Barker for his insightful commentary. All italicized terms are in Indonesian unless noted otherwise.

1 Of these terms, *banci* is the best known but is somewhat derogatory, so I use the preferred term *waria* (an amalgam of *wanita* [woman] and *pria* [man]). I italicize the term *gay* throughout to distinguish it from the English term "gay," to which *gay* is related but distinct. For consistency I italicize *lesbi* and *normal* as well. Data on the Kaliurang incident is compiled from PlanetOut.com, November 13 and 14, 2000; Detik.com November 30, 2000; *Kompas*, November 12 and 14, 2000; *GAYa Nusantara 77*; and direct testimony from witnesses.

2 According to witnesses, some of the motorcycles driven by the attackers also had stickers from the Muslim United Development Party or the Anti Immorality Movement (Gerakan Anti Maksiat or GAM) (Detik.com, November 14, 2000). The Ka'bah is the holy shrine at the center of the Great Mosque of Mecca.

3 The statement was allegedly in Javanese ("Lanang kok dandan wedok, banci metu;" in Indonesian this would be "Laki-laki kok dandan perempuan, banci keluar") (Detik.com, November 14, 2000).

4 Detik.com, November 13, 2000.

5 *GAYa Nusantara* 77:16–17, 23.

6 While *lesbi* women groups and correspondents participate in this network, it is dominated by *gay* men.

7 Because of difficulties with attendance, this congress was renamed a National Working Meeting (Rapat Kerja Nasional, shortened to Rakernas) and scheduled

for September 10–11 so as to coincide with September Ceria (Joyous September), a large *gay* event held annually near the city of Solo (Central Java).

8   Two leaders of the groups, Hasan Mulachela and Boyamin, stated that "as citizens of Solo we cannot accept these practices a la Sodom and Gomorrah to take place in Solo. If the Lesbian and Gay National Meeting takes place in Solo that would publicize those practices" (*Kompas*, September 11, 1999). Mulachela also threatened to bring out "thousands of the Islamic community" to force the congress to be cancelled (*Bernas*, September 11, 1999; Mulachela is also a member of the Pembaruan PRD party faction).

9   Many *gay* (also *lesbi* and *waria*) Indonesians who know of these two incidents see them as watershed moments when, for the first time, nonnormative masculinity became the target of publicly articulated hatred and physical assault.

10 In a review article, Carol Nagengast noted that "until relatively recently, few anthropologists examined violence and conflict between groups and the state and among groups within states" (Nagengast 1994:110). Nagengast identified anthropology's focus on ostensibly self-contained communities at the expense of the nation as one reason for this lack of attention to violence outside domains of custom and tradition (112; see also Riches 1986). Also in 1994, John Pemberton presented anthropology with the image of Javanese peasants shoving each other aside over pieces of a cooked chicken in a *rebutan* or "struggle" (Pemberton 1994:18, 213). By counterpoising this vignette to Geertz's use of the tranquil *selamatan* feast as master metaphor for Javanese culture (Geertz 1960), Pemberton indexed the growing number of ethnographically informed studies of violence in Indonesian societies (e.g., George 1996; Robinson 1995; Siegel 1998; Tsing 1993). More recently, scholars of Indonesia have responded to new and resurgent forms of violence following Soeharto's fall (e.g., Anderson 2001; Barker 1998; Rafael 1999; Stasch 2001; Wessel and Wimhofer 2001). Some of this scholarship provides insights on everyday violence, including domestic violence and its linkages to state violence (Berman 2000; Butt 2001; Idrus 2001). The primary emphasis, however, has been on "political violence."

11 I am grateful to Joshua Barker for this turn of phrase, which originates in his insightful commentary on an earlier version of this chapter, given at the meetings of the American Anthropological Association in 2001.

12 See, inter alia, Aripurnami 1996; Blackwood 1995b; Brenner 1998, 1999; Hatley 1997; Robinson 1989; Sen 1998; Tiwon 1996.

13 It is therefore not surprising that *tomboi* call themselves *hunter* in some regions of Indonesia, particularly south Sulawesi. They use this term because they "hunt" feminine women as potential partners; they consider the act of initiating contact masculine.

14 Ann Stoler notes her own "long-term and failed efforts" to find any significant discussion of homosexuality in the colonial Dutch East Indies (Stoler 1995:129).

15 See, for instance, "In Indonesia, Once Tolerant Islam Grows Rigid," *New York Times*, December 29, 2001.

16 See, for instance, the coverage of the incident in *Forum Keadilan*, May 25, 1995, 12–20. Since most *gay* men marry women, Ave's bachelor status at fifty-one years of age was noteworthy.

17 This new political homophobia in Indonesia is thus quite different from (though not entirely unrelated to) the arrest and conviction in Malaysia of Anwar Ibrahim, former deputy prime minister, on charges of sodomy and corruption.

18 Dédé Oetomo, personal communication.

19 For an example, see *Serambi Indonesia*, June 29, 1999. My thanks to Dédé Oetomo and Edward Aspinall for respectively bringing the Bali and Aceh incidents to my attention.

20 I thank Karl Heider for bringing this article to my attention.

8

Homo Hauntings

Spectral Sexuality and the Good
Citizen in Barbadian Media

David A. B. Murray

During a number of research trips to Barbados between 2002 and 2005, I was struck by the saturation of local media coverage of homosexuality.[1] Homosexuality was
being discussed in a variety of Barbadian media sites ranging
from newspapers to the Internet and radio. During my long-
est visit, from September 2004 to April 2005, I cut out and
filed every news item from the *Nation* (one of Barbados' two
daily newspapers) that included the words *homosexual* or
gay. By the end of that seven-month period, my file folder
had 355 clippings, which amounted to approximately 1.5
news items per issue. In retrospect, perhaps I shouldn't have
been so surprised. Gays and lesbians were hot news topics in
many media outlets around the world at this time. Much of
the news in the *Nation*, on local radio talk shows like *Down
to Brass Tacks*, and on Internet sites such as JustBajan.com
focused on same-sex rights and justice struggles occurring
elsewhere around the globe, such as the same-sex marriage
debates in Europe, Canada, and the United States; various
Christian denominations' battles over the ordainment of gay
and lesbian priests and ministers; and the ongoing battle
against HIV/AIDS. What I found interesting was how these
"overseas" affairs were "localized" through letters to the editor, radio talk show callers' comments, newspaper editorials,
op-ed columns, and online bulletin boards where opinions

were expressed about these events and their potential effects on Barbadian society.

However, homosexuality was a regular component in local news as well. In 2004–2005, three public forums were held by the National HIV/AIDS Commission to elicit feedback on Professor Mickey Walrond's *Report on the Legal, Ethical and Socio-Economic Issues Relevant to HIV/AIDS in Barbados* (2004). The report (commissioned by the attorney general's office) made numerous suggestions pertaining to HIV/AIDS; among them was support for the decriminalization of homosexuality in order to reduce stigma and fear associated with the virus.[2] These forums generated a great deal of coverage on the talk radio airwaves and in the op-ed and letters to the editor sections of the *Nation*.

In this chapter, I refer to these sites as "feedback media," which, taken together, form a hegemonic public discourse of sexuality. Much (but by no means all) of this feedback media, whether internationally or locally focused, valued homosexuality negatively: "wrong," "immoral," "danger-ous," "corrupt," "perverted," and "sin" were some of the more common descriptors used in discussing same-sex identities and practices.[3] In all this media talk, no voice of a "homosexual" from Barbados was to be found. No letters to the editor, online bulletin board postings, or op-ed columns were signed by anyone who said that he or she was "gay," "homosexual," or "lesbian."[4] Such was the case for the radio talk shows as well. Furthermore, there were no organized associations or groups dedicated primarily to sup-porting gay and lesbian rights in Barbados which reporters and/or editors could turn to for a response.[5]

In this chapter, I want to focus primarily on feedback media in Barbados; through critical discourse analysis of this delimited public arena of "talk," I think we can gain some insight into why homosexuality appears to be a problem in contemporary Barbados. This will allow us to see beyond the "negative" positioning of homosexuality—the antigay rhetoric—into the factors influencing the formation of the representational frameworks through which homosexuality comes to be signified. However, I will also try to show that it is important to locate these frameworks in relation to knowl-edge of Barbados' colonial history and its current, somewhat marginal position in a larger global ecumene celebrating neoliberal democracy and free-enterprise capitalism. In particular, I am interested in the gendered and sexual effects of current sociopolitical, cultural, and economic configurations in Barbados as they are located within larger historical and global flows. I will argue that hegemonic discourses against homosexuality in Barbadian feedback media are produced through a heterosexual patriarchal logic originating in a first wave form of globalization known as colonialism but which has been reproduced *and challenged* through the turbulent, uneven processes of economic, political, and cultural globalization over the past twenty years.

These discourses, combined with the absence of local gay and lesbian voices in the media, result in what I call a "spectral" sexuality that haunts the Barbadian mediascapes, where a threatening, perverted, and/or sick sexualized body or group of bodies are continually incarnated in discourse but never fully instantiated in the flesh. These deviant ghostly bodies haunt the dominant media discourse of a national body imagined to be heterosexual and masculine, which is perceived to be under attack from outside and inside forces (Mosse 1985; Alexander 1994, 1997). This is a haunting produced by global political, economic, and social forces that contribute toward a greater socioeconomic chasm between a small elite business class, a stressed and fragile middle class, and a growing class of working poor and/or unemployed in Barbados and around the world (Kimmel 2003). These perceptions and experiences of destabilization increase the surveillance of and concern about who and what are the sources of this socioeconomic instability. For a variety of historically contextual reasons, "homosexuals" have come to be, for some Barbadians, the bogeymen of a turbulent and stressful modernity in the new millennium, absorbing and representing all that is wrong with contemporary social life in a developing nation located on the margins of Euro-American nation-states' economic and political programs.

It is important to note that in this chapter I am focusing only on the ways in which homosexuality is discussed in a particular media genre (opinion or feedback media). This material should not be interpreted as indicative of how homosexuality is viewed by all Barbadians, nor is it reflective of "a" cultural belief system about (homo)sexuality. Media discourses, as noted by numerous media studies analysts, are particular sites in which information is structured by and through local, national, and global social, political, and economic forces (Hall 1980; Henry and Tator 2002; MacDonald 2003; Van Dijk 1988). As Debra Spitulnik has noted, exploring the social circulation of media discourse outside the contexts of direct media consumption can reveal diverse, creative reworkings of media discourses (1997). In other words, while it is important to understand how and why certain discourses are privileged—the goal of this chapter being to understand the "logic" of privileged homophobic discourses—we must not forget that there are multiple subjective lenses through which these discourses may be interpreted, resisted, and/or transformed. Suffice to say, I spoke with many Barbadians from a variety of different social backgrounds (age, gender, education, class) who did not agree with the opinions presented in the media. How and why these individuals have come to hold different opinions and beliefs about homosexuality (and why they did not call or write in to Barbadian feedback media sites) merits further interrogation that is beyond the scope of this chapter. Nevertheless, in a small island society like Barbados, the prevalence and uniformity of opinion on a particular topic across a variety of media sites speaks to the ways in which public negotiations of (sexual) morality circulate and appear to coalesce as acceptable representations of "a" Barbadian position. The question I now turn to is why a particular position emerged in this arena of public talk at this particular point in time.

I begin by exploring some of this media talk in a bit more detail, providing three examples which highlight some of the key frames through which homosexuality was negatively articulated. Following them, I analyze some of their common themes in relation to the gendered and sexualized contours of local and global social, economic, and political dynamics.

"The system is saying let everything go . . ."

The first example is drawn from a news, current affairs, and entertainment website for Barbadians (www.justbajan.com/opinion/) which carries a discussion forum where the Web server posts questions and people are invited to respond. A large number of comments (over 1,300 in May 2004) were posted in reaction to the question "Should gay people be allowed to get married?" The majority of comments were not supportive and in many cases included commentaries about homosexuality more generally. One posting seemed a bit out of place but generated some interesting responses: an individual named "Lost Boy," who self-identified as an American male, said he was planning to visit Barbados and wanted to know if gay tourists were welcome (leading me to assume he was not a Barbadian citizen). He received numerous responses. One reply came from Mr. X, twenty-five, who self-identified as a Barbadian male from Oistins (a town in the south of the island): "Would you welcome someone in your own country whose be-havior you consider to be immoral? . . . Would you welcome the Taliban to your home and if not why not? I hope you get the point. Gay people are not welcome by the majority of Bajans (Barbadians)." Another response came from "Assassin," who self-identified as a Barbadian male from Bridgetown (the capital city of Barbados):

> People like you might think our law against homosexuals is wrong but if you respect our laws and by extension the people of this country you will abide by the laws of this country. You seem to be of the opinion that the "poor, pitiful, uneducated" people of Barbados should be down on our hands and knees kissing the ground tourists like yourselves walk on just because you are willing to come and spend money in our country. . . . Keep that pro-homosexual propaganda drivel in your own country, we don't condone it here. Why should anyone listen to what America has to say about other countries' laws? Have you ever really sat down and analyzed the moral morass that your country currently exists in? Do you really believe that a sovereign nation should take hints and legal advice from a country like that?

The second example comes from a Caribbean Broadcasting Corporation (CBC) daily radio talk show in November 2004. The topic of the day was "Has Barbados become an immoral society?" which the host, Chester Con-nell, elaborated on: "Are we too tolerant of homosexuality, prostitution, and other so-called perverted trends now evident in Barbados?" The vast major-ity of the callers to the show agreed that Barbados was indeed becom-ing immoral, and that immorality could be defined primarily in terms of homosexuality and prostitution. During the program, some callers pro-vided explanations of why this type of "immorality" was taking over Bar-bados. One caller asserted, "There is a global agenda to legalize everything which was taboo before. This is something that is being pushed a lot in the state, to make everything that we consider wrong right . . . in other words the system is saying let everything go, whatever you wanna do, do: My position on prostitution and homosexuality is that God does not approve of it." Another caller identified a different reason for these problems: "At the core we've become selfish . . . it's a direction we've been going in progres-sively . . . there's the consumerism that is driving most of the issues relating to the economy . . . it's leading us down the path to perversion." A third caller made a similar comment: "[Men and women are] involved in all this kinky sex because it's a reflection of where we are in this society . . . it's this consumerism. People have big houses, nuff (enough) money, they're bored, don't know what to do with themselves, so this is what they do."

The third example is from one of the flurry of letters to the editor of the *Nation* between December 2004 and March 2005 responding to the just-published Walrond report's recommendation to decriminalize homosexuality and prostitution. Alicia Smith (a pseudonym) began her letter this way: "It was the former United States Surgeon General, Dr Benjamin Koop, who cautioned that the anal canal is not intended for use as a sexual orifice, given its very thin and fragile lining. This together with the disease profile and early death of homosexuals through hepatitis, liver disease, gastro-intestinal parasites, sexually transmitted diseases . . . [the list goes on] should be of particular concern to Professor Walrond who should oppose homosexuality on purely medical grounds. . . . We must not forsake our enduring Christian morality for the bigotry of secularism. . . . It will be tyrannical of the government to support [this recommendation]" (*Nation,* January 12, 2005).

Themes of Feedback Media

It should be noted the media were often quoted as the source of information in feedback media: in other words, writers and callers often began their statement by noting they had read something in the news, or heard something on the radio, and wanted to comment on it immediately. In a space with a relatively limited local mediascape (one local television station, two daily newspapers, and eight AM/FM radio stations owned by three companies) it is perhaps not too surprising that local news and talk about news circulates rapidly through these media circuits, generating more media coverage. For example, a number of callers to the radio talk show mentioned that they had read about the Walrond report forums in the *Nation* that morning; letters to the editor often mentioned a discussion that the writer had just heard on the radio. Media is thus a regular source of information in feedback media discussions: what is notable in Barbados is the relative uniformity of opinion across the various feedback media genres.

Feedback media comments and letters during this period conveyed at least five frequently repeated and related themes about homosexuality. First, many referred to Barbadian law as "proof" of the illegitimacy of homosexuality.[6] Second, the law was claimed to be representative of the nation's (Christian) morality.[7] The third theme was often found in relation to the second, comparing the moral health of Barbados to that of other nations and often finding the latter to be inferior, as for example in Assassin's reference to the United States being in a "moral morass" primarily because of its "pro-homosexual" stance (which of course is an interesting interpretation of American public discourses on homosexuality given George W. Bush's repeated assertions throughout his presidency that heterosexual marriage is the bedrock of civilization). Sometimes the nation of Barbados was positioned against a less specified, more global consortium of powerful nations and interests, as demonstrated in the comments of the CBC radio program caller who identified the "global agenda to legalize everything which was taboo before." In either case, the nation of Barbados was being compared to politically and economically powerful but morally corrupt nations.

In contrast to the third theme, the fourth theme located sources of immoral behaviors like homosexuality *within* Barbados. However, these sources were, at the same time, recognized as being produced or impacted by global influences. So, for example, we heard the radio show callers who noted the rise of "rampant consumerism" as the generator of "bad" behaviors such as selfishness, boredom, and listlessness, which then lead to "kinky sex" practices like homosexuality and visits to prostitutes. Finally, many of these commentaries explicitly described the homosexual body as a "diseased" body, through references to HIV/AIDS, other health problems like alcoholism, and/or "unclean" sexual practices like anal sex, and then claimed that homosexuality is thus a "lifestyle" or "behavior" that is unhealthy and therefore dangerous to Barbadian society.

In order to understand how and why these themes were popular in feedback media, it is necessary to identify a series of changes occurring in Barbados over the past twenty to twenty-five years that are related to historical and contemporary global economic and social transformations. The first of these transformations is political-economic. Jacqui Alexander's groundbreaking work on the sociosexual and political effects of tourism on Bahamian and Trinidadian nationalist discourses provides a key foundation for thinking about how Barbadian feedback media talk about homosexuality has emerged. Alexander demonstrates how homosexuality has been a central factor in structuring nationalist discourses of identity through modes of criminal spectacularization and/or erasure as governments try to lure transnational capital investments (1994, 1997). I argue that a similar situation exists in Barbados where the effects of internationally influenced local political and economic strategies are reshaping gendered and sexual relations, such that the "male homosexual" is quickly becoming the internal "other" for certain sectors of the Barbadian population—he has become a figure who threatens the legitimacy and order of the Barbadian nation-state, the one who represents all that is imposed, colonial, and unjustly empowered in a society undergoing rapid socioeconomic change.[8] In line with Patton's (1997) and Yingling's (1997) powerful analyses of how early discourses around HIV/AIDS contributed to moral panics reinforcing het-eronormative, racially exclusive, and deeply classed nationalisms, I am ar-guing that Barbadian feedback media discourses about the "homosexual" are indicative of a moral panic among some Barbadians that is produced in relation to rapid internal and external social, political, and economic trans-formations which reinforce for some, but not all, a long-standing percep-tion of marginality and powerlessness in their own society and abroad. This marginality may be perceived in terms of race, gender, political, and/or economic status and reflects a colonial legacy of racial, economic, and political subordination. A sense of increasing marginalization within a na-tion that is locally and internationally touted as a Caribbean success story in terms of its wealth, political stability, and social infrastructure (as avowed repeatedly by former prime minister Owen Arthur and in popular inter-national reports such as the U.S. Department of State Country Profiles) may lead certain factions of the population to scapegoat and stigmatize particu-lar groups whose different ideas and practices can be blamed for contribut-ing to what is wrong with their world.[9] For this sector, moral decay is linked to the "feminization" of the economy and public life, domains which are perceived to be traditionally heterosexual and masculine.

This line of thinking requires further inquiry into economic and political changes and the symbolic framing of those changes as they are occurring in Barbados. Carla Freeman, in her account of women working in the rapidly growing employment sector of "informatics" (data entry and call service centers) in Barbados, notes that Caribbean countries like Barbados have been marginalized by transnational economic treaties like NAFTA (North

American Free Trade Act) and the EEU (European Economic Union), resulting in ever increasing dependency on a service-based economy where informatics and tourism are two of the leading employment sectors (Freeman 2000:23,31). These arenas employ increasing numbers of women in low-wage jobs and are thus often classified as "feminized" economic sectors (Freeman 2000:44).

Furthermore, Freeman notes how popular discourses (as well as more esoteric theories) of globalization are couched in masculinist, heteronormative frames; for example, we hear talk of the importance of "penetrating virgin" markets. These are narratives in which power operates in masculinized acts of nonreciprocal penetration. Expressions of globalization valorize the norms of global finance, telecommunications, production, and trade which are associated with Western capitalist masculinity. And in many of the globalization discourses, "the local" is a developing country with no choice but to "submit" to the power of the developed nations and the inevitable "righteous" force of capitalism and its attendant social policies. In other words, high-level global restructuring is constructed as a masculinized domain characterized by high tech mobility, autonomy, and challenging opportunities, but local labor forces situated mostly in developing nation-states are feminized through their servitude, powerlessness, and lack of personal space and autonomy (Freeman 2001:1014–1016; see also Kimmel 2003:604). In nation-states with a history of colonization, these are gendered and racialized tropes of powerlessness that resonate with a not too distant past, but the old transparent discourse of the colonizing civilizations' "natural" superiority (rendering them easily identifiable as the villain) has been replaced by more opaque liberal rhetoric of free markets, individual freedom, and equal opportunity, rhetoric which is endorsed by the government of Barbados,[10] making it more difficult to explain why it is so hard to make ends meet and/or who is to blame.

I am suggesting that in light of an economy which is perceived to be increasingly more "feminine," exploitative, and subservient in its labor practices, some Barbadians feel that there are fewer and fewer "appropriate" (masculine) employment opportunities available to them. The shift to a service-sector economy not only creates the perception of a more feminized economy but also feminizes (in a patriarchal interpretation whereby "feminized" is associated with a subordinated, "please the master" status) national identity. A nation-state which accepts homosexuality is, from this perspective, proof of a powerless, penetrated, emasculated loser on the world stage. This is what I sense in some of the antihomosexual comments like those of Assassin, when, for example, he asks if Americans like Lost Boy assume Bajans are "submissive" because they rely on tourism and will accept homosexuals just because it's okay to do so in the United States.

When Assassin tells Lost Boy to "keep that pro-homosexual propaganda drivel in your own country. . . . Do you really believe that a sovereign nation should take hints and legal advice from a country like that," or when the caller on the CBC radio program discusses how "there is a global agenda to legalize everything which was taboo before," there lies both recognition and critique of a postcolonial society's place in the contemporary global ecumene. These Barbadians are aware of gay and lesbian activism around the world, but it is localized, that is, rendered meaningful in relation to local sociosexual issues through particular moral lenses. This overseas activism is often referred to as part of a gay rights agenda, or a progay system that is supported by (or controls) the political leaders of Euro-American nations, who are very powerful and are trying to impose their economic, political, and moral interests on the government and people of Barbados.

This perspective should not be summarily dismissed as a conspiratorial fantasy. Pressure to reform laws against homosexuality in numerous Caribbean nation-states is brought to bear by organizations like Amnesty International, Human Rights Watch, and the International Lesbian and Gay Association that critique nations' governments vis-à-vis human rights principles and agreements developed through supranational bodies like the United Nations.[11] The developed nations once again use their political and economic force to bully a developing nation into adopting their social and political agendas. The reactions from Assassin and other Barbadian feedback media contributors indicate a similar perception of and rhetorical resistance to forced submission to Western political, economic, and moral agendas which emasculate and thus humiliate their nation's status.[12]

However, a feminized "submissive" national economy and identity forcibly created by an external power (which reproduces tropes of colonial relations of power) is not the only way in which the homosexual comes to stand for social decay of the nation: a different, albeit related, connection between morality, homosexuality, and the national economy appears via the "problem" of vulgar materialism within contemporary Barbados, as we may recall in the response of the radio show caller who asserted that "consumerism . . . is driving most of the issues relating to the economy . . . it's leading us down the path to perversion." Commentaries such as this one are critical of an internal national material practice (consumption) resulting from a government-induced shift to a free-market, individualist, and privatized economy; they see uncontrolled consumption creating a more selfish, decadent, and amoral nation. These commentaries are different from Assassin's in two ways: (a) they see the homosexual threat as coming from or produced *within* Barbados rather than existing as an external threat. Thus there is tacit acknowledgment of homosexuality as an already existing phenomenon in Barbadian society; and (b) they employ a form of nationalist nostalgia, in which a "proper," heterosexual, family-oriented, Christian, and communal Barbadian nation of the past is compared to an "immoral" consumer-driven, privatized, secular, and pansexual Barbados of the present. Socioeconomic change is evaluated via a kind of sexual barometer where the possibility of accepting (homo)sexual practices by the minders of the nation-state indicates a precipitous fall from an imagined national past of heterosexual, familial unity. Scholars of nationalism elsewhere have noted the importance of nationalist nostalgia: myths in terms not of their (in)authenticity but rather the ways in which they are related to perceptions of racial, economic, and/or political (dis)empowerment by those who circulate them (Hage 2000; Mackey 2002; Povinelli 2002). The consensus of these nationalist narratives is usually the same—the moral decay of the nation—although there are different indexes or measurements of that decay. In the case of these Barbadian commentators, the clearest sign is sexual perversion, which ranges from "kinky sex acts" to state legitimization of homosexuality.

Notably, these commentaries focus almost exclusively on male homosexuality—I found very few references to lesbianism in feedback media. This is not surprising; as numerous scholars have noted, since most nationalisms are constructed through heterosexual, fraternal, and patriarchal frameworks, men who want to have sex with men are construed as the greatest internal threat to the (re)productive fantasies of the nationalist imaginary (Mosse 1985; Parker et al. 1992; Yuval-Davis 1997). From this perspective, women are supposed to occupy the private, domestic familial spaces of the national imaginary, and their sexuality is imagined only as heterosexually reproductive, submissive, and receptive to their husband's needs and desires. While female homosexuality is seen by nationalists as a corruption of femininity, it is nevertheless powerless and nonthreatening to men and less a challenge to heteropatriarchy than male homosexuality (Kempadoo 2004:47). Or to put it in the context of Alicia Smith's letter to the *Nation*, lesbians appear to be no threat to the fragile (male) anus.

These online commentaries, phone calls, and letters to the editor thus contribute to a hegemonic public discourse in which the internal or external male homosexual serves a particular semiotic strategy, acting as the key indicator of downward movement of the social respectability of the nation. Yet this is a spectral homosexual, a depersonalized, unnamed entity who is observed to be demanding and gaining rights in powerful, wealthy but morally corrupt Euro-American nations, and whose existence is now acknowledged in Barbadian public arenas, but only in one particular incarnation: a feminized male body which infects the legitimate heteromasculine national body of Barbados indexing the fall from a phantasmatic patriarchal past national unity. These spectral sexual deviants are critical components of nationalist imaginaries. As Marilyn Ivy notes in her analysis of Japanese nationalism, the nation can never be fully realized; it is a phantasmatic structure itself that produces, indeed requires, inscriptions of its own marginality in its narratives of cultural unity and homogeneity: the figure of the ghost "spectrally embodies . . . the recalcitrance of representation itself, the impossibility of stabilizing meaning . . . ghosts are haunting precisely because they reveal an inability to control representation" (1995:165). In Barbados media discourses, we often find the homosexual haunting the words of some Barbadians who desire an ideal of national cultural and economic solidarity yet who simultaneously reveal their own social, economic, and political marginality through their identification of the villains, the sexualized bogeymen, who ostensibly control "the system." Their own sense of disempowerment, however real or imagined, is produced through the prism of a nationalist political economic myth which promises prosperity and equality for all citizens who embrace the values of free-market capitalism and blames the individual who does not prosper in such a climate.

That this spectral homosexual is occupying mainstream media discourses at this particular point owes to not only the unpredictable effects of a global hegemonic heterosexualized masculinity in local contexts (Kimmel 2003) but also its presence in other gendered and sexed discourses circulating through global and local media coverage over the past fifteen to twenty years. As noted above, these include increased reporting on international gay and lesbian activism in many nation-states that Barbadians have emigrated to, and the ongoing presence of HIV/AIDS, still identified as a "gay" disease in parts of Barbados (Voelker 2001; Walrond 2004). Furthermore, HIV/AIDS education and prevention strategies, which include suggestions like that of the Walrond report to decriminalize homosexuality in order to reduce stigma, which will result in more men being educated about and tested for HIV, may in fact work to reinforce heterosexist norms. As Andil Gosine notes, Barbadian HIV/AIDS discourses which support the rights of homosexuals do so in terms of containing the threat of the virus spreading to the entire nation. The effect is to maintain the link between homosexuality and disease, a link that, as Alicia Smith points out, the government of Barbados should remind people about, instead of supporting their "rights" (Gosine 2007).

Another notable gendered and sexed discourse which influences opinions on homosexuality is Christianity. The regular allusions to the Bible, God, and Christian values in Barbadian feedback media discussions of homosexuality indicate the significant presence of religious values in public discourses assessing acceptable gendered and sexual behavior. According to the Barbadian census of 2000, the majority of Barbadians (of the total island population of approximately 275,000) identify themselves as belonging to a Christian denomination (Barbados Statistical Service 2000:34).[13] Until recently, the majority of Christian Barbadians were Anglican, but the increasing popularity of American-based Pentecostal charismatic Christianity has been noted locally in the media and anecdotally by many of my Barbadian interviewees (see also Robbins 2004). As Constance Sullivan-Blum points out in this volume, evangelical and fundamentalist Christians have focused energetically on organizing and communicating their position on the question of the sin of homosexuality and gay marriage and are increasingly sophisticated in their political influence, knowledge of media formats, and control of media technologies.

There are numerous additional circuits of public talk about gender and (homo)sexuality beyond the scope of this chapter, such as the lyrics of popular music styles like dancehall, calypso, and ragamuffin, which interact with, reflect, and influence feedback media opinions (see Gutzmore 2004 and LaFont, this volume). Once again, it is important to keep in mind that these various discourses on sex and gender in the media are, of course, always unstable and always intersecting with other kinds of social, political, and economic talk, rendering the positioning of gendered and sexed identities unstable themselves. However, in the early years of the new millennium, it was clear that differentially located and temporally generated discourses circulating through Barbadian feedback media had coalesced to produce a relatively uniform moral positioning on homosexuality, with the cumulative effect of further marginalizing it from the position of respectable citizenship.

Conclusion

As Henry and Tator note, "We cannot ignore the media's crucial role in influencing and reinforcing attitudes and opinions" (2002:7). In this chapter, I have tried to examine why there is a relatively consistent positioning of the homosexual as a threat to Barbadian society in feedback media. I have argued that Barbados is facing a turbulent moment in its history. It is facing major economic challenges in relation to its marginal position to other political economic alliances such as NAFTA and the EEU; it is also facing regional challenges through its participation in the Caribbean Single Market Economy (similar to the EEU in its objectives to create stronger, more globally competitive economies amongst participating Anglo-Caribbean nations), all of which are bringing about significant changes in the socio-economic fabric of life, resulting in what some might argue is a submissive, subordinated, or "feminized" (defined through a heteropatriarchal lens) economy. Like many other smaller societies, Barbados is also undergoing rapid technological changes through the increasing presence of computer, television, and mobile communication technologies, which in turn link Barbadians to multiple, globally circulating ideas, values, and identities relating to sexuality. Yet these changes and challenges are not necessarily all that new for Barbados (or the rest of the Caribbean for that matter), as indeed these are societies that have been forged through the transnational commerce of colonialism, migration of different ethnic groups, and exposure to multiple and often competing value systems for over five hundred years. Questions about what is "natural" or "unnatural" sex have been present in these societies from their colonial inception, but in recent years a particular incarnation of the "homosexual" has become the most visible index of (im)morality and social (in)stability in particular media discourses. This silent, spectral, yet ever-present entity has become the new pariah among individuals and groups unhappy with the current socio-economic situation, who strive to return to a mythic past of a communal, heterosexual, and homogenous (Christian) society.

Although these opinions dominate feedback media, there are notable exceptions challenging antigay sentiment which are authored by Barbadians ranging from Anglican ministers to laypersons. Assuming a uniform societal or national position on homosexuality based on patterns emerging through a particular media genre is deeply problematic; more research is necessary into the ways in which (homo)sexuality is positioned in relation to gender in everyday talk among families, networks, and diverse communities in Barbados. We must also, I think, create research frameworks which acknowledge the possibility of multiple, contextually generated moral frameworks operating throughout different communities and networks in Barbados.

Further research is also necessary on the organization of these media corporations: owners, managers, and editors of Barbadian media make decisions about what goes into print and onto airwaves, computer, and television screens. They may make their choices based on their own political and ideological agendas or what they perceive to be their readership's position. The negative positioning of the homosexual in Barbadian media does not reflect a consistent, uniform trait of a culturally homogenous nation, so we must continue to examine how and why this spectral sexuality occupies a central role in public discourses on citizenship and the state.

Notes

1 I made a total of four trips over this period, ranging in duration from one to seven months.
2 The report noted that there are laws in the Criminal Code of Barbados which are interpreted as antihomosexual. These laws refer to sodomy—strictly speaking, this means that heterosexual sodomy is outlawed as much as homosexual, but in almost all contemporary discussions these laws are utilized as primary examples of the state's criminalization of homosexuality. As some legal analysts have pointed out, it could be argued that homosexuality is not illegal in Barbados, only certain sexual positions are. Nevertheless, the report advocated for the removal of these laws.
3 See Murray 2006 for discussion on the diversity of perspectives on homosexuality in Barbados.

4   In one interview in the *Nation*, the president of United Gays and Lesbians against Aids in Barbados (see note 5) acknowledged he was gay, but I do not include this as I am focusing on opinion in feedback media.

5   In December 2001, the group United Gays and Lesbians against Aids in Barbados (UGLAAB) was formed to promote HIV/AIDS education, eliminate discrimination against lesbians and gays with HIV/AIDS, and defend the rights of persons living with HIV/AIDS. UGLAAB has organized informal discussion groups in Bridgetown, HIV/AIDS prevention workshops, and other outreach programs throughout the island. Their president told me that while they are dedicated to fighting for lesbian and gay rights, they are primarily focused on the impact of HIV/AIDS on the gay and lesbian community in Barbados.

6   See note 2 above.

7   While some callers/writers stated explicitly that Barbados is a "Christian" nation, others spoke of the "morality" (or moral decay) occurring throughout the nation and referred to the Bible as the source of proper morality, thus implicating national identity with Christian values.

8   As can be seen from the examples I have presented, most discussions of homosexuality focus on sex between men. Lesbians are notably absent from the majority of this media talk. I address this absence below.

9   http://www.state.gov. Accessed November 21, 2005.

10 See, for example, " Economic and Financial Policies of the Government of Barbados," presented March 14, 2007, by then-finance minister Owen Arthur (http://www.nationnews.com; accessed July 28, 2007).

11 However, as Matthew Engelke has observed, international human rights activism can have mixed results. Engelke notes how discourses of "human rights" are wound up in complex political and cultural dynamics that are simultaneously local and transnational and often carry within them the accumulated effects of colonial relations perpetuated through unequal economic and social outcomes of recent forms of globalization (1999). Engelke suggests that one of the reasons that President Mugabe of Zimbabwe was so persistent in identifying homosexuality as "un-African" and not defensible as a "right" was to buttress his party's claim to be the only moral authority able to rescue a society "under threat" from the political, social, and economic legacies of colonialism.

12 Suzanne LaFont makes a similar point about Jamaica in chapter 6 of this volume.

13 Barbados is by no means entirely Christian. The 2000 census recorded 1,657 Muslims, 2,859 Rastafarians, 1,293 belonging to other "Non-Christian" denominations, and 43,245 people who listed themselves as having no religious affiliation (or at least none listed on the census) (Barbados Statistical Service 2000:34).

9

Lucknow Noir

Lawrence Cohen

OCCASIONALLY I am asked to be an expert witness. The cases usually involve persons from India seeking asylum in the United States. The claim for asylum in most of these cases is made on the basis of what the court understands as sexuality, specifically homosexuality. I am asked because I teach and write on homosexuality and politics at a university (making me an expert) and because much of my scholarly research is based in India (making me a witness). Specifically, claimants attest that they face serious threats to life and liberty because they are gay or lesbian. These claimants are frequently same-sex partners of American citizens or permanent residents: marriage is not an option for citizenship. The immigration lawyer or agency that contacts me needs to know if I can testify that state-mediated conditions for lesbians or gay men are sufficiently oppressive in India to make a case for asylum. Getting someone through the homophobic apparatus of U.S. immigration, in other words, requires sworn testimony that the United States offers a haven against the homophobia of her benighted native land.

I was naturalized as an American citizen in 1979, and among other things that I was required to swear to at that time was that I was not a homosexual. That form of border policing may have ceased, but in 1990 I was unable to get a visa for a boyfriend from India to visit. Single men from

India, an immigration lawyer told me, are less likely than married men to be granted entry. I have lived in India for extensive periods since 1983: though my visas have never been predicated on my claiming heterosexuality, I have had required HIV tests because I was American. Over the subsequent two and a half decades, I have lived and worked as a gay man in both countries.

Comparing conditions for "lesbians and gay men" between the two nations is difficult. Only a minority of persons with strong same-sex attachments in India identify as something like gay or lesbian; gender and class may be much more germane to the distribution of conditions than does presumptive sexual identity alone. Extramarital sex of any kind for many women, and resisting marriage for both women and men, may present more salient economic and social risks. The policing of sex between men through arrests, blackmail, sex on demand, and rape is ubiquitous in many Indian towns and cities, but no massively organized public apparatus of homophobic punishment, interdiction, and shame exists in India to the extent it has in the United States over the last half century.

Though I have done what I can, when I accept such cases, to construct a good-faith narrative to keep an asylum claimant in the United States, particularly in the face of the markedly racialized and heterosexist policies of the Immigration and Naturalization Service and of its post-9/11 successors, I am in effect asked to do the impossible. That is, I am asked to frame something called India as a site of monumental "homophobia," rooted in this case in tradition and its illiberalism. The sensibility I am routinely incited to project is like that found in a review in the *New York Times* of the French philosopher Bernard-Henri Lévy's book on the killing of the American reporter Daniel Pearl, to wit, "cities of South Asia, suffused with the 'stench of the apocalypse,' as Lévy puts it" (Kaplan 2003).

So I was wary when asked to contribute to a collection on homophobia, particularly as some of the accounts I want to explore as ethnographer and archivist can all too easily be reduced to some equally glib variant of Lévy's stench. This chapter centers on the rape and murder of six young men in 1994 in the north Indian city of Lucknow, capital of the populous, powerful, and poor state of Uttar Pradesh. Some years ago, as I was assembling the beginnings of the argument that I will engage here, I noted a proliferation of North American novelistic accounts of the serial killing of young Indian queers, either gay men or transgendered *hijras* (eunuchs): in particular, Paul Mann's *Season of the Monsoon* (1992) and Leslie Forbes's *Bombay Ice*

(1998). The similarities between the two mystery novels, in which the violent death of young queer sex workers becomes in some ways a metonym for the poverty and inhumanity of India itself, are notable enough that one of these authors unsuccessfully sued the other for plagiarism. Via the Internet, I interviewed Mann on why he had chosen the serial killing of homosexuals for his plot, wondering if he knew of the Lucknow murders in 1994. Mann responded that he did not know about any real killings. He wanted to pick as victims for his story the most socially abject class of persons he could imagine. The effort was to give a sense of the cheapness of life in the place he was trying to depict: again, apocalyptic stench.

In my own framings of the Lucknow murders, given the incitement to immodest accusation bundled up in the juridical instruments that asylum claimants, attorneys, and I struggle to manipulate to best advantage, the danger is in reproducing some similar version of already-spoken-for abjection, in which the possibility of a conversation through events is limited by the popular dissemination of a priori interpretive claims on the forms deployed. The purpose of the chapter that has emerged in response to the invitation to be included in this volume is therefore neither that of *audit* (the murders as a forensic accounting of human rights violations, over there) nor some feel-good anthropological *counternarrative* (the murders somehow reinscribed or rendered irrelevant to the broader scheme of things, enabling an account of tolerance and homo-utopia, over there). To the extent that what Eve Sedgwick termed the homosexual/heterosexual binarism (1990) and the historical emergence of male homosexual panic more generally (1985) do not secure the same terrain among even the transnational urban elites of contemporary South Asia as they do in the United States (Seabrook 1999; Khan 2001, 2003), homophobia as such may not be what is at stake in accounting for specific institutions and practices that punish persons recognizable under the globalizing gaze of LGBT/queer.

It is a useful premise among some of the arguments in this volume that the specific psychological or sociological premises of many working theories of homophobia often presume too much, but it is not my intent to discount the relevance either of behavioral and psychodynamic factors and theorizations thereof or of structural accounts of stigma, bias, and violence. I presume that the motivations behind the rape and killing of these young men in Lucknow are as multiple as are the analytic measures that might help one understand the events in question. But the apparent ease with which person after person was violently attacked and killed in this case, I will argue, had little to do with the putative identification of the victims' erstwhile pleasures. "Homosex," to use the vernacular term that moves between Hindi, Urdu, and English in the city, was less the object of panic: it was, rather, the preeminent figure of the political *tout court*. Thus "homophobia," which presumes a series of operations by which the homosexual is consolidated as the constitutive outside (Butler 1993) of sexual normality, may not be the most helpful or at least not the only generative concept to organize our thought. What is at stake, in the first instance, is what I will call "the feudal."

The Feudal as Sexual Orientation

The feudal is a ubiquitous figure in contemporary political reportage in India, in English, Hindi, and other languages. It signifies all that is not cosmopolitan and is often synonymous with the equally omnipresent accusation of backwardness. Temporally, it has a double referent, past and future. On the one hand, the feudal as a contemporary problem calls to mind the persistent landlordism of the various colonial systems of tax farming and the ornamentalism of indirect rule: it suggests both libertine rapaciousness and foppish decadence as figures of a despotism that cannot limit either its desire or its presentation of self. This mode of the feudal is predominantly retrospective, a depiction of an obsolete political aesthetic. As a depiction of extant forms, it is used to characterize social relations in "backward areas" (the organization of power in more remote districts, for example) and in stereotypically delineating social relations among urban Muslims. One of its ubiquitous characteristics is pederasty. "*Navabi shauk*" in north India literally figures princely desire and usually signifies *londebaazi*, taking pleasure in young men.

The feudal is not only a referent of the archaic, however, but of an emergent norm of violence that is taken as threatening to undo the civil promise of liberal nationalism. It often implies land mafia or other lumpen elements—rural or small town "vested interests" or urban underworld "dons," and the *goondas* or thugs who constitute their hired muscle—who are seen to stand against progress and outside civil society. Such "feudal elements" are usually framed as signs of imminent creeping rot, often in spatial as well as temporal terms. Thus the "backward" state of Bihar, east of

Uttar Pradesh where Lucknow is situated, represents a feudal environment that is seen to be extending throughout India, and news articles speak of the *Biharization* of civil society at "the center" (in the capital of New Delhi and for the cosmopolitan more generally). Or both Bihar and Uttar Pradesh along with the neighboring "Hindi-belt" states of Madhya Pradesh and Rajasthan are figured collectively as the acronym BiMaRU, meaning "sick," a disease not only unto itself but a threat precisely in their "feudal" character to the rest of the country. The feudal in this second sense does not draw upon the form of decadence as an excess of courtly culture but implies a set of rural or urban milieus in which insufficiently cultured beings may rise to prominence.

Both temporal stances of the feudal are frequently figured in terms of homosex. One sign of the decadence or the rapaciousness of the courtly feudal (rendered either as abject or dangerous depending on context) is the libertine desire for eunuchs or boys, taken not as a different object choice but a sign of the excess of desire: not just a wife but women, not just women but boys, not just boys but eunuchs.[1] Traveling through rural eastern Uttar Pradesh and western Bihar over the past twenty years and entering into conversations on the norms and forms of *zamindari* (landlord, feudal) life, I was surprisingly often told of some doting old raja or despotic zamindar in the next district whose politics were somehow encapsulated in his desiring not only women but additionally or primarily young men, *londa*s. And the new incivility of lumpenized politics may also be marked by *londebaazi* as a desiring form that renders the presumptive violence of the anticosmopolitan as sexual predation between men. This latter form became central to local readings of the Lucknow murders.[2]

Psychopathic Homosexual Killer

By the discovery of the fifth body, the engines of publicity were in full gear. In the metros, the large cities defined by their sizeable English-speaking publics, the relatively new private video and cable channels framed the deaths and the forensic apparatus that had grown up around them as a political scandal in the making. *Newstrack*, the television news magazine produced from the late 1980s through mid-1990s as a videocassette by the English print magazine *India Today*, did a feature story. The videography alternated between shots of darkness and light. As the anchor Manoj Raghuvanshi began to speak, shots of a car speeding through the night appeared behind him. It was an Ambassador model, with the red siren on top that marked it as a politician's vehicle. Slowly, the photos of four of the disfigured teenage heads appeared on the screen while Raghuvanshi introduced the story. "In the last month, Lucknow the capital city of Uttar Pradesh has been paralyzed with fear. A psychopathic homosexual killer whose identity is yet to be established is on the loose. Between the twelfth of February and the twentieth of March, five bodies of teenage boys were found in VVIP [Very Very Important Person] areas, all sodomized and strangled. The evidence suggests the use of a U.P. government car in transporting these bodies. This strengthens the suspicion of the involvement of someone with official connections" (*Newstrack* 1994).

The reporter's voice now takes over, leading us through what was becoming the dominant narration of the serial killer, in which madness and homosexuality were being superseded by rumors of a government secret for what defined the terror of the nocturnal moment. "It is past midnight. An Ambassador car with a red VIP light flashing on top stops in an affluent colony in Lucknow, Butler Palace, and parks there for a while. The area's chowkidar [the watchman] suspects nothing. The next morning, an unidentified body of a boy is found at the spot, sodomized and strangled."

The camera pans the spot and then a police photo of the first victim appears, taken in death. A resident describes finding the boy, and then we see the Ambassador again, at night. Then the unfolding horror continues. "After five days of this incident, the suspected psychopathic homosexual killer struck again. On the eighteenth of February, the naked body of another unidentified teenage boy was found, this time in the parking area of the State Government Guest House. After a gap of another five days, two more bodies were found strangled on the twenty-third of February, one in a park in Nahira, and the other in the Lal Bagh Officers' Residential Complex."

The camera pans each of the crime scenes and their VVIP environs. Then it cuts again to cars roaming at night, and then to the Secretariat building of the state assembly, the Vidhan Bhawan, still clothed in darkness. The scene brightens into daytime. "On the twentieth of March, the killer stalking the city chose the state Secretariat to dump his fifth victim, thirteen-year-old Mohammed Asif, son of a police constable. His body was found underneath an Ambassador car, which belongs to a finance department official. He was sodomized and his genitals were smashed before he was strangled. Now, as each new victim surfaces the tide of panic rises." The chief minister at the time, Mulayam Singh Yadav, is interviewed. Yadav's concern appears to be the *janata*, something variously subtitled for *Newstrack's* metropolitan audience as "people" and "public." The producers translate his response into English: "Because of all these murders, the people are naturally getting agitated, but the government has taken a serious view of these incidents."

The reporter then shifts focus to what this "agitation" has entailed:

> It was only after the recovery of the fifth body in the Secretariat that the police actually woke up and took serious action. The Uttar Pradesh government constituted a high-level team, headed by an inspector-general of police to investigate the case. A massive manhunt was launched. What do the police have to start with? What are the clues? What do all the victims have in common? Preliminary investigations reveal that all these male victims came from identical backgrounds, economically weaker sections, their age between thirteen and eighteen years. All the crimes were committed in one police station area, Hazratganj. All the bodies were sodomized. All the bodies were found naked from waist downwards. All the bodies were transported in a VIP car and dumped in VVIP areas. Although the police claim to have identified numerous witnesses, and even identified the kind of car used, the registration number of the car was not given out. The question being raised by many people is, with so many witnesses, why don't the police have the car number? And if they do, are they trying to shield a VIP?

In the elite media, the deaths of the young men begin to fade into the background as the real crime of the event appears to be a police and government cover-up. Sodomy becomes a sign of something else. For the anchor, it suggests the possibility of cosmopolitan diagnosis—homosexuality juxtaposed with psychopathy—but for both his reporter and the janata the sodomitical figures a political malaise and the secret that alternately contains or reveals it.

Gay as Forensic Explanation

By 1997, when I was living in Lucknow for several months, the serial killings had been all but forgotten, the case hung up in the courts and local news media devoting no space or time to it. I learned of the serial killer when I was interviewing Deepak Sharma, a reporter for the English paper *Pioneer*, after he had written a story about another and more recent murder. Frederick Gomes was a well-known sports coach and teacher at the city's most famous private school, La Martinière. After he was shot, rumors of all kinds circulated. Sharma pulled them together: Gomes was killed because he was involved with drug smuggling, because he was a womanizer, because of an argument with a well-placed student, and because he was "a gay." The last came to stand for the whole set: "Gomes Was a Gay" highlighted in large type and boldface drew readers' attention to Sharma's article.

By "gay as forensic explanation," I mean that no further elaboration was necessary to connect the possible fact of Gomes being a gay to the event of his violent death. The biographical picture reconstituted was of a man with fiery and excessive appetites: women, crime, money, and young men. The pederastic was enfolded with the rest, with no hint of a homo/hetero opposition or an exceptional category of bisexuality, and it came to stand for the whole. That Gomes was a gay was less the suggestion of an abjection that could be extended to the logic of his killing than that of a poorly delimited desire that located him in equally voracious and ultimately lethal company.

I interviewed Sharma. He said he was less interested in suggesting that Gomes was a gay than in making a comment on the extraordinary proliferation of rumors. But when I pushed him on why "the gay" could serve as a metonym for criminality, he told me that the whole matter boiled down to the noxious influence of the neighboring town of Malihabad on the aristocratic mores of Lucknow. I asked how.

Malihabad was historically a Pathan town, settled long ago by those Afghan tribesmen famous, Sharma reminded me, for their boy loving. Pathans were involved in all manner of organized crime in India, he went on. In this region, Pathans specialized in the production and movement of heroin from Afghanistan and Pakistan into India, where it was processed and then sent out and elsewhere through porous ports. Heroin money had transformed this sleepy town heretofore known more for its mangoes, and Malihabad Pathans were moving in to Lucknow, sending their children to La Martinière, and transforming the famed politesse of Lucknow's courtly society dating from the city's eighteenth- and nineteenth-century heyday as the capital of the kingdom of Oudh. Pederasty, primitivism, and new wealth composed an indivisible set under the twin signs of culture and history. "Gomes Was a Gay" figured a much larger reconfiguration and redistribution of value.

As Sharma and I were discussing the Pathan thing, his editor came into the room. He called me into his larger and air-conditioned office and told me that Pathans and culture had nothing to do with the murders. The editor was a Marxist sociologist by training, from the Jawaharlal Nehru University in New Delhi, a center for left-leaning scholarship in the social sciences. It's all about land tenure, he said. He was from Punjab, he went on, and his wife was from Bengal, places where unlike u.p. and neighboring Bihar this sort of thing, homosex, was not something so often encountered. The reason for the local ubiquity of homosex, he said, was the long-term effects of the regional specificity of the British rule of property, the creation of specific regimes of land and taxation in colonial India through the adaptation of different practices of landlordship and tenancy. The *zamindars* or landlords of u.p. and Bihar were particularly "feudal" in the regime of terror and abjection the local rule of property allowed them to sustain, even after the reforms of the postcolonial state. The question of Gomes and of the specific local movement of capital and heroin was suspended for a *longue durée* account of modes of production and their effects. "Gay" here for my colleague signified a generalized state of feudal violence, the desire of the powerful for total control over the landless.

In neither case, the conversation with the reporter or that with his boss, did the "gay" ever circulate out to the person or body of the one presumptively violated. These latter were, in the words of the *Newstrack* reporter covering the serial killings in 1994, the "economically weaker sections," and violence directed against *them* was self-explanatory.

The Feudal, Lucknow-Style

With the serial killings, the police force's inability to find a killer—many men were arrested, interrogated, and eventually released—was increasingly laid at the door of a high-level cover-up. Initially, the psychopathic homosexual killer was thought to be a leading politician who used boys sexually and then had them killed to prevent word getting out. A member of the state cabinet, Reoti Raman Singh, was identified as the likely culprit, though this claim circulated among journalists and political cognoscenti in the capital primarily by word of mouth. In 1996, two years after the killings, many women and men I interviewed in the city had heard the rumors and presumed Singh was somehow implicated, though by that time the case had dropped from sight.

At least two glosses might be offered to locate the logic of the accusations of Singh's guilt and of subsequent events, each drawing on the general category of the feudal as the chronotope of backwardness and its close association with pederastic form.

The feudal, version 1: Lucknow, for its publicists, is steeped in a particular mixture of elegy and politesse, a sense of *lakhnavipan*, Lucknow-ness, which circulated widely from the 1950s through the 1970s through a genre of popular Hindi film set in or linked to the city and simultaneously celebrating and lamenting the exquisite manners and pleasure/pain of the *tawaif* or courtesan. The counterpart to the courtesan in such narratives was the *nawab* or prince, famed in both the colonial and nationalist historiographies of British India for cultivation to the point of dissolution, a state narratively framed as an incessant desire for an object other than the nation or the people: courtesans, boys, eunuchs, pigeons, poetry, drink, dress, festivals, food, or, in the version of the writer Premchand and later the filmmaker Satyajit Ray, chess. The figure of the nawab drew both on widely circulating colonial historiography (thus the globally distributed language of elite, effete "nabobs" in the later nineteenth century and the dispersed invention of place names like San Francisco's Nob Hill) and, more specifically, on efforts in north India to create a national and Hindu vehicle out of Hindi by setting it against an increasingly Islamicized Urdu identified with the sexual excess of the nawab and tawaif (King 1992; Dalmia 1997).

In some registers, this *navabi shauk*, princely desire, is constitutively sodomitical in its abjection and excess, and such shauk is part and parcel of the received account of Laknavi cultivation. In later print and electronic media revisions of the Lucknow serial killings following on subsequent and apparently unrelated incidents of sodomitical violence, both local and nationally based journalists asked "what is it about Lucknow?"—and navabi shauk was at least one proffered answer, holding within it the implicit association of navabi culture and Islam and thus a second and far broader kind of accusation.

Accounts of navabi shauk linked to murder were not unfamiliar to contemporary forensic imagination in the city: the parallel though less public case in Lucknow in the early 1990s of the death of a handsome British heir to a biscuit-manufacturing fortune, allegedly at the hands of Jimmy, the Raja of Jehangirabad, and his alleged murderous lover and estate agent Ram Prasad, was often mentioned to me by the *talukdar*s, the city's gentry. Jimmy's elegant if appropriately crumbling mansion, visited by Princess Elizabeth and Jacqueline Kennedy, was used as the set for one of the most famous courtesan films of the 1970s, *Umrao Jan*.

The feudal, version 2: Yet in the case of the killings of the young men in 1994, no such account of obsessive cultivation circulated in the city, not the least because Reoti Raman Singh was neither from Lucknow nor emblematic of its fading cultivation. "Lucknow," one journalist told me, "is being Bihar-ized." Bihar, to the east of Uttar Pradesh, had for most metropolitan publics by the 1980s become synonymous with corruption and the failure of both the state and civil society. Bihar, according to many in the Uttar Pradesh cities of Banaras, Allahabad, and Lucknow where I lived for some time, was full of rapacious *zamindar*s, landlords, who I was told particularly love a beautiful boy. *Londebaazi* is the desire for boys, and the equation was often made between landlordism and londebaazi, with or without a historical gloss like that provided by the Marxist editor.

Again, these various geographies of rot and their consistent sexualization are predicated on a piece of local knowledge: that the feudal, that backward order that nationalists had tried unsuccessfully to reform and was now reclaiming more and more of India, was not only omnivorous in its desire but fervently and at times violently pederastic. The ability to *extinguish* another in the satisfaction of one's desire, the exercise of hierarchy without *jajman* or *dan* (the gift of the lord establishing the ethic of his superiority), were not only represented by asymmetrical homosexuality but enacted by it. Whether from Bihar or Malihabad next door, this latter sense of the feudal was sharply distinguished from the cultivation of navabi shauk. Whether in the local press or in nationally circulated media based in Delhi or Mumbai (Bombay), the dominant figure of the feudal was that of the anticivility of large peasant interests progressively eroding the metropolitan culture of Nehruvian India. This, the dominant feudal, was rapacious, never effete.

In such an imaginable chronotope of feudal expansion and state and civil decline, Reoti Raman Singh's alleged actions at first read as part and parcel of the spread of the feudal and its constitutive desire. People in Lucknow described him, or other politicians variously fingered as the serial killer, as representative of the new criminalized legislature and its exemplification of "the feudal."

But this characterization, too, didn't hold, in part as Singh was not the archetypical goon (the word comes from the Hindi and contemporary Indian English *goonda*, as in ruffian, bully, hired muscle, or to use another and parallel borrowing, thug, implying a violence already spoken for) but a deft and aggressive politician, a master rather than an exemplar of the feudal as a mode of reason.

The story that began, over the second half of 1994, to take root was therefore less an account of excess than of the *citation* of excess: that Singh had had the rape-murders committed *in order to represent the state as feudal* and in so doing to precipitate a crisis of law and order. Singh's alleged intent was to bring down his party boss, the then chief minister Mulayam Singh Yadav. Yadav's persona was isomorphic with that of his party, the Samaj-wadi (Socialist])Party (the SP), a regional power largely limited to U.P. and throughout the 1990s in shifting and at times segmentary opposition to the nationally dominant and Hindu-identified Bharatiya Janata Party (the BJP) and the low caste Bahujan Samaj Party (the BSP). There was apparent friction between the two men. Reoti Raman Singh had earlier defected from the SP but returned to help Mulayam achieve his latest victory. A second story that also took root, though I could only find it in the Congress-tilted English paper *Asian Age* at a time when Congress was courting the BSP, suggested that it was not Reoti who had committed the murders to bring down Mulayam but the reverse: that Mulayam had put events in motion to frame Reoti with trying to frame him.

I recall rumor and reportage at length here to underscore the obvious and never questioned ground of debate: that what I am calling sodomitical violence was necessarily, even constitutively, an index of the political, that it was ubiquitous not only in textual mediation but in the corporeal citation of terror and forensic response. The predicates of this index are multiple, and one I would argue is that unwanted sex from the mildly to the violently coercive was a feature of everyday trouble for socially marginal men. The marginality that might make one particularly vulnerable to sodomitical address includes, as for the Lucknow victims, class, caste, religion, age, and migrant status, but it often also included "feminine" or "third" gendered presentation.

There are multiple caveats in any foregrounding of the feudal, not the least of which is its complicity with a dominant if not hegemonic sensibility, particularly among metropolitan elites identifying with the terms (if not the structure) of homosexual/heterosexual binarism, that homosexuality was inevitably a matter of excessive desire and resulting coercion. "Gays have no self-control," a then-unmarried friend from Calcutta told me in 1987. "I can't meet girls here the way you can in the States, but you don't see me going after guys. I have self-control." Again and again, dominant metropolitan discourse then and now frames the "gay" as a position of elite desire and a synonym for predation, set against the poor or otherwise marginal partner of "the gay," who either bears his abjection quietly or recognizes its fungibility and cultivates it through feminine or third gendered presentation.

Nor is my effort to foreground the practice and representation of male-male rape as constitutively political at the expense of an attentiveness to the rape of women and the symbolic work the latter violation does in recasting passionate attachments. The two rapes, male-male and male-female, are as it were bound up together in the constitution of the political, and bound as well to the possibility of pleasure and care after, in spite of, against, and alongside violent events. A growing literature has documented the use of the abduction and rape of women, and of the representation of these acts, in the constitution of national and communal—Hindu, Muslim, and Sikh—publics, during the Partition violence of 1947 and during the Hindu right–sponsored communal violence of the 1990s and the present decade (Bacchetta 1994; Agarwal 1995; Butalia 1995; Das 1995). But if the act and citation of male-female abduction and rape addresses and demands a split, "communal" public (Hindus versus Muslims, in the most common case),[3] the act and citation of male-male rape and killing in the Lucknow murders addresses a unified, localized public (residents of the city, or state, or nation) set not against itself but against the apparently feudal excess of the political regime.

I draw attention to the Lucknow murders neither to suggest that they constitute a norm of sexualized violence or that they are some structural equivalent to what may be more or less usefully framed as homophobia elsewhere. Punishing action against women and men who desire and constitute their gender against the grain is certainly not foreign to the places and times addressed here, and the very *idiom* of the sodomitical in north India—the punishing or joking language of the *gandu* ("bugger" or "faggot," but with the vehemence or familiarity of "cock-sucker")—presumes the abject and shameful state of being the penetrated male. Whether the transnational movement of a concept of homophobia will in the future mobilize individuals and institutions in the intensified normalization of such punishment is an open question. Certainly, any accounting of punishment and response would require a thick sociology of bodily comportment, questions of marriage, mappings of the licit, trackings of colonial and national regulation, and delineations of the moments when the West's spectral presence demands particular punishments for certain gender trouble.

I draw attention to the murders to underscore the ubiquity of the feudal and its citation as a critical site and moment in the constitution of a certain knowledge of sexual difference and punishment and of a possible forensics thereof. I turn next to an event that occurred in 2001, again situated primarily in Lucknow, that has been read as indicative of Indian state homophobia today and which I have, at times, been urged to cite in asylum cases, framing the event in relation to the knowledge of the feudal absent from metropolitan and global reports.

Activists Remain Jailed

Internationalism in arenas marked as gay has since the 1990s been mediated by publicists like Rex Wockner, whose syndicated newsfeed appears in newspapers and websites and claims for itself the developmental role of advancing institution building in the former Eastern Bloc and Third World: "If someone in an organization with 14 people in a Third World country reads a story about hundreds of thousands of people marching in a pride parade in Los Angeles, they could get the idea that if they stick with it, they might make it. . . . That's really why I do this." Fair enough. But though Wockner is read by many of the peripheral activists he cites as his ideal public, the dominant flow of information is not surprisingly from the political periphery to the center. Thus a cyberjournalist admiringly notes that "Wockner's international coverage has brought the struggles of emerging sexual-freedom movements in places like Zimbabwe to the attention of an international readership" (Silberman 1998). It is worth noting, in the article cited, that the "international" public constituted by Wockner's news is set against "places like Zimbabwe."

Within such a global dispensation, India may fall in the latter camp, a "place like Zimbabwe" and not simply an example of the unmarked international. Several of Wockner's pieces on India over the 1990s and into the present have focused on the city of Lucknow. The article of his I cite is multiply distributed across paper and electronic archives. The version I cite, off the commercial erotica site Badpuppy.com, is titled "Activists Remain Jailed in Lucknow, India" (Wockner 2001). The text is juxtaposed with a file photograph of the Taj Mahal, located several hundred kilometers away from Lucknow in Agra. Wockner articles archived on the Badpuppy site are divided fairly neatly into international stories with accompanying photos of the persons or events depicted, and stories of places like Zimbabwe, with touristic metonyms like the Taj. The observation is neither that surprising nor compelling, but it is of a piece with the genre the article exemplifies.

The article notes that employees of two AIDS organizations in Lucknow, Naz Foundation International (NFI) and Bharosa, remain in jail on charges of "conspiracy to commit 'unnatural sexual acts.'"

> A judge refused the arrestees' bail requests on July 11, accusing them of "polluting the entire society by encouraging the young persons and abating [*sic*] them to committing the offence of sodomy." The AIDS work of both organizations has been supported by the Uttar Pradesh State AIDS Control Society and India's National AIDS Control Organization. The International Gay & Lesbian Human Rights Commission denounced the arrests on July 25. "The use of police force to raid agencies and arrest staff engaging in government-sanctioned HIV/AIDS prevention activities—the conflation of this educational activity with abetting, spreading, and conspiring to commit sodomy—reflects ignorance and prejudice masquerading as enforcement of the law," IGLHRC said. Section 377 of the Indian Penal Code punishes sodomy with up to 10 years in prison.

As a brief summary of events, the account is fairly accurate, though the outcry of many activists and NGO (nongovernmental organization) representatives throughout India goes unmentioned while the U.S.–based IGLHRC's denunciation receives pride of place. Wockner's account has all the elements of GLBT internationalism—reference to punitive laws, the suggestion of the backwardness of non-Western societies, the heroic role of Western NGOs—that Martin Manalansan classically delineated (1995).

The arrests themselves were less the campaign of an AIDS-phobic state apparatus than the result of a contingent assemblage of political forces. The two AIDS organizations were run by a charismatic British South Asian activist, Shivananda Khan, who was investing foundation and bilateral health promotion capital in AIDS organizations targeting men who have sex with men (MSM) across the subcontinent. Khan had in effect taken over a small gay group in Lucknow known as Friends India, hiring one of the two main founders of that group to run Naz Foundation International (his umbrella NGO supporting research and development in MSM-focused AIDS prevention among Asians globally) and oversee Bharosa (the local Lucknow-based heir to Friends India). Khan was seen by many in the AIDS and gay movement worlds in India as the rival of a prominent Mumbai gay and AIDS activist and journalist Ashok Row Kavi. Both men courted controversy at times and both arguably were empire builders: each had a distinct vision of how best to prevent AIDS among MSM populations (Cohen 2005). In such a context, rumors proliferated as to why Khan's organization was attacked and his outreach workers and chief officer arrested.

There were two primary sets of rumors. One set circulated among a number of cognoscenti in the gay movement and blamed either Row Kavi or Khan for events leading up to the arrest. One story was that the other founder of Friends India, the one not brought in by Khan to run NFI, was resentful at being passed over and sought out Row Kavi's assistance, leading to the spread of unfounded accusations against Khan including that he somehow was supporting Pakistan. Khan and the remaining founder of Friends India (who was arrested) were Muslims, as were most of the arrested outreach workers, and the accusation of pro-Pakistan sentiment (if ever made) suggested the mobilization of anti-Muslim bias among the Lucknow police. Row Kavi, a former Hindu monk, is noted for expressing arguably pro-Hindu and anti-Muslim and Christian sentiments on the air and online, leading some of his liberal opponents to accuse him of being part of the Hindu right.

Row Kavi and his alleged Friends India accomplice strongly denied accusations that they had anything to do with the arrests, however, and in turn suggested that these accusations were fomented as a matter of dirty tricks by Khan and an ambitious human rights lawyer who was one of his supporters. In media pronouncements, however, both Khan and Row Kavi were tireless and united in challenging the illegality and stupidity of the arrests and of charges that safer-sex videos and a dildo used for condom demonstrations constituted sexual pandering.

The second set of rumors suggested that the outreach workers arrested were engaging in sex work themselves. If so, and there is no solid evidence for the claim, it reflects less the specificity of these Lucknow NGOs and more the structure of Indian AIDS prevention. Many outreach workers to MSM populations across the country have been sex workers or former sex workers, in part because these men often have the contacts and skills to do effective outreach.

The outreach workers faced taunts, violence, and extraordinarily difficult conditions in jail; they were released several weeks later on bail, but as of this writing several years later their trials are in some cases still underway. The U.P. police have not attempted similar arrests elsewhere, and despite the picture offered by Wockner and IGLHRC the Lucknow affair does appear to involve NGO infighting over strategy and resources, with blame to be had on all sides. It also involves a local police administration particularly invested in arresting "homosexuals" as variously constituted (foreign, Islamic) threats to the nation, and therefore eager to capitalize on the accusations circulating among NGOs in competition for AIDS capital. Whether the "homophobia" of the Lucknow police is a sign of the intensified normalization of antigay punishment under contemporary globalization is an open question: as of this writing, Lucknow remains the exception.

After the arrests, the city's reporters began to link them to previous forensic engagements with the gay, and principally to the serial killer from 1994, never brought to justice and hitherto all but forgotten in the press. But accounts of political secrets or stratagems that saturated the media in 1994 were missing. What is it about Lucknow, the press again asked. The Islamicized specter of navabi shauk was again invoked, but here with no sense of high culture (however decadent) and a new hint of accusation, against Khan. Other criminal cases—Gomes, Raja Jimmy—were alluded to. The sense of creeping rot was trebly framed: the violent feudal, the Muslim feudal, and a new element not present in the reportage of 1994: the decadence of the West, as exemplified in the culture of NGOs, the supporters of

Naz. Over the subsequent months and years, this equation of the violent feudal, Islam, and the threat of NGO governance was repeated. The stakes in forensic imagination, and in the mobilization of the gay, were shifting.

Coda: The Limits to the Beautiful

Through the second half of the twentieth century and into the current era of the global security state, two figurations of same-sex eroticism were predominant within north Indian public culture, despite their arguable salience either to emergent metropolitan queer institutions or more generally to the lives of persons constituting their gender or sexual practice against the grain. I have elsewhere described these figurations in the terms of violence and beauty (1995a, 2002). My current work engages the relation between them as a general problem. Most of the preceding comments have focused on the violent: the ways the feudal and the sodomitical can come to stand in for one another. If there is a signature field of human endeavor that the violent in these terms invokes, it is of course politics. If there is a signature commodity that follows accounts of the sodomitical-political, it is heroin, as in Sharma's discussion of the Malihabadization of Lucknow through Pathan heroin money.

The other dominant figuration has not been touched on here, but it merits brief mention in closing. Many English- and Hindi-language discussions of the postliberalization era of globalizing investment and ownership in India have linked an emerging commodity aesthetics to the idea of "the gay." Advertisements may feature same-sex couplings (Cohen 2002; Vanita 2002); discussions of the new middle-class male may frame him as reliant on gay style; and the fashion industry, consistently thematized as "gay," has become a ubiquitous site in the production of celebrity, middle-class careers, and reflexive attention to the new consumption. The gay explicitly offers a mode of desire set against marriage and paternal authority, and as such it is seen to configure the stakes in a broader moment of individualist consumption and experimental self-making, This mode is distinct from that of the feudal, the latter rooted explicitly not only in the political but in the local, the nonmetropolitan, the informal traffic in goods at the margins of the law, and the phallic economy of circulating penetration. "India," staged or imagined as a relation between the metropolitan and the rural (Shukla 1992), between the civil and the political (Chatterjee 2004), or between the sublime and Hobbesean Warre (Hansen 1999), becomes a problem of the relation of the cosmopolitan gay to the sodomitical.

What I am calling the beautiful frames these stakes in liberalized consumption and self-making in relation to an earlier moment also figured as in some sense gay, that of national planned development.[4] The development state has far from disappeared in India, even under the uneven track of neoliberal reform, but it is like a dreamworld after the fact in the Benjaminian sense, apparent as fragmented series (Buck-Morss 1989, 2000). One such series is that of *swadesi*, of Gandhian self-reliance and the project of homespun cotton; another frames the "Nehruvian," specifically the nationalist leader and first Indian prime minister Jawaharlal Nehru's linked commitments to science, secular humanism, and the beautiful. Thomas Hansen has described these projects as marking off a sublime realm of *satyagraha* (Gandhian nonviolent practice) or of modernist planning set against the violence of quotidian engagement: I would suggest they marked themselves and are still registered as claims for the beautiful. Nehru famously noted that an emergent India "should not tolerate ugliness." In multiple projects and media, the remains of development as a dream of self and societal remaking are reworked in the terrain of cosmopolitanism and fashion.

The stakes in this reworking are perhaps most evident in the divergent curricula of the National Institute of Design in Ahmedabad and the National Institute of Fashion Technology in Delhi, where variant and experimental approaches to the relation between the possibilities of market form and the ethical remainders of both Gandhian and Nehruvian claims on the social are assayed. The latter institution in particular is both in imaginary and real terms a site where meanings and uses of "the gay" are produced. These stakes are also evident in the role of foreign NGOs as paradoxical executors of earlier nationalist and state promises of both self-reliance and progress in the replacement of violence by beauty. Since the mid-1990s, NGOs have been accused—particularly but not exclusively by the Hindu right—of importing non-Indian or non-Hindu practices and values, either sexual or Christian or Muslim or all three, into both metropolitan and small-town public culture. The attacks on Khan and the Bharosa workers exemplify the pattern. Similarly, the well-known attacks on both Deepa Mehta's film *Fire* and Karan Razdan's *Girlfriends* linked the two "lesbian films" to non-Indian and anti-Hindu NGO values denigrating women. Such attacks drew on a body of reference linking a putative Gandhian betrayal of the Hindu nation, Nehruvian secularism, and contemporary foreign influence.

It is in this context that I offer my final example, the most publicized case of violence against queers in recent Indian history (Cohen 2007), far outstripping reportage on the Lucknow serial killer. In August 2004, a World Health Organization employee and U.S.–trained MBA, Pushkin Chandra, along with a second man variously described in the press as Vishal or Kuldeep and as Chandra's associate, boyfriend, friend, lover, male companion, so-called companion, partner, or gay partner, were found dead, evidently murdered, at the former's home in a wealthy Delhi neighborhood not far from the National Institute of Fashion Technology. The two had gone with two other men, a taxi or school van driver, Rajesh, and his "accomplice," Moti, to a farewell party for a Danish health researcher well known in both elite gay and NGO circles in Delhi, Mumbai, and elsewhere in the country. The quartet apparently later returned to Pushkin's place, a *barsati* or separate apartment on his family's property. Television, newspaper, and Internet reports of the murders stressed and in some cases manufactured lurid details: the gay pornography tape still playing on the television, the photos of nude men scattered everywhere, the particularly violent disposal of the bodies. Forensic accounts from local police were quickly disseminated: these stressed the likelihood that the NGO manager Chandra was a marketer of pornographic photos whose plans had gone terribly awry when his intended victims—the absconding murderers—had reacted violently to being photographed while having sex. Chandra's relative foreignness and apparent renunciation of his family—his American degree, his NGO job, his refusal of marriage and open life as a gay man, and his living in the barsati as opposed to in the main building with his parents—were cited, as was the fact that the Danish researcher had left the country (it was, after all, his farewell party). A plot was intimated linking the exploitation of young men as sexual models with the NGO circuit and the gay as a new mode of living. Other details—the stolen car, camera, computer, and considerable other property, the identity and prior history of the killers, Pushkin's own character and his actual relation with his family and his friends, and any discussion of the other murder victim—were downplayed or missing in many accounts. Activists associated with AIDS-prevention NGOs and others responded angrily to the reportage. In response, the columnist Swapan Dasgupta wrote a scathing rebuke, "Not with Gay Abandon," attacking "gay activists and rent-a-cause liberals" for attempting to turn "perversity into victimhood."

Dasgupta's comments were widely circulated on the Internet, particularly among Indians abroad. Like elite media efforts to turn the Lucknow affair into the depredations of a "psychopathic homosexual," they drew on both globally intensifying grammars of a homosexual-heterosexual binarism and a particularly Indian feudal equation of violence and the sodomitical. But the earlier event did not reverse the victimhood of murderer and murdered. Dasgupta went far beyond such a reversal, suggesting that not only were any claims of "gay bashing" in India entirely fictitious but that the "Pushkin case" was linked to international child pornography rings and "a nexus between employees of international aid agencies and the gay underworld." NGOs were serving as covers for criminal networks (Dasgupta 2004).

The Pushkin case is a Delhi story. As Dasgupta and other journalists noted, South Delhi parties in which well-off gay men paid admission and nonelite men were present primarily as sex workers are frequent, though the farewell party was not a sex-for-hire venue. Less asymmetrical or more hybrid spaces for sex, care, and community than the usual parties are few, as opposed, for example, to Mumbai or Chennai. The class morphology of Delhi gay parties reflects the class morphology of Delhi and the growing marginalization of the city's working class and poor. What men do with and through these venues, however, is not necessarily the account of simple exploitation that Dasgupta imagines. The erasure of Kuldeep from the newspaper stories prevents a different accounting.

Most representations of same-sex eroticism between men in contemporary India have been focused either on the sodomitical political, the order of violence and the feudal, or on the "gay" commodity aesthetics of global capital refiguring the fragments of progress and self-reliance, the order of beauty and the cosmopolitan. With few exceptions until the Pushkin case, the world of fashion and metropolitan consumption iteratively marked as gay has not elicited phobic or punishing accounts. Where such accounts have marked the cosmopolitan has been in the occasional and short-lived effort of the Hindu right to mobilize political capital around the "lesbian film." Everyday incidents of violence targeting same-sex desire are frequent, of course, but these cluster around the beating or extortion of men who have sex with men by the police or others and are usually encompassed within the logic of the expansive feudal along with many other norms and forms of violent action.

The Pushkin case may offer a different moment, or it may be a kind of exception. What it appears to suggest is a growing critique of the claims of beauty and their current idioms of transnationalism, image production, and NGO governance in which the gay and the sodomitical are less opposed orders of civil versus political society than a "nexus," in Dasgupta's phrase, in which such difference becomes incoherent. There is a suggestion, in Dasgupta's bromide, of creeping rot from both sides now, from the violence of Malihabad and Lucknow and from the beauty of the West. That such an imagined zone of indistinction authorizes the punishment of same-sex desire is worth attending to.

Notes

Versions of this chapter were given as talks at the University of California Irvine, the University of California San Diego, the University of Chicago, and San Francisco State University: I am grateful for all suggestions, and for those of David Murray and the anonymous reviewers. Donald Moore first alerted me to the appearance of the serial killing of male and transgendered female sex workers in India as a staple of detective fiction. This draft was written while I was enjoying the hospitality and intellectual fellowship of the School of American Research in Santa Fe.

1   I use the English *eunuch* for persons who might in different contexts be described as *hijra*s, *kinnar*s, or *koti*s in part as many hijras themselves use the term for self-reference, and in part as it suggests the particular coding of a trans-gendered presence in South and Central Asian courtly forms (see Cohen 1995b 2004, 2005).

2   The origins of the feudal as pederastically constituted are probably multiple: in *longue durée* representations of Indian sovereignty through figures of *bhogi* or libertinage (Madan 1987); in the importance of eunuchs and cross-dressing to the central Asian, Persian, and Turkish courtly forms that transform the organization of sovereign representation; in the local incorporation of colonial understandings of pederasty as a dominant form of Oriental despotism; in the intensification of violence, including homosocial rape, as a feature of the stratification consequent upon colonial tax farming; in the courtly cultures of princely states within a colonial regime inciting decadence; in the centrality of obscene referent, including pederasty, to the emerging print cultures of the late nineteenth and early twentieth century (Gupta 2001); and in the forms of progressive social critique (colonial and anticolonial) of the twentieth century that utilize the pub-

licity of this print culture to attack the feudal as both misogynist and pederastic (Vanita 2006).

3   "Communal" in India usually signifies religious nationalism and interreligious conflict.

4   That the order of practice and reason popularly spanning the Gandhian nationalist and Nehruvian statist eras of the Congress Party was figured as sexually nonnormative is an essay unto itself; here I will only draw attention to the Gandhian aesthetics of transgendered or "bisexual" self-fashioning (Nandy 1983), to the dandyism by which Nehru is taken to have supplemented Gandhian sartorial asceticism, and to the various criticisms, in Hindi and Bhojpuri literature and satirical media, of the Congress body—in my reckoning, the order of the beautiful—as sodomitically available for penetration by its opposite number, the order of the violent (see Cohen 1995a for a discussion of related materials).

Epilogue: What Is to Be (Un)Done?

David A. B. Murray

I HAD TO LEAVE Kampala quickly. I had finished my social work degree and was developing a support group for young kuchus [gay men]—about twenty of us met regularly at homes and sometimes bars around the city. But over the last few months, the police had begun to call me on my cell phone, and I even had to meet with an officer who basically told me that they had information on me to prove that I was engaged in immoral activities and would publish my name in the newspapers "unless . . ."—which meant I would have to pay them a lot of money. I didn't have that kind of money. Luckily, I had just received acceptance of my paper and a plane ticket to the International Conference on LGBT Rights in Montreal, so I decided to get out of Uganda before things got worse and seek protection in Canada.

I had never been on a plane before and I kept wondering if they might stop me at the airport in Kampala, but I made it through. When the plane finally touched down in Montreal, I was nervous about Canadian customs, but when I told the customs officer I was here for the LGBT Rights Conference he just nodded and stamped my book. I was expecting someone from the conference would be there to meet me, but there was no one. I was confused, and started asking people for directions to the conference, but nobody spoke English, nobody seemed to know anything about it. I walked outside, and saw a taxi.

I asked the driver if he knew about the conference, and he said, in broken English, yes, but go to Toronto, it's in Toronto. I didn't know exactly where Toronto was—I thought it might be near to Montreal, so I said okay and got in the taxi. We drove a few kilometers until the driver stopped and said, "Here for Toronto." It was a train station. I thought, okay, I need to get on the train to go to Toronto. I was surprised at the price of the ticket, but I had heard that things cost more here.

I was so confused by the time I got to Toronto. When I emerged from the train station I started to ask people about the location of the LGBT conference, but they ignored me until finally a friendly black man said I must be meaning the International HIV/AIDS conference that would be starting in two weeks. By this point, I wasn't sure what I was here for, so I said yes, and could he help me find protection and somewhere to stay. He said he knew a place which allowed "people like me" to stay and they would help me. He took me to a brick building, and a nice man showed me a room and gave me the address of an office which he said I should go to immediately.

I went the next day, and was surprised to see it was a lawyer's office (I thought I would need to go to the police). When we met he asked if I wanted to apply for refugee status, I asked why—I didn't think I was a refugee. He explained to me that in Canada I could apply to stay here as a refugee if I was being persecuted or threatened back in Uganda based on my sexual orientation. I thought, yes, this is what was happening to me. Then it was so simple. I went to a government office the next day and explained to the officer what was happening to me in Uganda. He took my passport and when he gave it back to me I was suddenly on my way to being a refugee!—Edward, twenty-seven

Stories like this one abound in Toronto these days. Edward was most likely counted as one of the 150 delegates from the 2006 International AIDS conference in Toronto who filed for refugee status. In fact, Canada appears to have developed a reputation as a haven for "gay refugees." Between 2000 and 2003, nearly 2,500 people from 75 different countries sought asylum on the basis of sexual orientation (Jimenez 2004). According to a newspaper report, the largest number of these refugees came from Mexico and Costa Rica, two countries that are not at the top of most "homophobic hotspots" lists. Of the 602 Mexican claims made between 2000 and 2003 on the basis of sexual orientation, 71 were accepted, 67 were rejected, 415 await hearings, and 50 were abandoned or withdrawn. The Canadian Immigration and Refugee Board (IRB) received so many cases from self-professed Costa Rican homosexuals that it issued jurisprudential guidelines concluding that homosexuals do not face persecution in Costa Rica (Jimenez 2004).

Immigration lawyers specializing in these kinds of refugee cases must thus help their clients prove to the IRB that (a) they are homosexual and (b) they will face persecution in their country if they return. As one lawyer stated, this area is a very complex one: "I used to call it Gay 101. Immigration and Refugee Board members ask claimants what day the Gay Pride parade was on, where the gay bars in Toronto are located and whether they were in a relationship. . . . But what does that prove? Members have to have gaydar [gay radar], and rely on their gut instinct. But it is also a subjective area" (Jimenez 2004).

As the chapters in this volume have demonstrated, homosexuality and homophobia are, to say the least, practices which involve subjectivity. We might add that subjectivity also applies to immigration and refugee boards' policies defining homosexuality and other nation's cultural attitudes toward sexual practices and treatment of sexual minority groups. But Edward's story is also a reminder of the reality of "homo hatred" and its effects, generating the migration of many to new and unfamiliar places. Their claims speak to the centrality and urgency of better understanding how same sex sexual practices are being debated, supported, denied, condemned, or negotiated within and across national borders.

Homophobia is no longer an issue that lies hidden in the crevices and shadows of public culture(s). The contributors to this volume have demonstrated that varying incarnations of the homosexual, for better or for worse, are now occupying the center stage of local, national, and international discussions of citizenship, rights, development, health, morality, family values, and criminality. As noted by Hoad (1999), Giorgi (2002), Larvie (1999), and others, gays and lesbians have become, in some cases, the new model citizen embraced by a number of nation-states (and not just northern, Euro-American ones), reflecting the progressive, liberal, democratic, multicultural states' tolerance of diversity and concomitantly, some would argue, their moral superiority over and against those nation-states that continue to criminalize, persecute, and criticize homosexuality (see Martin Manalansan's chapter in this volume for an example of this moral superiority within mainstream white American gay activist circles). State-sanctioned violence against gays and lesbians has become the target of numerous international human rights campaigns (albeit quite recently) and, increasingly, international development funding is predicated on the recipient country's promise to recognize the rights of their sexual minorities. At the same time, we have seen throughout this volume that the transnational circulation of this "model gay/lesbian citizen=modern nation-state" discourse has, not surprisingly, generated a hostile reaction in many religious and political arenas, both north and south of the equator.

Yet we have also seen that this globally circulating construction of gayness has many manifestations and many effects. As some of the contributors here (Boellstorff, Cohen, Murray, and LaFont) have noted, in some places, it appears to (re)create, contribute to, and/or perpetuate unequal relations between former colonizing and colonized societies, the latter of which continue to be politically, economically, and socially marginalized as the former trumpet their "successes" of democracy, globalization, free trade, and prosperity. In these settings, "gay" comes to represent just another imposition of imperial political, economic, and moral power that has been in place since colonial times. "The gay/lesbian" may also simultaneously come to signify the immorality, corruption, and unfairness of these imperialist regimes and their modernizing projects and is accused of "diluting" or "polluting" traditional values, cultures, and communities. At the same time, in these places, but for differently positioned groups, "lesbian/gay" may be a relatively new way of making conceptual connections between sexual desire, gender, and identity, connections that are quite different from other sex/gender/desire relations that have been circulating locally or regionally. Being "gay" or "lesbian" may become an additional or supplemental way of thinking about oneself as a sexual, gendered, and social being, or it might be rejected as strange, irrelevant, and dangerous. It may introduce a means through which to politicize and organize against discrimination, utilizing international rights discourses as a weapon against national discourses (and laws) of improper, immoral citizenship, or it may introduce new ways to discriminate. As "gay" gains symbolic capital as a form of legitimate citizenship in certain powerful, national and international discourses, it may simultaneously construct its heterosexist and homophobic other through its intersections with historically constituted political, social, religious, and economic relations of inequality.

Other contributors focusing on European or settler societies like Greece, America, and Australia (Manalansan, Riedel, Angelides, and Sullivan-Blum) have analyzed how homophobic discourses are a critical component of the production of moral universes which are in turn built on nationalist, ethno-racial, or religious "logics," which are in turn being affected, challenged, and transformed by social, economic, and political changes within and beyond the nation. These linkages are complex, twisted, and compulsory for understanding how homophobia, or preferably *homo hatred*, is generated and sustained.

The most dangerous outcome of studying these rapidly changing sexual "ideoscapes" (Appudurai 1996) would be for political, juridical, and cultural pundits to reduce the complexity and intensity of these debates as they occur at every level: whether local, national, or international, within the church or temple, at a rally or at a moment in the past, we have seen throughout this volume that there is never just one position within any social, religious, or political domain toward homosexuality. In other words, the presence (arrival, statement, or development) of homosexuality does not always simply or only induce a phobia: it may generate everything from hatred to curiosity to indifference, from tolerance to celebratory embrace. And all of this within the borders of any community, whether it be local, national, transnational, religious, ethnic, racial, sexual, age-based, virtual, or physical. Even when there appears to be uniform opposition to the homosexual, it is undergirded by diverse sentiments and logics which must be understood in order to challenge and dismantle it.

I want to draw attention to the plurality of locations and the density of debate within and between borders that these chapters convey in order to illustrate the discursiveness through which homosexuality and homophobia continue to be debated, rethought, and created anew. It is in immigration and lawyers' offices, courts and parliaments, police bureaus and activist networks, church halls, kitchens, bedrooms, and computer screens that these discussions occur. By recognizing the multiplicity and density of these discussions we can begin to dismantle the "naturalness" of homophobia that is often invoked in its presentation. No nation, no culture, no group, no individual is traditionally, essentially, permanently, *naturally* homophobic. Homo hatred arises out of historical confluences of diverse political, economic, and cultural dynamics; it does not sit uniformly, timelessly, or completely within any cultural, sociopolitical, or economic formation, although it most certainly occupies a privileged or legitimized position within some of them. It doesn't exist everywhere and may in fact only arise in places where the "homosexual/gay" has emerged as a form of sociosexual identification. And, to repeat, in these "gay" places, there are by no means uniform perspectives on the position of the "gay" person in that community or society.

This may not appear to be good news for Edward or Edward's lawyer, who has to "prove" to the Immigration and Refugee Board that Edward is a homosexual and that Uganda is a place where this category of person is discriminated against in order to help Edward begin the process of obtaining Canadian citizenship. Nor is it good news for the IRB, a bureaucracy embedded in a legal and political framework that locates and demarcates culture, sexual identity, and morality within national borders. Needless to say, this nation=culture=sexuality framework creates conceptual misrepresentations, perpetuates stereotypes, and erases the complexity of social life in any context. It may do much damage to individuals like Edward even as it purportedly works to protect him. Edward may get to live in Canada as a gay Ugandan refugee but a number of Costa Ricans don't because their nation is "tolerant" of homosexuals, according to the IRB. But what if they are gay and HIV positive? Gay and poor? Gay and black? Gay and from an evangelical Protestant family? Lesbian? Transgendered? Does the IRB's pronouncement recognize the impact of differently positioned subjects in the multiple hierarchies of oppression of any nation-state?[1]

When we factor in the hegemony of antigay discourses as national, cultural, or religious "truths" in some locations, and the effective enforcement of these "truths" through rhetorical, institutional, or physical violence, we are able to perhaps move toward a position that does not reduce the complexity of sexual ideoscapes anywhere but recognizes their positioning in relation to the discursive production and circulation of power, its attendant (im)moral frameworks, and the effects of these "truth" regimes on those who are created as problematic, polluted, or unworthy due to their sexual practices. The chapters in this volume are a step in that direction, yet they are only a first step. Ongoing critical inquiry and ethnographic analysis of the creation and circulation of homo hatred, as well as resistance to it—its doing and undoing, in other words—is of critical importance as social, political, and economic conditions rapidly transform in locations around the world, creating new heroes, new pariahs, and new marginalities.

Note

1 For an excellent overview of the complexity involved in developing and implementing international or global policies and programs to end social discrimination in a related area—violence against women—see Merry 2006.

Agarwal, Purshottam
1995   Surat, Savarkar, and Draupadi: Legitimising Rape as
            a Political Weapon. *In* Women and the Hindu Right.
            Tanika Sarkar and Urvashi Butalia, eds. Pp. 29–57.
            New Delhi: Kali for Women, 1995.
Ahmed, Sara
2004   The Cultural Politics of Emotion. London: Routledge.
Alexander, M. Jacqui
1994   Not Just (Any)Body Can Be a Citizen: The Politics
            of Law, Sexuality and Postcoloniality in Trinidad
            and Tobago and the Bahamas. Feminist Review
            (Autumn 1994):9.
1997   Erotic Autonomy as a Politics of Decolonization:
            An Anatomy of Feminist and State Practice in the
            Bahamas Tourist Economy. *In* Feminist Genealogies,
            Colonial Legacies, Democratic Futures. M. J. Alex-
            ander and C. T. Mohanty, eds. Pp. 63–100. New York:
            Routledge.
Alexander, Jacqui, and Chandra Mohanty, eds.
1997   Feminist Genealogies, Colonial Legacies, Democratic
            Futures. New York: Routledge.
Alexandrakis, Othon
2003   Between Life and Death: Violence and Greek Roma
            Health and Identity. M.A. thesis, University of West-
            ern Ontario.
Alisjahbana, Sutan Takdir
1966   Indonesia: Social and Cultural Revolution. Kuala
Lumpur: Oxford University Press.

Alliance of Revolting Feminists

1984   Alliance of Revolting Feminists Manifesto. Melbourne Women's Lib-
            eration Newsletter (1984):12–13.

Ammerman, Nancy

1991   North American Protestant Fundamentalism. *In* Fundamentalism
            Observed. Martin E. Marty and R. Scott Appleby, eds. Pp. 1–65. Chi-
            cago: University of Chicago Press.

Amnesty International

2000   Jamaican Deaths in Prison. Report. Electronic document, http://
            web.amnesty.org, accessed March 29, 2006.

Anderson, Benedict

1983   Imagined Communities: Reflections on the Origins and Spread of
            Nationalism. London: Verso.

Anderson, Benedict, ed.

2001   Violence and the State in Suharto's Indonesia. Ithaca, NY: Southeast
            Asia Program Publications, Cornell University.

Anderson, Patricia

1986   Conclusion: Women in the Caribbean. Social and Economic Studies
            35:291–325.

Angelides, Steven

2004   Feminism, Child Sexual Abuse, and the Erasure of Child Sexuality.
            GLQ: A Journal of Gay and Lesbian Studies 10(2):141–177.

2005   The Emergence of the Paedophile in the Late Twentieth Century. Aus-
            tralian Historical Studies 36(126):272–295.

Anonymous

2006   Gayness in the Caribbean—A Personal Experience. New Reports, Jan-
            uary 23. Electronic document, http://www.globalgayz.com, accessed
            April 1, 2006.

Apostolidou, Anna

2004   Kaleidoskopiká sómata: Diaseksoualikótita kai i kataskeví enallaktikís
            thulikótitas sti sínchroni Elláda (Kaleidoscopic bodies: Transsexuality
            and the construction of alternative femininities in modern Greece).
            Unpublished MS.

Appadurai, Arjun

1996   Modernity at Large: Cultural Dimensions of Globalization. Min-
            neapolis: University of Minnesota Press.

Aripurnami, Sita

1996   A Feminist Comment on the Sinetron Presentation of Indonesian
            Women. *In* Fantasizing the Feminine in Indonesia. Laurie Sears, ed.
            Pp. 249–258. Durham: Duke University Press.

Armstrong, Karen

2000   The Battle for God. New York: Alfred A. Knopf.

Asselberghs, Herman, and Dieter LeSage
2003   Homo Politicus Pim Fortuyn: A Case Study. www.makeworlds.org.
Austin, Diane J.
1984   Urban Life in Kingston Jamaica. New York: Gordon and Breach Science Publishers.
Bacchetta, Paola
1994   All Our Goddesses Are Armed: Religion, Resistance, and Revenge in the Life of a Militant Hindu Nationalist Woman. *In* Against All Odds: Essays on Women, Religion, and Development in India and Pakistan. Kamla Bhasin, Ritu Menon, and Nighat S. Khan, eds. Pp. 133–156. Delhi: Isis International and Kali for Women.
Baker, Paul
2002   Polari: The Lost Language of Gay Men. New York: Routledge.
Barbados Statistical Service
2000   Population and Housing Census. Bridgetown: Government Printing Department.
Barker, Joshua
1998   State of Fear: Controlling the Criminal Contagion in Suharto's New Order. Indonesia 66:7–44.
Bergling, Tim
2001   Sissyphobia: Gay Men and Effeminate Behavior. New York: Southern Tier Editions.
Berman, Laine
2000   Surviving on the Streets of Java: Homeless Children's Narratives of Violence. Discourse and Society 11(2):149–174.
Binnie, Jon
2004   The Globalization of Sexuality. London: Sage.
Blackwood, Evelyn
1995a   Falling in Love with an-Other Lesbian: Reflections on Identity in Fieldwork. *In* Taboo: Sex, Identity and Erotic Subjectivity in Anthropological Fieldwork. Don Kulick and Margaret Willson, eds. Pp. 51–75. London: Routledge.
1995b   Senior Women, Model Mothers, and Dutiful Wives: Managing Gender Contradictions in a Minangkabau Village. *In* Bewitching Women, Pious Men: Gender and Body Politics in Southeast Asia. Aihwa Ong and Michael G. Peletz, eds. Pp. 124–158. Berkeley: University of California Press.
Boellstorff, Tom
1999   The Perfect Path: Gay Men, Marriage, Indonesia. GLQ: A Journal of Gay and Lesbian Studies 5(4):475–510.
2002   Ethnolocality. Asia Pacific Journal of Anthropology 3(1):24–48.
2003   Dubbing Culture: Indonesian Gay and Lesbi Subjectivities and Ethnography in an Already Globalized World. American Ethnologist 30(2):225–242.

2005   The Gay Archipelago: Sexuality and Nation in Indonesia. Princeton: Princeton University Press.

2007a   A Coincidence of Desires: Anthropology, Queer Studies, Indonesia. Durham: Duke University Press.

2007b   Queer Studies in the House of Anthropology. Annual Review of Anthropology 36:17–35.

Bolton, Ralph

1995   Tricks, Friends and Lovers: Erotic Encounters in the Field. *In* Taboo: Sex, Identity and Erotic Subjectivity in Anthropological Fieldwork. Don Kulick and Margaret Willson, eds. Pp. 140–167. London: Routledge.

Boswell, John

1980   Christianity, Social Tolerance, and Homosexuality: Gay People in Western Europe from the Beginning of the Christian Era to the Fourteenth Century. Chicago: University of Chicago Press.

Boukli, Evi, and Panagiotis Kappas

2004   Ypóthesi Spices (The Spices Case). Unpublished MS, Department of Sociology, Panteion University, Athens.

Boyne, Ian

2004   Time for Serious Gay Debate. Jamaica Gleaner Online, December 5. http://www.jamaica-gleaner.com, accessed April 1, 2006.

Braithwaite, Edward

1971   The Development of Creole Society in Jamaica 1770–1820. Oxford: Clarendon Press.

Brenner, Suzanne

1998   The Domestication of Desire: Women, Wealth, and Modernity in Java. Princeton: Princeton University Press.

1999   On the Public Intimacy of the New Order: Images of Women in the Popular Indonesian Print Media. Indonesia 67:13–37.

Buck-Morss, Susan

1989   The Dialectics of Seeing: Walter Benjamin and the Arcades Project. Cambridge: MIT Press.

2000   Dreamworld and Catastrophe: The Passing of Mass Utopia in East and West. Cambridge: MIT Press.

Bunzl, Matti

2004   Symptoms of Modernity: Jews and Queers in Late-Twentieth-Century Vienna. Berkeley: University of California Press.

Burnett, Richard

2004   What Happened to "One Love"? August 19. Electronic document, http://www.hour.ca, accessed April 2, 2006.

Butalia, Urvashi.

1995   Muslims and Hindus, Men and Women: Communal Stereotypes and the Partition of India. *In* Women and the Hindu Right. Tanika Sarkar and Urvashi Butalia, eds. Pp. 58–81. New Delhi: Kali for Women.

Butler, Judith

1990   Gender Trouble. New York: Routledge.

1993   Bodies That Matter: On the Discursive Limits of "Sex." New York: Routledge.

Butt, Leslie

2001   KB Kills: Political Violence, Birth Control, and the Baliem Valley Dani. Asia Pacific Journal of Anthropology 2(1):63–86.

Cage, Ken

1999   An Investigation into the Form and Function of Language used by Gay Men in South Africa. M.A. thesis, Rand Afrikaans University.

Cameron, Deborah

1997   Performing Gender: Young Men's Talk and the Construction of Heterosexual Masculinity. In Language and Masculinity. Sally Johnson and Ulrike Hanna Meinhof, eds. Pp. 47–64. Oxford: Blackwell.

Campaign

1986 [1976]   Age of Consent: Should be Lowered to 14. Campaign (May):4.

Carr, Adam

1983–1984   Delta Squad's "Child Sex Ring." Outrage (December/January):6.

Chanock, Martin

2000   "Culture" and Human Rights: Orientalising, Occidentalising and Authenticity. In Beyond Rights Talk and Culture Talk. Mahmood Mamdani, ed. Pp. 15–36. New York: St. Martin's Press,

Chatterjee, Partha

2004   The Politics of the Governed: Reflections on Popular Politics in Most of the World. New York: Columbia University Press.

Chauncey, George

1994   Gay New York: Gender, Urban Culture, and the Making of the Gay Male World, 1890–1940. New York: Basic Books.

Chodorow, Nancy J.

1999   Homophobia—American Psychoanalytic Foundation Public Forum. Electronic document, http://www.cyberpsych.org, accessed July 29, 2003.

Christgau, Robert

1993   Africanist Abomination: Homophobia as a Business. Village Voice. Electronic document, http://www.robertchristgau.com, accessed July 31, 2003.

Clarke, Edith

1957   My Mother Who Fathered Me. London: George Allen and Unwin.

Cohen, Cathy J.

1997   Punks, Bulldaggers and Welfare Queens: The Radical Potential of Queer Politics? GLQ: A Journal of Lesbian and Gay Studies 3:437–465.

Cohen, Lawrence

1995a   Holi in Banaras and the Mahaland of Modernity. GLQ: A Journal of Lesbian and Gay Studies 2(4):399–424.

1995b   The Pleasures of Castration: The Postoperative Status of Hijras, Jan-
             khas, and Academics. *In* Sexual Nature, Sexual Culture. Paul Abram-
             son and Steven Pinkerton, eds. Pp. 276–304. Chicago: University of
             Chicago Press.

2002   What Mrs. Besahara Saw: Reflections on the Gay Goonda. *In* Queer-
             ing India: Same-Sex Love and Eroticism in Indian Culture and So-
             ciety. Ruth Vanita, ed. Pp. 149–160. New York: Routledge.

2004   Operability: Surgery at the Margins of the State. *In* Anthropology in
             the Margins of the State. Veena Das and Deborah Poole, eds. Pp. 165–
             190. Santa Fe: School of American Research Press.

2005   The Kothi Wars: AIDS Cosmopolitanism and the Morality of Clas-
             sification. *In* Sex in Development: Science, Sexuality, and Morality
             in Global Perspective. Vincanne Adams and Stacy Leigh Pigg, eds.
             Pp. 269–303. Durham: Duke University Press.

2007   Song for Pushkin. Daedalus 136(2):103–115.

Collins, Elizabeth Fuller, and Ernaldi Bahar

2000   To Know Shame: Malu and Its Uses in Malay Societies. Crossroads:
             An Interdisciplinary Journal of Southeast Asian Studies 14(1):35–69.

Comstock, Gary, David

1996   Unrepentant, Self-Affirming, Practicing: Lesbian/Bisexual/Gay Peo-
             ple within Organized Religion. New York: Continuum Publishing
             Company.

Constantine-Simms, Delroy

2001   Is Homosexuality the Greatest Taboo? *In* The Greatest Taboo:
             Homosexuality in Black Communities. Delroy Constantine-Simms,
             ed. Pp. 76–87. Los Angeles: Alyson Books.

Coontz, Stephanie

1992   The Way We Never Were: American Families and the Nostalgia Trap.
             New York: Basic Books.

Cornwall, Andrea, and N. Lindisfarne, eds.

1994   Dislocating Masculinity. London: Routledge.

Cowan, Jane

1990   Dance and the Body Politic in Northern Greece. Princeton: Princeton
             University Press.

Cowan, Jane, ed.

2000   Macedonia: The Politics of Identity and Difference. London: Pluto
             Press.

Cozijn, John

1983   Is Boy Love a Gay Issue? Campaign (June):12–13.

Crew, Louie

1997   Changing the Church: Lessons Learned in the Struggle to Reduce In-
             stitutional Heterosexism in the Episcopal Church. *In* Overcoming
             Heterosexism and Homophobia: Strategies that Work. James T. Sears

and Walter Williams, eds. Pp. 341–353. New York: Columbia University Press.

Cruz-Malave, Arnaldo, and Martin Manalansan, eds.
2002   Queer Globalizations: Citizenship and the Afterlife of Colonialism. New York: New York University Press.

Daily, Oread
2002   Words Kill. One People's Project. Electronic document, http://www.onepeoplesproject.com, accessed August 10, 2003.

Dalmia, Vasudha
1997   The Nationalization of Hindu Traditions: Bharatendu Harischandra and Nineteenth-century Banaras. Delhi: Oxford University Press.

Danforth, Loring
1995   The Macedonian Conflict: Ethnic Nationalism in a Transnational World. Princeton: Princeton University Press.

Das, Veena
1995   National Honor and Practical Kinship: Unwanted Women and Children. *In* Conceiving the New World Order: The Global Politics of Reproduction. Rayna Rapp and Faye D. Ginsburg, eds. Berkeley: University of California Press.

Dasgupta, Swapan
2004   Not with Gay Abandon. Pioneer, August 23. Electronic document, http://www.dailypioneer.com, accessed June 8, 2009.

Davies, Christie
1997   Religious Boundaries and Sexual Morality. *In* Que(e)rying Religion: A Critical Anthology. Gary David Comstock and Susan E. Henking, eds. Pp. 39–60. New York: Continuum.

Davis, Garwin
2003   Homophobia Remain High. Jamaica Gleaner Online, July 26. Electronic document, http://www.jamaica-gleaner.com, accessed July 31, 2002.

Davis, Garwin, and Pat Roxborough
2000   Gay Cruises in Question. Jamaica Gleaner Online, September 9. Electronic document, http://www.go-jamaica.com, accessed February 22, 2002.

Dawes, Mark
2004   Don't Bow to Gay Pressure. Jamaica Gleaner Online, November 20. Electronic document, http://www.jamaica-gleaner.com, accessed, March 30, 2006.

DeCecco, John, ed.
1985   Baiters, Bigots: Homophobia in American Society. New York: Harrington Press.

Delaney, Samuel
1999   Times Square Blue, Times Square Red. New York: New York University Press.

Douglas, Mary

1983   The Effects of Modernization on Religious Change. *In* Religion and America: Spiritual Lives in a Secular Age. Mary Douglas and Steven Tipton, eds. Pp. 25–43. Boston: Beacon Press.

Dover, Kenneth James

1978   Greek Homosexuality. Cambridge: Harvard University Press.

Dubisch, Jill, ed.

1986   Gender and Power in Rural Greece. Princeton: Princeton University Press.

Ellison, Marvin M.

1993   Homosexuality and Protestantism. *In* Homosexuality and World Religions. Arlene Swidler, ed. Pp. 149–179. Valley Forge, PA: Trinity Press International.

Elliston, Deborah A.

2004   A Passion for the Nation: Masculinity, Modernity and Nationalist Struggle. American Ethnologist 31(4):606–630.

Emerson, Jody

1982   Women and Paedophilia. Gay Community News (November):30–31.

Engelke, Matthew

1999   We Wondered What Human Rights He Was Talking About. Critique of Anthropology 19(3):289–314.

Equal Opportunity Board

1987   Report of the Equal Opportunity Board for the Year ended 30 June 1987. Papers presented to Parliament, Session 1987–1988. Equal Opportunity Board and Commissioner for Equal Opportunity— Reports, 1986–1987:82–105.

Errington, Shelly

1989   Meaning and Power in a Southeast Asian Realm. Princeton: Princeton University Press.

ExcesS Weekend

2001   Ooh La Laa, "Some questions nuh fi answa." January 24. Kingston, Jamaica.

Faubion, James

1993   Modern Greek Lessons: A Primer in Historical Constructivism. Princeton: Princeton University Press.

Faul, Michael

1999   "Paradise" Can be an Ordeal for Gays. Associated Press, June 13. Electronic document, http://www.sodomylaws.org, accessed March 25, 2006.

Ferguson, Roderick

2004   Aberrations in Black: Toward a Queer of Color Critique. Minneapolis: University of Minnesota Press.

Figgou, Lia, and Susan Condor
2006   Irrational Categorization, Natural Intolerance and Reasonable Dis-
            crimination: Lay Representations of Prejudice and Racism. British
            Journal of Social Psychology 45:219–243.
Fih, Barbara
1983   Sex Talk Teacher Taken from Class. The Age, November 12:3.
Fih, Barbara, and Stephanie Bunbury
1983   I Didn't Call for Lower Sex Age: Teacher. The Age, November 11:3.
Finkelhor, David
1984   Child Sexual Abuse: New Theory and Research. New York: Free Press.
Floyd, Kory
2000   Affectionate Same-Sex Touch: The Influence of Homophobia on
            Observers' Perceptions. Journal of Social Psychology 140(6):774–788.
Fone, Byrne.
2000   Homophobia: A History. New York: Metropolitan Books.
Foner, Nancy
1973   Status and Power in Rural Jamaica. New York: Teachers College Press.
Forbes, Leslie
1998   Bombay Ice. New York: Farrar, Straus and Giroux.
Fortune, Marie M.
1995   Love Does No Harm: Sexual Ethics for the Rest of Us. New York:
            Continuum.
Fortuyn, Pim
1997   Tegen de islamisering van onze cultuur: Nederlandse identiteit als
            fundament. Rotterdam: A. W. Bruna.
Foucault, Michel
1978   The History of Sexuality: An Introduction. New York: Random
            House, Inc.
1990a [1976] The History of Sexuality, vol. 1: An Introduction. Robert Hurley,
            trans. New York: Vintage.
1990b [1984] The History of Sexuality, vol. 2: The Use of Pleasure. Robert Hurley,
            trans. New York: Vintage.
Franklin, Sarah
1997   Embodied Progress: A Cultural Account of Assisted Conception. New
            York: Routledge.
Freeman, Carla
2000   High Tech and High Heels in the Global Economy: Women Work and
            Pink Collar Identities in the Caribbean. Durham: Duke University Press.
2001   Is Local:Global as Feminine:Masculine? Rethinking the Gender of
            Globalization. Signs 26(4):1007–1037.
Freund, Kurt et al.
1972   The Female Child as a Surrogate Object. Archives of Sexual Behavior
            2(2):119–133.

Fulkerson, M. M.

1997   Gender—Being It or Doing It? The Church, Homosexuality, and the Politics of Identity. *In* Que(e)rying Religion: A Critical Anthology. Gary D. Comstock and Susan E. Henking, eds. Pp. 188–201. New York: Continuum Publishing Company.

Garvey, Tom

2004   Beenie Man Concert Tour Caves under Gay Pressure. Windy City Media Group. Electronic document, http://www.windycitymedia group.com, accessed March 20, 2006.

Gavanas, Anna

2001   Masculinizing Fatherhood: Sexuality, Marriage and Race in the U.S. Fatherhood Responsibility Movement. Ph.D. dissertation, Department of Anthropology, Stockholm University.

Geertz, C.

1960   The Religion of Java. Glencoe, Ill.: Free Press.

1973   Person, Time and Conduct in Bali. *In* The Interpretation of Cultures. Pp. 360–411. New York: Basic Books.

1980   Negara: The Theatre State in Nineteenth-Century Bali. Princeton: Princeton University Press.

1990   "Popular Art" and the Javanese Tradition. Indonesia 50:77–94.

Gender Public Advocacy Coalition (GPAC)

2002   GPAC Condemns Murder of DC Transgendered Teens. Archive News, August 14. Electronic document, http://www.gpac.org, accessed August 8, 2003.

George, K.

1996   Showing Signs of Violence: The Cultural Politics of a Twentieth-Century Headhunting Ritual. Berkeley: University of California Press.

Gilmore, David

1982   Anthropology of the Mediterranean Area. Annual Review of Anthropology 11:175–205.

Ginsburg, Faye D.

1989   Contested Lives: The Abortion Debate in an American Community. Berkeley: University of California Press.

Giorgi, Gregori

2002   Madrid in Transito: Travelers, Visibility and Gay Identity. GLQ: A Journal of Lesbian and Gay Studies 8(1–2):57–80.

Goldstein, Richard

2003   Get Back: The Gathering Storm over Gay Rights. Village Voice, August 6–12:32–34.

Gorman, E. M.

1997   A Special Window: An Anthropological Perspective on Spirituality in Contemporary U.S. Gay Male Culture. *In* Que(e)rying Religion: A Critical Anthology. Gary David Comstock and Susan E. Henking, eds. Pp. 330–337. New York: Continuum Publishing Company.

Gosine, Andil
2007   Reading Mia Mottley's Statement on (Homo)Sex: An Interrogation of
            HIV/AIDS scripts on Sexuality. Unpublished MS.
Graf, E. J.
1999   What Is Marriage For? Boston: Beacon Press.
Greenberg, David
1988   The Construction of Homosexuality. Chicago: University of Chicago
            Press.
Groth, A. N., and H. J. Birnbaum
1978   Adult Sexual Orientation and Attraction to Underage Persons.
            Archives of Sexual Behavior 7:175–181.
Gupta, Charu
2001   Sexuality, Obscenity, Community: Women, Muslims, and the Hindu
            Public in Colonial India. New Delhi: Permanent Black.
Gutzmore, Cecil
2004   Casting the First Stone: Policing of Homo/Sexuality in Jamaican Pop-
            ular Culture. Interventions 6(1):118–134.
Hage, Ghassan
2000   White Nation: Fantasies of White Supremacy in a Multicultural
            Society. New York: Routledge.
Halkias, Yiannis
2002   Yiatí filioúndai oi "brátsoi" stin Eliá? (Why do the "musclemen" kiss
            on Elia?). NITRO, October, 40–42.
Hall, Billy
2003   Firestorm Threatens Anglican Unity. Jamaica Gleaner Online,
            August 10. Electronic document, http://www.jamaica-gleaner.com,
            accessed August 8, 2003.
Hall, Stuart, ed.
1980   Culture, Media, Language: Working Papers in Cultural Studies, 1972–
            79. Birmingham: Hutchinson in association with the Centre for Con-
            temporary Cultural Studies, University of Birmingham.
1996   Representation: Cultural Representations and Signifying Practices.
            London: Sage.
Halperin, David
1990   One Hundred Years of Homosexuality and Other Essays on Greek
            Love. New York: Routledge.
Hammonds, Evelyn
1994   Black (W)holes and the Geometry of Black Female Sexuality. Differ-
            ences 6(2–3):126–147.
Hansard
1982   New South Wales Parliamentary Debates. Hansard. March 9:2231.
1986   Victorian Parliamentary Debates. Legislative Assembly. Hansard
            385:3022–3028.

Hansen, Thomas Blom
1996   Recuperating Masculinity: Hindu Nationalism, Violence and the Exor-
            cism of the Muslim "Other." Critique of Anthropology 16(2):137–172.
1999   The Saffron Wave: Democracy and Hindu Nationalism in Modern
            India. Princeton: Princeton University Press.
Harding, Susan F.
2000   The Book of Jerry Falwell: Fundamentalist Language and Politics.
            Princeton: Princeton University Press.
Harrison, Faye V.
1997   The Gendered Politics and Violence of Structural Adjustment. *In* Sit-
            uated Lives: Gender and Culture in Everyday Life. Louise Lamphere,
            Helena Ragon, and Patricia Zavella, eds. Pp. 451–468. New York:
            Routledge.
Hatley, Barbara
1997   Nation, "Tradition," and Constructions of the Feminine in Modern
            Indonesian Literature. *In* Imagining Indonesia: Cultural Politics and
            Political Culture. Jim Schiller and Barbara Martin-Schiller, eds.
            Pp. 90–120. Athens: Ohio University Press.
Hefner, Robert W.
2000   Civil Islam. Princeton: Princeton University Press.
Heiloudaki, Tzeni
2002   Oi Ángeloi den Éhoun Fílo (The angels have no gender). Athens:
            Ombros Publications.
Henry, Frances, and Carol Tator
2002   Discourses of Domination: Racial Bias in the Canadian English Lan-
            guage Press. Toronto: University of Toronto Press.
Herek, Gregory
2003   Definitions: Homophobia, Heterosexism, and Sexual Prejudice. Elec-
            tronic document, http://psychology.ucdavis.edu, accessed July 29,
            2003.
Herzfeld, Michael
1985   The Poetics of Manhood: Contest and Identity in a Cretan Mountain
            Village. Princeton: Princeton University Press.
1987   Anthropology through the Looking-Glass: Critical Ethnography in
            the Margins of Europe. Cambridge: Cambridge University Press.
1991   A Place in History: Social and Monumental Time in a Cretan Town.
            Princeton: Princeton University Press.
Hoad, Neville
1999   Between the White Man's Burden and the White Man's Disease. GLQ:
            A Journal of Lesbian and Gay Studies 5(4):559–584.
Howells, K.
1981   Adult Sexual Interest in Children: Considerations Relevant to Theo-
            ries of Etiology. *In* Adult Sexual Interest in Children. M. Cook and
            K. Howells, eds. Pp. 55–94. New York: Academic Press.

Human Rights Watch (HRW)

2004   Hated to Death: Homophobia, Violence and Jamaica's HIV/AIDS
Epidemic. November (16)6. Report. Electronic document, http://
hrw.org, accessed March 20, 2006.

Hunter, James Davidson

1991   Culture Wars: The Struggle to Define America. New York: Basic
Books.

Idrus, Nurul Ilmi

2001   Marriage, Sex, and Violence. In Love, Sex, and Power: Women in
Southeast Asia. Susan Blackburn, ed. Pp. 43–56. Clayton, Australia:
Monash Asia Institute.

Institute for Modern Greek Studies

2006   Lexikó tis Koinís Neoellinikís (Dictionary of Modern Greek). Thessaloniki, Greece: Aristotle University of Thessaloniki Press.

International Gay and Lesbian Human Rights Committee (IGLHRC)

2000   Support the Inclusion of Sexual Orientation as a Protected Category
in the Jamaican Constitution. World Watch. Electronic document,
http://www.ilga.org, accessed August 20, 2003.

Ivy, Marilyn.

1995   Discourses of the Vanishing: Modernity, Phantasm, Japan. Chicago:
University of Chicago Press.

Jackson, Peter A.

1999   Tolerant but Unaccepting: The Myth of a Thai "Gay Paradise." In
Genders and Sexualities in Modern Thailand. Peter A. Jackson and
Nerida M. Cook, eds. Pp. 226–242. Chaing Mai: Silkworm Books.

Jakobsen, Janet R., and Ann Pellegrini

2003   Love the Sin: Sexual Regulation and the Limits of Religious Tolerance.
New York: New York University Press.

Jamaica Gleaner

2001   Sexuality and the Law. Jamaica Gleaner Online. Electronic document,
http://www.jamaica-gleaner.com, accessed March 27, 2006.

Jamaican Cave

n.d.   Log On Lyrics—Elephant Man. Report. Electronic document, http://
www.jamaicancaves.org, accessed March 28, 2006.

Jamaican Friends of Lesbians and Gays (J-FLAG)

2001   About Us. Organization website. Electronic document, http://
www.jflag.org, accessed March 30, 2006.

Jamaican National HIV/AIDS Prevention and Control Program (JN HIV/AIDS
PCP)

2004   Facts and Figures, HIV/AIDS Epidemic Update 2004. Report. Electronic document, http://www.moh.gov.jm, accessed March 29, 2006.

Jamaican News Reports (JNR)

2005–2006   Tragic End to Attempted Gay-Bash in Kingston. Globalgayz. Electronic
document, http://www.globalgayz.com, accessed March 30, 2006.

Jaynes, Gary
1998   Young Gay and Proud—20 Years On. Unpublished MS, Australian
            Lesbian and Gay Archives.
Jimenez, Maria
2004   Gay Refugee Claimants Seeking Haven in Canada. Globe and Mail,
            April 24.
Jorstad, Erling
1993   Popular Religion in America: The Evangelical Voice. Westport, CT:
            Greenwood Press.
Kandiyoti, Deniz
2002   Pink Card Blues: Trouble and Strife at the Crossroads of Gender. *In*
            Fragments of Culture: The Everyday of Modern Turkey. Deniz Kan-
            diyoti and Ayşe Saktanber, eds. Pp. 277–293. New Brunswick, NJ:
            Rutgers University Press.
Kantor, Martin
1998   Homophobia: Description, Development, and Dynamics of Gay
            Bashing. Westport, CT: Praeger.
Kantsa, Venetia
2002   "Certain Places Have Different Energy": Spatial Transformations in
            Eresos, Lesvos. GLQ: A Journal of Lesbian and Gay Studies 8(1–2):
            35–55.
Kaplan, Robert D.
2003   The Books of Daniel. New York Times, September 21: 18.
Karayianni, Evthimia, and Pantelis Tolis
1998   Omofilofilía kai Koinonikí Pragmatikótita (Homosexuality and social
            reality). Undergraduate thesis, Department of Sociology, Irakleio,
            SEYP School.
Katz, Jonathan Ned
1983   The Lesbian/Gay Almanac: A New Documentary. San Francisco:
            Harper Collins.
Keeler, Ward
1983   Shame and Stage Fright in Java. Ethos 11(3):152–165.
Keiser, Elizabeth
1997   Courtly Desire and Medieval Homophobia: The Legitimation of Sex-
            ual Pleasure in *Cleanness* and Its Contexts. New Haven: Yale Univer-
            sity Press.
Kempadoo, Kamala
2004   Sexing the Caribbean: Gender Race and Sexual Labor. New York:
            Routledge.
Kempf, Edward J.
1920   Psychopathology. St. Louis: C.V. Mosby Company.
Khan, Shivananda
2001   Culture, Sexualities, and Identities: Men Who Have Sex with Men in
            India. Journal of Homosexuality 40(3/4):99–115.

2003   Questions and Thoughts. Pukaar 42(July):3, 27.

Khayatt, Didi.

2002   Toward Queer Identity. Sexualities 5(4):487–501.

Kimmel, Michael

1996   Manhood in America: A Cultural History. New York: Free Press.

2003   Globalization and its Mal(e)contents. International Sociology
            18(3):603–620.

King, Christopher

1992   Images of Vice and Virtue: The Hindi-Urdu Controversy in Two
            Nineteenth Century Hindi Plays. *In* Religious Controversy in British
            India: Dialogues in South Asian Languages. Kenneth W. Jones, ed.
            Pp. 123–148. Albany: State University of New York Press.

Kinsman, Gary

1996   The Regulation of Desire: Homo and Hetero Sexualities. Montreal:
            Black Rose Books Ltd.

Kirtsoglou, Elisabeth

2003   "O Erotas Eínai Thilykó": Oi Erotikés Diaforés kai i Epílysí tous se
            mia Ellinikí Eparhía ("Love is Female": Erotic conflicts and their
            resolutions in a Greek province). *In* Otan Gynaíkes Ehoun Diaforés:
            Antithéseis kai Syngroúseis Gynaikón sti Synchroni Elláda (When
            women have differences: Women's oppositions and conflicts in con-
            temporary Greece). Christina Vlachoutsikou, ed. Pp. 219–250.
            Athens: Medusa Press.

2004   For the Love of Women: Gender, Identity and Same-Sex Relations in a
            Greek Provincial Town. New York: Routledge.

Kitzinger, Celia

1987   The Social Construction of Lesbianism. Newbury Park, CA: Sage
            Publications.

Kulick, Don

1998   Travesti: Sex, Gender, and Culture among Brazilian Transgendered
            Prostitutes. Chicago: University of Chicago Press.

Kulick, Don, and Charles Klein

2003   Scandalous Acts: The Politics of Shame among Brazilian Travesti
            Prostitutes. *In* Recognition Struggles and Social Movements: Con-
            tested Identities, Agency and Power. Barbara Hobson, ed. Pp. 215–238.
            Cambridge: Cambridge University Press.

LaFont, Suzanne

1996   The Emergence of an Afro-Caribbean Legal Tradition in Jamaica.
            Bethesda, MD: Austin and Winfield Press.

2000   Gender Wars in Jamaica. Identities: Global Studies in Culture and
            Power 7:233–260.

2001   Very Straight Sex: The Development of Sexual Morés in Jamaica.
            Journal of Colonialism and Colonial History 2(3). Electronic docu-
            ment, http://muse.jhu.edu, accessed August 15, 2003.

Lancaster, Roger N.

1992   Life Is Hard: Machismo, Danger, and the Intimacy of Power in
            Nicaragua. Berkeley: University of California Press.

1995   That We Should All Turn Queer. *In* Conceiving Sexuality. Richard G.
            Parker and John H. Gagnon, eds. Pp. 135–156. New York: Routledge.

Lancaster, Roger, and Micaela di Leonardo, eds.

1997   The Gender/Sexuality Reader. New York: Routledge.

Larvie, Sean Patrick

1999   Queerness and the Specter of Brazilian National Ruin. GLQ: A Journal
            of Lesbian and Gay Studies 5(4):527–558.

Lawrence, Bruce

1989   Defenders of God: The Fundamentalist Revolt against the Modern
            Age. Columbia: University of South Carolina Press.

1998   Shattering the Myth: Islam beyond Violence. Princeton: Princeton
            University Press.

Leap, William, and Ellen Lewin, eds.

1996   Out in the Field: Reflections of Lesbian and Gay Anthropologists.
            Chicago: University of Illinois Press.

Levy, Bronwen, and Alison Thorne

1985   Politics, Paedophilia and Free Speech: The Witch Hunt Continues.
            Hecate 11(2):66.

Lewis, Linden

2000   Nationalism and Caribbean Masculinity. *In* Gender Ironies of
            Nationalism: Sexing the Nation. Tamar Mayers, ed. Pp. 261–281. Lon-
            don: Routledge.

Lienesch, Michael

1993   Redeeming America: Piety and Politics in the New Christian Right.
            Chapel Hill: University of North Carolina Press.

Loizos, Peter, and Evthymios Papataxiarchis

1991   Gender, Sexuality, and the Person in Greek Culture. *In* Contested
            Identities: Gender and Kinship in Modern Greece. Peter Loizos and
            Evthymios Papataxiarchis, eds. Pp. 221–234. Princeton: Princeton
            University Press.

Long, R. E.

1997   The Sacrality of Male Beauty and Homosex: A Neglected Factor in the
            Understanding of Contemporary Gay Life. *In* Que(e)rying Religion:
            A Critical Anthology. Gary David Comstock and Susan E. Henking,
            eds. Pp. 266–285. New York: Continuum.

Lyons, Andrew, and Harriet Lyons

2004   Irregular Connections: A History of Anthropology and Sexuality. Lin-
            coln: University of Nebraska Press.

MacDonald, Myra

2003   Exploring Media Discourse. Cornwall, UK: Arnold Publishers.

Mackey, Eva

2002   House of Difference: Cultural Politics and National Identity in Can-
            ada. Toronto: University of Toronto Press.

Madan, T. N.

1987   Non-Renunciation: Themes and Interpretations of Hindu Culture.
            New Delhi: Oxford University Press.

Maiti, Prasenjit

2001   On Black Narratives and White Meanings: Revisiting Frail Descrip-
            tions of Virile Power. Electronic document, http://65.107.211.206/
            post/poldiscourse/maiti/3.html, accessed July 30, 2003.

Manalansan, Martin IV

1994   Disorienting the Body: Locating Symbolic Resistance among Filipino
            Gay Men. Positions: East Asia Cultures Critique 2(1):73–90.

1995   In the Shadows of Stonewall: Examining Gay Transnational Politics
            and the Diaspora Dilemma. GLQ: A Journal of Lesbian and Gay Stud-
            ies 2(4):425–438.

2002   A Queer Itinerary: Deviant Excursions into Modernities. In Out in
            Theory: The Emergence of Lesbian and Gay Anthropology. Ellen
            Lewin and William L. Leap, eds. Pp. 246–263. Chicago: University of
            Illinois Press.

2003   Global Divas: Filipino Gay Men in the Diaspora. Durham: Duke Uni-
            versity Press.

Mann, Paul

2002   Season of the Monsoon. New York: Fawcett Columbine.

Marty, Martin E., and R. Scott Appleby

1992   The Glory and the Power: The Fundamentalist Challenge to the Mod-
            ern World. Boston: Beacon Press.

Mason, Gail

2002   The Spectacle of Violence: Homophobia, Gender and Knowledge.
            London: Routledge.

Mason, Gail, and Anna Chapman

2003   Defining Sexual Harassment: A History of the Commonwealth Legis-
            lation and its Critiques. Working Paper No. 27, Center for Employ-
            ment and Labor Relations Law (March):1–25.

Massad, Joseph

2002   Re-Orienting Desire: The Gay International and the Arab World.
            Public Culture 14(2): 361–385.

May, Henry

1983   Ideas, Faiths and Feelings: Essays on American Intellectual and Reli-
            gious History (1952–1982). Oxford: Oxford University Press.

McConaghy, Neil

1970   Penile Response Conditioning and its Relationship to Aversion
            Therapy in Homosexuals. Behaviour Therapy 1:213–221.

1993   Sexual Behaviour: Problems and Management. New York: Plenum
Press.

McGeorge, John

1964   Sexual Assaults on Children. Medicine, Science and the Law 4:245–
253.

Melbourne's Star Observer

1986a   Melbourne's Star Observer, November 21:3.

1986b   Cain to Outlaw Thorne. Melbourne's Star Observer, December 5:1.

Melhuus Marit, and Kristi Anne Stølen, eds.

1996   Machos, Mistresses, Madonnas: Contesting the Power of Latin American Gender Imagery. London: Verso.

Merry, Sally E.

2006   Human Rights and Gender Violence: Translating International Law
into Local Justice. Chicago: University of Chicago Press.

Messing, Gordon M.

1981   Tsinganos and Yiftos: Some Speculations on the Greek Gypsies.
Byzantine and Modern Greek Studies 7:155–167.

Miami Herald

2007   Gay Travel: Make Sure Islands Will Welcome You. Electronic document, http://www.miamiherald.com, accessed September 21, 2007.

Miller, Neil

1995   Out of the Past: Gay and Lesbian History from 1869 to the Present.
New York: Vintage.

Mohanty, Chandra

1988   Under Western Eyes: Feminist Scholarship and Colonial Discourses.
Feminist Review 30:61–88.

Moore, Roland

1995   Gender and Alcohol Use in a Greek Tourist Town. Annals of Tourism
Research 22(2): 300–313.

Mosse, George

1985   Nationalism and Sexuality. New York: H. Fertig.

Murray, David A. B.

2002   Opacity: Gender, Race, Sexuality and the "Problem" of Identity in
Martinique. New York: Peter Lang.

2006   Whose Right: Human Rights, Sexual Rights and Social Change in Barbados, Journal of Culture, Health and Sexuality 8(3):267–281.

Murray, Stephen O.

1995   Latin American Male Homosexualities. Albuquerque: University of
New Mexico Press.

2000   Homosexualities. Chicago: University of Chicago Press.

Nagengast, Carole

1994   Violence, Terror, and the Crisis of the State. Annual Review of
Anthropology 23:109–136.

Nandy, Ashis
1983   The Intimate Enemy: Loss and Recovery of Self under Colonialism.
            Delhi: Oxford University Press.
Newstrack
1994   Serial Killer Terrorizes Lucknow as Five Teenage Boys Found Sod-
            omized and Strangled. Newstrack, April.
Newton, Esther
1993   My Best Informant's Dress: The Erotic Equation in Fieldwork. Cul-
            tural Anthropology 8(1):3–23.
2000   Margaret Mead Made Me Gay: Personal Essays, Public Ideas. Dur-
            ham: Duke University Press.
Nugent, Robert, and Jeanine Gramick
1990   Homosexuality: Protestant, Catholic and Jewish Issues: A Fishbone
            Tale. Journal of Homosexuality 18(3–4): 7–46.
Olafson, Erna
2002   When Paradigms Collide: Roland Summit and the Rediscovery of
            Child Sexual Abuse. In Critical Issues in Child Sexual Abuse: Histori-
            cal, Legal, and Psychological Perspectives. Jon R. Conte, ed. Pp. 71–
            106. London: Sage.
Outrage
1984   Faction Dispute Threatens Conference. Outrage 15 (August):5.
1985   Thorne "Not Fit To Teach": Cain. Outrage 20 (January):5.
1986   Vic Child Sex Report Exonerates Gays, Slams Pedophiles. Outrage 37
            (June):7.
1987   Teaching Deal Ends Three-year Thorne Saga. Outrage 44 (January):8.
Parker, Andrew, Mary Russo, Doris Sommer, and Patricia Yaeger, eds.
1992   Nationalisms and Sexualities. New York: Routledge.
Parrinder, Geoffrey
1998   Sexual Morality in the World's Religions. Oxford: Oneworld
            Publications.
Patsalidou, Nikki
1982   I Omofilofilía stin Kipriakí Koinonía: Koinonikí Proséngisi
            (Homosexuality in Cypriot society: A social approach). In
            Omofilofilía, Omilíes kai sizitíseis pou éyinan sto seminário
            I Omofilofilía (Homosexuality: Speeches and discussions that
            occurred in the seminar "Homosexuality"). Pp. 43–55, March.
Patton, Cindy
1997   From Nation to Family: Containing African AIDS. In The Gender/
            Sexuality Reader. Roger Lancaster and Micaela di Leonardo, eds.
            Pp. 279–288. New York: Routledge.
Peacock, James
1968   Rites of Modernization: Symbolic and Social Aspects of Indonesian
            Proletarian Drama. Chicago: University of Chicago Press.

Pemberton, John
1994   On the Subject of "Java." Ithaca, NY: Cornell University Press.
Peristiany, John George
1966   Honor and Shame: The Values of Mediterranean Society. Chicago:
            University of Chicago Press.
Petridis, Alexis
2004   Pride and Prejudice. The Guardian digital edition. December 10. Elec-
            tronic document, http://arts.guardian.co.uk/, accessed March 28,
            2006.
Petropoulos, Elias
1993 [1971] Kaliarndá: An Etymological Dictionary of Greek Homosexuals' Slang.
            Athens: Nefeli Press.
Pharr, Suzanne
1988   Homophobia: A Weapon of Sexism. Little Rock, AK: Chardon Press.
Phellas, Constantinos N.
2002   The Construction of Sexual and Cultural Identities: Greek-Cypriot
            Men in Britain. Aldershot: Ashgate Publishing Limited.
Pitter, Eugene
2001   Culture or Creativity? Jamaica Gleaner Online, January 11. http://
            www.jamaica-gleaner.com, accessed July 31, 2003.
Poorthuis Frank, and Hans Wansink
2002   De islam is een achterlijke cultuur, February 9, Electronic document,
            http://www.volkskrant.nl, accessed May 4, 2004.
Povinelli, Elizabeth A.
2002   The Cunning of Recognition: Indigenous Alterities and the Making of
            Australian Multiculturalism. Durham: Duke University Press.
Povinelli, Elizabeth, and George Chauncey
1999   Thinking Sexuality Transnationally: An Introduction. GLQ: A Journal
            of Lesbian and Gay Studies 5(4):439–450.
Powell, Dorian
1984   The Role of Women in the Caribbean. Social and Economic Studies
            33:97–122.
Prieur, Annick
1998   Mema's House, Mexico City: On Transvestites, Queens and Machos.
            Chicago: University of Chicago Press.
Pruitt, Deborah, and Suzanne LaFont
2004   Romance Tourism: Gender, Race, and Power in Jamaica. *In* Tourism
            and Tourists. Sharon Gmelch, ed. Prospect Heights, IL: Waveland
            Press.
Puar, Jasbir K.
2006   Mapping U.S. Homonormativities. Gender Place and Culture
            13(1):67–88.
2007   Terrorist Assemblages: Homonationalism in Queer Times. Durham:
            Duke University Press.

Rafael, Vicente L., ed.

1999   Figures of Criminality in Indonesia, the Philippines, and Colonial Vietnam. Ithaca, NY: Cornell Southeast Asia Program.

Rich, Adrienne

1980   Compulsory Heterosexuality and Lesbian Existence. Signs: A Journal of Women in Culture and Society (Summer):631–657.

Riches, David

1986   The Phenomenon of Violence. *In* The Anthropology of Violence. David Riches, ed. Pp. 1–27. Oxford: Basil Blackwell.

Robb, Carol S.

1995   Equal Value: An Ethical Approach to Economics and Sex. Boston: Beacon Press.

Robbins, Joel

2004   The Globalization of Pentecostal and Charismatic Christianity. Annual Review of Anthropology 33:117–143.

Robinson, Geoffrey

1995   The Dark Side of Paradise: Political Violence in Bali. Ithaca, NY: Cornell University Press.

Robinson, Kathryn

1989   Choosing Contraception: Cultural Change and the Indonesian Family Planning Programme. *In* Creating Indonesian Cultures. Paul Alexander, ed. Pp. 21–38. Sydney: Oceania Publications.

Robinson, Paul, and Owen Wood

1983   "Sex-at-10" Teacher Outrage. Sun, November 10:1–2.

Rodgers, Susan

1995   Telling Lives, Telling History: Autobiography and Historical Imagination in Modern Indonesia. Berkeley: University of California Press.

Rodriguez, E. M., and S. C. Ouellette

2000   Religion and Masculinity in Latino Gay Lives. *In* Gay Masculinities. Peter Nardi, ed. Pp. 101- 129. Thousand Oaks, CA: Sage Publications, Inc.

Roof, Wade Clark

1982   America's Voluntary Establishment: Mainline Religion in Transition. Daedalus 111 (Winter):165–184.

Roof, Wade Clark, and William McKinney

1987   American Mainline Religion: Its Changing Shape and Future. New Brunswick, NJ: Rutgers University Press.

Rubin, Gayle

1984   Thinking Sex: Notes for a Radical Theory of the Politics of Sexuality. *In* Pleasure and Danger: Exploring Female Sexuality. Carole S. Vance, ed. Pp. 267–319. London: Pandora Press.

Schlee, Gunther, ed.

2002   Imagined Differences: Hatred and the Construction of Identity. New York: Palgrave.

Schneider, David
1980   American Kinship: A Cultural Account. Chicago: University of Chicago Press.
Seabrook, Jeremy
1999   Love in a Different Climate: Men Who Have Sex with Men in India. London: Verso.
Sedgwick, Eve Kosofsky
1985   Between Men: English Literature and Male Homosocial Desire. New York: Columbia University Press.
1990   Epistemology of the Closet. Berkeley: University of California Press.
Seizer, Susan
1995   Paradoxes of Visibility in the Field: Rites of Queer Passage in Anthropology. Public Culture 8(1):73–100.
Sen, Krisna
1998   Indonesian Women at Work: Reframing the Subject. *In* Gender and Power in Affluent Asia. Krishna Sen and Maila Stivens, eds. Pp. 35–62. London: Routledge.
Seremetakis, C. Nadia, ed.
1993   Ritual, Power and the Body: Historical Perspectives on the Representation of Greek Women. New York: Pella Publishing Company.
Shepard, William
1987   Islam and Ideology: Towards a Typology. Journal of Middle East Studies 19:307–336.
Shukla, Shrilal
1992   Raag Darbari. Gillian Wright, trans. New Delhi: Penguin.
Siegel, James
1997   Fetish, Recognition, Revolution. Princeton: Princeton University Press.
1998   A New Criminal Type in Jakarta: Counter-Revolution Today. Durham: Duke University Press.
Silberman, Steve
1998   Wiring the Gay World. Wired, August 5. Electronic document, http://www.wired.com, accessed March 2, 2008.
Silvera, Makeda
1996   Man Royals and Sodomites. *In* Lesbian Subjects. Martha Vicinus, ed. Pp. 167–177. Bloomington: Indiana University Press.
Silvester, John
1983   The Kids on Our Streets: "Delta" Probe Shock. Sun, March 30:1–2.
Simey, T. S.
1946   Welfare and Planning in the West Indies. Oxford: Clarendon Press.
Simpson, George Eaton
1978   Black Religions in the New World. New York: Columbia University Press.

Sims, Bruce
1982   The Nuclear Family Explodes. Gay Community News (March):26.
Sioubouras, Fotis
1980   Pezodrómio (Sidewalk). Athens: Kaptos Publications.
Smith, M. G.
1962   West Indian Family Structure. Seattle: University of Washington
            Press.
Smith, Raymond T.
1988   Kinship and Class in the West Indies. New York: Cambridge Univer-
            sity Press.
Spitulnik, Debra
1997   The Social Circulation of Media Discourse and the Mediation of
            Communities. Journal of Linguistic Anthropology 6(2):161–187.
Spong, John Shelby
1994   Born of a Woman: A Bishop Rethinks the Birth of Jesus. San Fran-
            cisco: Harper.
1996   Liberating the Gospels: Reading the Bible with Jewish Eyes. San Fran-
            cisco: Harper.
Stasch, Rupert
2001   Giving Up Homicide: Korowai Experience of Witches and Police
            (West Papua). Oceania 72:33–52.
Steedly, Mary
1999   The State of Culture Theory in the Anthropology of Southeast Asia.
            Annual Review of Anthropology 28:431–454.
Stephens, Gregory
2002   A Culture of Intolerance. Jahworks.org. Electronic document, http://
            www.jahworks.org, accessed July 31, 2003.
Stoler, Ann Laura
1995   Race and the Education of Desire: Foucault's History of Sexuality and
            the Colonial Order of Things. Durham: Duke University Press.
Stolzoff, Norman C.
2000   Wake the Town and Tell the People: Dancehall Culture in Jamaica.
            London: Duke University Press.
Sullivan-Blum, Constance Rose
2003   "The Two Shall Become One Flesh": The Same-Sex Marriage Debate
            in Mainline Christianity. Ph.D. dissertation, Department of Anthro-
            pology, State University of New York, Binghamton.
Summit, Roland C.
1983   The Child Sexual Abuse Accommodation Syndrome. Child Abuse
            and Neglect 7:177–193.
Suryakusuma, Julia
1996   The State and Sexuality in New Order Indonesia. In Fantasizing the
            Feminine in Indonesia. Laurie Sears, ed. Pp. 92–119. Durham: Duke
            University Press.

Sydney Morning Herald

1983   Child Pornography: Nine Arrested. Sydney Morning Herald, November 7:2.

Szymanski, Dawn M., Y. Barry Chung, and Kimberly F. Balsam

2001   Psychosocial Correlates of Internalized Homophobia in Lesbians. Measurement and Evaluation in Counseling and Development 34(1):27–38.

Taktsis, Kostas

1989   To Foveró Víma (The fearful step). Athens: Exandas.

Tegopoulos-Fitrakis

1997   Mikró Ellinikó Lexikó (Pocket Greek dictionary). Athens: Armonia.

Teunis, Niels, and Gilbert Herdt, eds.

2007   Sexual Inequalities and Social Justice. Berkeley: University of California Press.

Theodorakopoulos, Loukas

1982   Omofilofília kai Pnevmatikí Dimiouryía (Homosexuality and spiritual creativity). In Omofilofília, Omilíes kai sizitíseis pou éyinan sto seminário I Omofilofília (Homosexuality: Speeches and Discussions That Occurred in the Seminar "Homosexuality"). Pp. 167–187, March.

Thompson, Tony

2002   Jamaican Gays Flee to Save Their Lives. Observer International. October 20. Electronic document, http://observer.guardian.co.uk, accessed October 26, 2002.

Thumma, Scott

1991   Negotiating a Religious Identity: The Case of the Gay Evangelical. Sociological Analysis 52:333–347.

Tin, Louis-Georges, ed.

2003   Dictionnaire de L'homophobie. Paris: Press of the Universities of France.

Tiwon, Sylvia

1996   Models and Maniacs: Articulating the Female in Indonesia. In Fantasizing the Feminine in Indonesia. Laurie Sears, ed. Pp. 47–70. Durham: Duke University Press.

Triandafyllidou, Anna

2000   The Political Discourse on Immigration in Southern Europe: A Critical Analysis. Journal of Community and Applied Social Psychology 10:373–389.

Tronto, Joan C.

1993   Moral Boundaries: A Political Argument for an Ethics of Care. New York: Routledge.

Tsiakalos, Georgios

2006   Greece: Xenophobia of the Weak and Racism of the Mighty. *In* The
              Globalization of Racism. Donaldo Macedo and Panayota Gounari,
              eds. Pp. 192–208. Boulder, CO: Paradigm Press.

Tsing, Anna L.

1993   In the Realm of the Diamond Queen: Marginality in an Out-of-the-
              way Place. Princeton: Princeton University Press.

1995   Empowering Nature, or: Some Gleanings in Bee Culture. *In* Natu-
              ralizing Power: Essays in Feminist Cultural Analysis. Sylvain
              Yanagisako and Carol Delaney, eds. Pp. 113–143. New York: Routledge.

Tully, Carol T.

2000   Lesbians, Gays and the Empowerment Perspective. New York: Colum-
              bia University Press.

United Nations

2000   The World's Women 2000: Trends and Statistics. New York: United
              Nations.

Vadasz, Danny

1983   For Love or Money? Behind the Headlines, Who's Screwing Whom?
              Outrage 2 (May):3–5.

1984   Court Dumps Delta in Conspiracy Case. Outrage 14 (June):5.

Valentine, David

2003   The Calculus of Pain: Violence, Anthropological Ethics, and the Cate-
              gory Transgender. Ethnos 66(1): 27–48.

Vance, Carole S.

1989   Social Construction Theory: Problems in the History of Sexuality. *In*
              Homosexuality, Which Homosexuality? Dennis Altman, Carole
              Vance, Martha Vicinus, and Jeff Weeks, eds. Pp. 13–34. Amsterdam:
              Schorer.

van der Veer, Peter

2006   Pim Fortuyn, Theo van Gogh, and the Politics of Tolerance in the
              Netherlands. Public Culture 18(1):111–124.

Van Dijk, T. A.

1988   News as Discourse. Hillsdale, NJ: Lawrence Erlbaum.

Vanita, Ruth

2002   Homophobic Fiction/Homoerotic Advertising: The Pleasures and
              Perils of Twentieth Century Indianness. *In* Queering India: Same-Sex
              Love and Eroticism in Indian Culture and Society. Ruth Vanita, ed.
              Pp. 149–160. New York: Routledge.

2006   Introduction. *In* Chocolate, and Other Writings on Male-Male Desire.
              Ruth Vanita, ed. and trans. New Delhi: Oxford University Press.

Vasilikou, Katerina

1998   Tautótita fílou, Epikindinótita, kai AIDS: Néoi ándres omofilófiloi kai
              diahírisi tou kindínou ékthesis ston ió tou AIDS (Gender identity,
              risk, and AIDS: Young men and the management of the danger of

exposure to the AIDS virus). M.A. thesis, Department of Sociology, National School of Public Health, Athens.

Vermeulen, Hans

1983   Urban Research in Greece. *In* Urban Life in Mediterranean Europe. Michael Kenny and David Kertzer, eds. Pp. 109–132. Urbana: University of Illinois Press.

Voelker, Rebecca

2001   HIV/AIDS in the Caribbean: Big Problems among Small Islands. JAMA 285(23):2961–2965.

Wahid, Abdurrahman

1999   Tuhan Tidak Perlu Dibela (God does not need to be defended) . Yogyakarta: LkiS Yogyakarta.

Walrond, E. R.

2004   Report on the Legal, Ethical and Socio-Economic Issues Relevant to HIV/AIDS in Barbados. Submitted to the National HIV/AIDS Commission, Bridgetown, Barbados.

Walters, Basil

2001   The "Unspeakable" Things about Staceyann Chin. Jamaican Observer. June 1. Electronic document, http://www.jamaicaob server.com, accessed October 26, 2002.

Weinberg, George H

1972   Society and the Healthy Homosexual. New York: St. Martin's Press.

Weismantel, Mary

2001   Cholas and Pishtacos: Stories of Race and Sex in the Andes. Chicago: University of Chicago Press.

Wessel, Ingrid, and Georgia Wimhofer, eds.

2001   Violence in Indonesia. Hamburg: Abera.

Weston, Kath

1991   Families We Choose: Lesbians, Gays, Kinship. New York: Columbia University Press.

1993   Lesbian/Gay Studies in the House of Anthropology. Annual Review of Anthropology 22:339–367.

1998   Long Slow Burn: Sexuality and Social Science. Chicago: University of Chicago Press.

White, Nicole

2001   Rhythm of Hatred: Anti-Gay Lyrics Reflect an Island's Intolerance. Miami Herald, August 5. Electronic document, http://www.geocities .com, accessed July 31, 2003.

Wickberg, Daniel.

2000   Homophobia: On the Cultural History of an Idea. Critical Inquiry 27:42–57.

Wignall, Mark

2004   Those Flaming Homosexuals. Daily Observer, June 17.

Willett, Graham

1981   New Masculinity. Gay Community News (September):24.

1999   "Proud and Employed": The Gay and Lesbian Movement and the Vic-
            torian Teachers' Unions in the 1970s. Labour History: A Journal of
            Labour and Social History 76 (May):78–94.

2000   Living Out Loud: A History of Gay and Lesbian Activism in Australia.
            St. Leonards: Allen and Unwin.

Williams, Eric

1970   From Columbus to Castro: The History of the Caribbean. New York:
            Vintage Books.

Williams, Lawson (pseudonym)

2000   Homophobia and Gay Rights Activism in Jamaica. Small Axe: A Jour-
            nal of Criticism 4:106–111. Repr. In Our Caribbean: A Gathering
            of Lesbian and Gay Writing from the Antilles. Thomas Glave, ed.
            Pp. 382–388. Durham: Duke University Press, 2008.

Williams, Walter

1992   Benefits for Nonhomophobic Societies: An Anthropological Perspec-
            tive. In Homophobia: How We All Pay the Price. Warren J. Blumen-
            feld, ed. Pp. 258–276. Boston: Beacon Press.

Wilson, Peter

1973   Crab Antics. New Haven: Yale University Press.

Winkler, John

1990   The Constraints of Desire: The Anthropology of Sex and Gender in
            Ancient Greece. New York: Routledge.

Wockner, Rex

2001   Activists Remain Jailed in Lucknow, India. Gay Today, August 8. Elec-
            tronic document, http://gaytoday.badpuppy.com, accessed March 2,
            2008.

Wright, Brett

1984   Child-Sex Task Force Snared in Legal Web. The Age, July 2:10.

Wright, L., H. Adams, and J. Bernat

1999   Development and Validation of the Homophobia Scale. Journal of
            Psychopathology and Behavioral Assessment 21(4):337–347.

Wright, Timothy

2000   Gay Organizations, NGO's, and the Globalization of Sexual Identity:
            The Case of Bolivia. Journal of Latin American Anthropology 5(2):
            89–111.

Yanagisako, Sylvia J., and Carol Delaney

1995   Naturalizing Power. In Naturalizing Power: Essays in Feminist Cul-
            tural Analysis. Sylvia Yanagisako and Carol Delaney, eds. Pp. 3–22.
            New York: Routledge.

Yanagisako, Sylvia, and Carol Delaney, eds.

1995   Naturalizing Power: Essays in Feminist Cultural Analysis. New York:
            Routledge.

Yiannakopoulos, Kostas

1998   Politikés sexoualikótitas kai igías tin epohí tou AIDS (The politics of
            sexuality and health in the age of AIDS). Sínhrona Thémata 66:76–86.

Yingling, Thomas

1997   AIDS and the National Body. Durham: Duke University Press.

Yip, Andrew K.

1997   Gay Male Christian Couples: Life Stories. Westport, CT: Praeger Pub-
            lishers.

Young-Bruehl, Elizabeth

1996   The Anatomy of Prejudices. Cambridge: Harvard University Press.

Younge, Gary

2005   Jamaican Gay Activist Shot Dead after Being Abducted. Guardian
            digital edition. Electronic document, http://www.guardian.co.uk,
            accessed March 30, 2006.

Yuval-Davis, Nina

1997   Gender and Nation. London: Sage.

Zarkia, Cornélia

1996   Philoxenia: Receiving Tourists—but not Guests—on a Greek Island. *In*
            Coping with Tourists. Jeremy Boissevain, ed. Pp. 143–173. Providence,
            RI: Berghan.

STEVEN ANGELIDES is a research fellow at Monash University Australia. He is the author of *A History of Bisexuality* (2001).

TOM BOELLSTORFF is an associate professor in the department of anthropology at the University of California, Irvine, and editor-in-chief of *American Anthropologist*. He is the author of *The Gay Archipelago* (2005); *A Coincidence of Desires* (Duke, 2007); and *Coming of Age in Second Life* (2008).

LAWRENCE COHEN is an associate professor of anthropology and South and Southeast Asian studies at the University of California, Berkeley. He is the author of *No Aging in India: Alzheimer's, the Bad Family, and Other Modern Things* (1998) and the coeditor of *Thinking about Dementia* (2006).

DON KULICK is a professor of anthropology in the department of comparative human development at the University of Chicago. His books include *Travesti: Language and Sexuality* (1998) (coauthored with Deborah Cameron); and *Fat* (2005) (coedited with Anne Meneley).

SUZANNE LAFONT is a professor of anthropology at Kingsborough Community College. She is the author of *Constructing Sexualities: Readings in Sexuality, Gender and Culture* (2003) and coeditor of *Unravelling Taboos: Gender and Sexuality in Namibia* (2007).

MARTIN F. MANALANSAN IV is an associate professor of anthropology and Asian American studies at the University of Illinois, Urbana-Champaign. He is the editor of several anthologies and is the author of *Global Divas: Filipino Gay Men in the Diaspora* (Duke, 2003).

DAVID A. B. MURRAY is an associate professor of anthropology and director of the graduate program in women's studies, York University. He is the author of *Opacity: Gender, Sexuality, Race and the "Problem" of Identity in Martinique* (2002).

BRIAN RIEDEL is the projects coordinator and lecturer for the Center for the Study of Women, Gender, and Sexuality at Rice University.

CONSTANCE R. SULLIVAN-BLUM is an independent scholar currently working as a public folklorist at the ARTS Council of the Southern Finger Lakes. Her publications include "The Natural Order of Creation: Naturalizing Discourses in the Christian Same-Sex Marriage Debate" in *Anthropologica* (2006).

Melbourne Women's Liberation, 72
Middle East, 100 n. 2
Misogyny, 28, 115
Moral superiority, 112
Morocco, 34
Mugabe, Robert, 20–21, 161 n. 11
Muslims. *See* Islam

Nagengast, Carol, 144 n. 10
NAMBLA, 64, 67
Nationalism, 6–9, 26–27, 153, 156–57
National masculinity, 142–43
Naz Foundation International (NFI), 176–79
Neoliberal state, 28
Netherlands, 27–28
New York City, 12, 34–47
Normative heterosexualities, 1, 73. *See also* Heterosexuality; Heterosexism
North American Free Trade Agreement, 150, 153
North American Man/Boy Love Association, 64, 67

Oetomo, Dédé, 124, 126, 141
Oral sex, 112
Organization for the Solidarity of Transsexuals and Travesti of Greece, 97, 101 n. 18
Orientalism, 28
Ostracism, 59

Papathanasiou, Valantis, 102 n. 19
Parenting, 71
Pederasty, 165, 169, 183 n. 2
Pedophilia, 13, 63, n. 12, 64–81, 81 n. 11
Pemberton, John, 144 n. 10
Phelps, Fred, 32 n. 1
Philippines, 42, 100 n. 2; Filipinos, 12, 32, 36, 40–44
Political homophobia, 22, 123–45
POP, 91, 99
Popular culture, 7
Pornography, 69

Postcolonial society, 6, 155
Prejudice, 3–4, 22, 86
Premarital sex, 53
Prostitution, 150–52, 98, 101 n. 18, 178, 182; courtesans, 171
Protestant churches, 48–63; evangelical and fundamentalist, 6, 12, 19, 21, 30, 32 n. 1, 49–52, 80 n. 2, 131, 158, 190; mainline, 9, 49, 51, 53, 58, 60; Westboro Baptist Church, 19, 32 n. 1
PSG, 13, 64–74, 81
Puar, Jasbir, 28, 31
Public behavior, 98
Public sex, 37–39

Queens, 44. *See also* Effeminate men; Gay men
Queers of color, 12, 23, 36, 38–39, 42, 44–46, 84, 130, 190

Race, 28, 36, 44, 85, 110, 152–53
Race-phobia, 24
Racial politics, 5
Racism, 23, 25, 39, 82–84, 92, 94, 102, 115
Rape, 69, 174
Refugees, 186–87
Religion, 5, 7, 14, 29, 50, 58–62, 110, 121, 134. *See also* Christianity; Islam
Reproductive choices, 53, 61
Respectability, 111–12
Reverse homophobia, 23
Roman Catholic Church, 61 n. 2, 63 n. 13
Row Kavi, Ashok, 177–78

Same-sex marriage, 12, 48–51, 54, 56, 63 n. 10, 146, 149, 163, 181
SATTE, 97, 101 n. 18
Sedgwick, Eve, 24, 164
Sex, public, 37–39
Sex education, 73–74, 77, 80 n. 8
Sexism, 23, 25
Sexophobia, 36–43
Sex Panic (activist group), 36, 39

DAVID A. B. MURRAY is an associate professor of anthropology at York University. He is the author of *Opacity: Gender, Sexuality, Race, and the "Problem" of Identity in Martinique.*

Library of Congress Cataloging-in-Publication Data

Homophobias : lust and loathing across time and space /
edited by David A.B. Murray.
p. cm.
Includes bibliographical references and index.
ISBN 978-0-8223-4582-4 (cloth : alk. paper)
ISBN 978-0-8223-4598-5 (pbk. : alk. paper)
1. Homophobia.
2. Homophobia in anthropology.
I. Murray, David A. B., 1962–
HQ76.4.H66 2009
306.76'6—dc22
2009030091